D1830470

POLITICS OF STATE AUTONOMY AND REGIONAL IDENTITY–JAMMU AND KASHMIR

POLITICS OF STATE AUTONOMY AND REGIONAL IDENTITY – JAMMU AND KASHMIR

Sunita
Kalindi Collage
University of Delhi

KALPAZ PUBLICATIONS
DELHI - 110 052

Politics of State Autonomy and Regional Identity – Jammu and Kashmir

Rs. 750
© Sunita
ISBN : 81- 7835 - 407-1

All rights Reserved. No Part of this book may be reproduced in any manner without written permission.

Published in 2006 in India by
Kalpaz Publications
C-30, Satyawati Nagar,
Delhi-110 052
Email : kalpaz@hotmail.com

Lasertype Setting by: Tact Computer Graphics, Delhi
Printed at: Salasar Imaging System, Delhi

Contents

Preface

It is not easy in India to write a book on Kashmir problem. Books have been written on the Punjab problem, Jharkhand problem and even on the situation of insurgency in the North-East. No one call them anti-national but it is easy to invite such an adjective on Kashmir. Till now anything that has been written or edited is basically of the 'Nationalist Type'.

Most of the writers hold the opinion that the situation of Kashmir worsened as its autonomy was not duly honoured. The second stream of Kashmir specialists is headed by people like Jagmohan. In their view not only Kashmir is an integral part of India, but it is such a part which has gone way-ward because of excessive love and affection. This section wants a military not a political solution. This is the most conservative stream of Indian Nationalism. Since independence a qualitative change has come not only in the Kashmir valley but in Indian politics as well. So new ideas are needed. This book entitled *Politics of State Autonomy and Regional Identity: jammu and kashmir* is a humble endeavour in this direction. In this an attempt has been made to establish that to be an Indian nationalist, does not mean to reject Kashmiri nationalism. Only a true nationalist can understand the pangs of another nationalist. The question of future of Kashmir is ultimately the question of future of Indian federalism. In the last fifty years a good deal of change has come about in the politics of Kashmir state as well as Centre. No problem can remain unchanged for so long. Kashmir problem has seen many ups and downs in these years. But one issue remained same; what should be the attitude of the Indian federalism toward Kashmiri people? What should be the relationship between these two? In a broad sense it is a question of distribution of power between the centre and the states. The objective of my book is to discuss the autonomy demand specifically for the state of Jammu and Kashmir. This is a demand that often generates tension between the Centre and the States of Kashmir. This book on the one hand is the description of the special status between Amritsar treaty of 1846 and 1947 under British rule and the other is the description of accession of Kashmir to the Indian federation upto demand aired by RSS to trifurcate Jammu and Kashmir into three states of Jammu, and Kashmir and Ladakh, in context of the relations between the Centre and Jammu and Kashmir.

My study is based on comparative, historical and systemic study of all three regions. This study is concerned with these major issues.

- The strategic importance of Jammu and Kashmir State.
- The nature and extent of this autonomy demand and its effect on the relationship of Centre State.
- The area of autonomy presently enjoyed by the state.
- State's role to increasing regional imbalance and regional autonomy demand.
- Fiscal position of the State.
- Internal political dynamics and socio-cultural and psychological pulls, that are behind many or region and sub-region urges in the state.

This book is divided into 9 chapters.

Chapter 1 gives a general introduction of the Indian federal system and a view of its specialties and outlook. The greatest problem of the Indian federalism (autonomy demand) has been dealt with emphasis.

Chapter 2 deals with multi-ethnic and multi-religious identity of the state. It gives general information regarding Kashmir state, its geography, history, culture, economy etc. This has been dealt with special condition of the state after its assimilation in 1846. It also described the special right and autonomy Kashmir used to enjoy under British Raj.

Chapter 3 deals with the accession of Kashmir to India. This chapter tries to find out that what was the aspiration of Kashmiri people behind acceding to India, and what was the aspiration of the Indian state. After Sheikh Abdullah's arrest and before the Sheikh Abdullah's return into politics in 1977, the relationship between Centre and the State have been dealt with in it.

Chapter 4 discusses the politics of the state from Sheikh Abdullah's accedences to power in 1977 to rise of insurgency and terrorist activities there.

Chapter 5 relates to terrorist activities and autonomy demand in decade of 90's. In this decade for the first time facts come to light, which were earlier repressed in the name of patriotism and blind nationalism. In the name of keeping terrorist at bay, central government came out with such laws that played havoc with the life and dignity of the Kashmiri people. These laws not only transgressed the autonomy of Kashmir but also frequently violated human rights. This chapter also deals with the BJP's outlook on Kashmir.

Chapter 6 has described the state assembly demand for autonomy of June 2000. Some questions have been addressed in this chapter: why the Government rejected it, and what were the reactions of different political parties, along with how this report has disastrous for the unity and integrity of the nation. It also deals with the trifurcation demand of July 2002 of Kashmir into Jammu, Kashmir and Ladakh.

Chapter 7 deals with the fiscal autonomy of the state of Jammu and Kashmir. This chapter focused on J&K's relation with the Indian Union in economic perspective. This chapter deals with some questions like what type of economic problems Kashmir is facing; How much money and grant were spent on the state from central assistance; where the hundreds of thousand crores of rupees invested in Kashmir have gone? What should be the basic of allocation of funds between and within the regional areas, population, backwardness. Why Jammu and Ladakh have very poor representation in revenue, police, judicial, education, agriculture and irrigation services.

Chapter 8 deals with the internal political dynamics and socio-cultural and Psychological pulls that are behind many of regional and sub-regional urges in the state. The focal point of this chapter is to trace the root causes of regional imbalance within the state. Whether the nature of imbalance and suffering is economic, cultural, political? Where lies the root the regional imbalance and how this regional imbalance influence autonomy demand. And how this regional autonomy demand creates tensions between centre and the state relationship. This chapter will carefully examine differentiation between three regions on the ground of ethnicity, language, religion culture, caste, ideology and how for these factors gives birth to regional political movement for the realization of socio-culture and politico-economic objectives. This chapter will focus on some questions. How is the valley seemed to dominate all discussion? Why having more population and area Jammu and Ladakh provinces have less seats in state assembly? Why a CM has always to be from the valley even if he derives his strength from the elected representation in the Jammu region? And how far state government is responsible for increasing regional imbalance like if the state Government can give subsidy to fruit growers in

Kashmir, it should also provide some assistance to vegetable growers of Ladakh, who are surviving against the most formidable odds, about 95 per cent to 98 per cent students fail to qualify in the matriculation examination due to state's biased language and education policy. Region's educational administrative and economic needs are being intentionally ignored by the state government. What state government has done to remove all discriminations will also be examined.

Chapter 9 is divided into four sections. The first section analyses the political development at the time of Kashmir's accession to India to July 2002 (when the demand of trifurcation was raised). The second section discussed the shortcoming of politics in the centre and in the state of Kashmir. In the third section, suggestions on Kashmir autonomy have been given. Fourth section proposes the future policy for Kashmir and describes the scope for further research.

This book is an attempt to examine the relationship Kashmir identity with the Indian Union, the regional identity of Jammu and Ladakh with the state; sub-regional identity with the regional centre. My prescriptions are deeply federal and decentralizing in nature, evolve in the spirit of bottom-up approach.

I believe that this book help the readers to understand the basic problems of Kashmiri politics. At the same time I am also conscious that inspite of my very limited aim the book would be having lots of shortcomings for which I would alone be responsible. Any critical suggestions or evaluation to make the book more meaningful and relevant to the readers will be most gratefully accepted and incorporated in the future editions of the book. I am deeply grateful to Dr. Veena Kukreja (Reader in Delhi University) Prof. M.P. Singh, Prof. Bidyut Chakravarty, Prof. Subrata Mukherji (Delhi University), Dr. K.K. Panda (Ex-Registrar of Delhi University), Dr. Sanghmittra (Dy. Director in ICHR), Dr. A.K. Raina (Kirorimal College), Dr. Renu Shetty (Reader in Gargi College), Madalsa Kundnani (Gargi College), for their cooperation and sharing their valuable time and thoughts with me.

I sincerely thanks all the well wishers, family members, scholars, colleagues in the discipline, and above all dear students who have always been the main inspiration behind this endeavour. My last word of thanks is reserved for my husband Pramod Kumar without his constant support and encouragement none of this would have happened.

1
Indian Federalism: Nature and Determinants

Federation, as an idea of multilevel government, is now widely acknowledged to be the best founding principle of the politics for multicultural societies. Federal principle are concerned with the combination of self rule and shared rule.

Federalism, that is to say the constitutional distribution of powers between a national government and a number of states or provincial governments is better known as working on different issues with the cooperation of others. Since federalism implies the co-existence of two sets of government, that is the national government and government of the constituent units, division of power between centre and the states is absolutely essential. Usually matters of national importance are assigned to the central government and matters of local importance are assigned to the government of constituent units.

The term federalism, has been used in a variety of contexts. Indeed, the extent of termological and conceptual abuse has obscured its meaning. Like the word 'Democracy', federalism tends to mean different things to different people.[1]

It is not easy to define federalism. There is a classical version and there are other versions. According to S. Rufus, an Australian scholar of federalism, there are as many as 44 kinds of federalism. These types of federalism are : Dual, orthodox, classic, polis, traditional, cooperative, bargaining, integrated, interdependent, creative, new permissive, functional, pragmatic, organic, pluralistic, competitive, centralised, decentralised, peripheralised, fused, corporate, national, social, oligarchic, unitary, constitutional, international military, political, monistic, polar, total, partial, contract, feudal, functional, incipient.[2] It is not easy to define federalism. In the classical sense, federalism was fairly closely defined. It meant the particular type of government practised with slight variation by the Americans, Australians, Canadian and the Swiss. The prominant features of these types of federalism are well known. The federal structure is the outcome of the merger of a number of separate states into a single sovereign state, with legislative and executive powers coordinately divided between federal and unit governments, each of which acts directly on the people. The classical or orthodox definitions of federalism are popularised by Freeman, Garren, Dicey and K.C. Wheare.

According to Prof. Dicey "Federalism means the distribution of force of the state among a number of coordinate bodies each originating in and controlled by the constitution."[3]

According to Freeman, a Federal state has the followed characteristics :

"On the one hand, each of the member of union must be wholly independent in those matters which concern each member only, on the other hand, all must be subject to a common power in those matters which concern the whole body of the members collectively..... Each member is perfectly independent within its own sphere."[4]

This characteristic of the 'Perfect independence' of constituent unit in a federation within a constitutionally demarcated sphere is also the distinctive feature of Wheare's definition of federalism, when he says, "By the federal principle I mean the method of dividing powers so that the general and regional government are each within a sphere, co-ordinate and independent."[5]

Professor K.C. Wheare, thus applies two tests for a true federation- coordination and independence.[6] Wheare one of the earliest students of modern federalism, called "general" and "regional" governments.[7] The terms "general" and "regional" governments are useful because they avoid those specific titles (e.g., state or province), which do not refer to all federations. (It is unfortunate that the term "region" has been adopted by the Europian community to describe something less territorially specific, namely areas within the various member states.)[8]

Wheare emphasized the importance between the sub-ordination of local government to the central government in a nation state and the more equal relationship between regions and general government in a federation. He characterized that relationship as one of "Coordinancy". He considered American constitution an ideal federalism.

Thus Wheare's definition of federalism which insists that the federal and unit governments are each, within its own sphere, have both coordinate and independent powers, uses the term 'quasi-federal' to denote constitutions and governments which deviate too much from its conceptual model. By applying such criteria, most of constitution of the new federations would be only quasi federal. The definition of federalism by K.C. Wheare could not fulfil the growing demands of modern times of the new federations. The most suitable definition of modern federalism is given by A.H. Birch. He amends Wheare as follows : "A federal system of government is one in which there is a division of powers between one general and several regional authorities, each of which, in its own sphere, is coordinate with the others, and each of which acts directly on the people through its own administrative agencies."[9] By this definition, the federal and regional governments are not required to be strictly independent of one another, as according to Wheare's definition they should be. Similarly, Bernard Schwartz also points to the inappropriateness of the classical concept of federalism in the modern times. "The classical concept of federalism, however, upon which the American system was based," says Prof. Schwartz, has not been able successfully to withstand the stresses of twentieth century political evaluation. Government in the United States, no less than government in other parts of the world has followed a trend-toward consistent concentration of authority in the centre of political structure.[10]

Ronald Watts defines federation as a form characterised by a constitutionally assigned and protected distribution of authority and resources between at least two orders of government within a single polity, within which each of the orders of government has some direct electoral and fiscal relationship within the citizens.[11] The emerging tendencies in federal system were realized by Livingston in 1956, when he says that the essential nature of federalism is to be sought for, not in the shadings of legal and constitutional terminology, but in the forces – economic, political, social, cultural-that have made the outward forms of federalism necessary. According to him, federalism, like most institutional forms, is a solution of or an attempt to solve, a certain type of problem of political organisation.[12] He pointed out that the essence of federalism lies not in the constitutional structure or institutional structure but in the society itself, federal government is not a devise by which the federal qualities of the society are articulated and protected.[13] In 1964, W.H. Riker pointed out that, "A constitution is federal if (i) two level of government rule the same land and people (ii) each level has atleast one area of action in which it is autonomous (iii) there is some guarantee (even-though merely a statement in the constitution) of the autonomy of each government in its own spheres."[14]

The modern age is the age of "cooperative federalism". The essential features of cooperative federalism is not coordination and interdependence between the federal and unit governments, but cooperation and interdependence among them. A.H. Birch rightly accepts the term 'Cooperative federalism' as indicative of the changing balance of forces whereby federation and unit government are ceasing to be rigidly independent of one other. In the similar way Prof. Reagon pleads that "federalism needs to be re-examined, not from the view-point of abstract conceptualization, but by close description and analysis of the major forms of constituing actual interaction, between the national state and local level of government." He summed up the difference between the old style and new style of federalism as follows:

"Old style federation described a non relationship between the centre and state governments. New style federalism refers to a multifaceted positive relationship of shared action. The meaning of federalism to-day lies in a process of joint action, not in a matter of legal status. It lies not in what governments are but what they do. It is a matter of action rather than structure. It is dynamic and changing not static and constant."[15]

However, whatever the definition of federalism, it should be understood as a phenomenon which represents some kind of compromise between its forces of regionalism and its forces of nationalism, or, in other words, between centrifugal and centripetal forces. It provides a constitutional device for bringing unity in diversity by harmonising the forces of centrifugal and centripetal trends in a country for the achievement of common national goals.

These distinctions or definitions were not always appreciated. A number of federations including Canada and India, in which powers were distributed between one general and several regional government, did not make the important distinction between subordination and coordination, or between decentralization and non-centralization. Regional government were treated as local governments subordinate to the centre, not as coordinate governments responsible to the constitution.

There are still "quasi-federations" (another of Wheare's terms) where the general government often behaves as a strong central government. India is one of these quasi federations; indeed, the Government of India is often referred to as "the centre". It may be that only in a classical federal system like that of United States, is non centralization taken for granted. Since the American System is usually taken as the model, we need to know what is it – and now it looks from the perspective of India. A perusal of the functioning of federalism of America, Australia, Canada and Swiss or elsewhere clearly reveal that the formal criteria for testing the presence of federalism set forth by Wheare has been rejected to a great extent. Now federalism is embracing a new workable meaning almost everywhere. It may be noted here that Indian federalism is no exception to this general tendency and developing phenomenon of federalism.

In recent years, researchers have tended to make a clear distinction between federalism and actual federalism. Federalism is now often treated as an "ism" comparable to nationalism or capitalism, that is to say a Philosophical concept. This was not always done in part, with the result that federalism has not received that treatment by political philosophers that has been given to other "isms".[16] Indeed the theory of federalism and actual practice were often confused.

Essential Characteristics of a True Federal Polity.

A federal system usually has the following five essential characteristics :

1. Division of Powers—The division of powers between two levels of government is an essential feature of federalism. Federalism means the distribution of powers of the state between the central and state government under the framework of the constitution. The basis of such distribution of power is that in matters of national importance, in which a uniform policy is desirable in the interest of the units, authority is entrusted to the centre, and matters of local concern remain with the states.

2. A Written Constitution—A federal constitution must almost be a written constitution. It will be practically impossible to maintain the supremacy of the constitution and division of powers between the centre and the states, unless the terms of the constitution have been reduced into writing. To base an arrangement of this kind upon understandings or conventions would be certain to generate misunderstandings and disagreements.[19]

3. Supremacy of Constitution—A Federal state derives its existance from the constitution. Therefore, every power, legislative, executive or judicial whether it belongs to the nation or to the individual state, is derived and is subordinate to and controlled by the constitution.[17] The constitution in a federal state constitutes the supreme law of the land. As Prof. Wheare rightly says "that these two institutions the supreme constitution and the written constitution are, then, essential institution to a federal Government. The supreme constitution is essential if Government is to be federal the written constitution is essential if government is to work well.[18]

4. Independence of Judiciary—In a federal state independent judiciary is essential for maintaining the federal system. The very nature of a federal state involves a division of powers between the centre and the state under the framework of the constitution. It is, therefore, essential to maintain this division of powers between the two levels of government. This must be done by some independent and impartial authority above the beyond ordinary bodies whether federal or state legislatures existing under the constitution. The judiciary thus has, in a federal polity, the final powers to interpret the constitution and guard the provisions of the constitutions. Hence an independent judiciary is a must under a federal constitution.

5. A Rigid Constitution—A natural corollary of a written constitution is its rigidity. In a rigid constitutions the procedure of amendment is complicated and difficult. But, this does not means that the constitution should be legally unalterable. It simple means that the power of amending the constitution should not remain exclusively with either the centre or the state. A constitution of a country is considered to be a permanent document. It is called the supreme law of the land. The supremacy of the supreme law of the land can only be maintained if the method of the amendment is rigid. At the same time it requires that a change in it should not become impossible.

If we apply these tests or characteristic on any constitution of the world, there can be no doubt that 'that country is a federation'. But not all federative systems are federation proper. The alternative, some old and some new, are listed below.[20]

1. Federation

The Canada of 1867 had been somewhat similar. Though the Canadians called their system a "confederation", it was far from being a confederacy like the India of 1950. Canada was then more like a quasi-federation, composed of a strong dominion government (to which many of the leading provincial politicians had gravitated) and relatively weak provincial governments, referred to by former Prime Minister Sir John A. Macdonald as "Local" governments. But unlike the Indian constitutions, the British North America Act of 1867 specifically stated in its principle that Canada was intended to be based on "the federal principle". K.C. Wheare in his book "Federal Government" says that "the Canadian constitution is quasi-federal in law but it is predominantly in practice".[21] Today, Canada is clearly a federation.

2. Quasi-Federal

The framers of the Indian constitution refrained from calling their new state with its strong "centre" a federation at all. Yet clearly, even if India was not to be a federation like the united state, it could hardly be transford into a unitary state on the British Model. When Wheare called India a "quasi-federation" he indicated that its form of government lay somewhere between a unitary state and a federation. In some ways India remains a quasi-federations.

3. Confederacy

Modern federaticns (or quasi-federations) are not to be confused with traditional confederacies, for centuries the most common form of "federation", the term being interchangeable. Only with the invention of the modern federation by the Americans in 1787, was a clear destination draw between them. Under the confederate system, major decisions had been left in the hand of the constituent units, thus making the relationship much looser than in modern federation. In other words, whereas in a "quasi federation" important decision were reserved for the general government, in a confederacy such decisions remained the responsibility of constituent unit. A corollary to this was that the general government had no authority over individual citizens. It could neither tax them nor conscript them. Only the constituent units had this authority.

Because of their failure to provide strong government, especially in time of fiscal or military crisis, confederacies came into disrepute. Before 1787, when America underwent a fiscal crisis, the state had been members of a confederacy, governed by the articles of confederation of 1781. Eight years later, the American south fought, and lost, the civil war as a confederacy. In each instance the inability of the confederate leadership to tax or conscript individual weakened the organization.

Yet confederacy still has its attractions for those who believe that general government have become too powerful. Since 1945 there have been several states' rights movements in the American south. Similar movements have arisen in India and Canada. From Kashmir to Quebec there have been those who would weaken the hold of the general government in Delhi or Ottawa but who do not wish to sever the connection with the general government altogether. What they have sought can be compared to confederacy.

4. Quasi-Confederacy

There have also been regional politicians who, while their public pronouncements are ostensibly federalists, have tried to enhance the power of their own regional government at the expense of the general government. In other words, they have promoted what can perhaps be called a quasi-confederate form of government.

5. Community

None of the form of government discussed so far, from unitary through quasi-federation and federation to quasi-confederacy, are new. What is new has been the attempt by the sovereign states of Europe to devise something they have called a community.

The community can be distinguished from the experience of federations like the United States, Canada and India by three of its characteristics. In the first place, the Europian states are not excolonies compelled by circumstances to seek some form of federations. Secondly they have not had to make an immediate decision on the form political union should take : they can let the European community evolve over several decades. Lastly, in creating a supranational authority they are challenging the nation-state, a form of polity invented and developed in Europe after the Renaissance, the Reformation; the French Revolution and the Industrial Revolution. The European community is therefore creating a novel form of government.

6. Sovereignty – Association

While the European community is something new, it may not be a useful model of secessionist minded people in Quebec, Punjab or Kashmir. Here what is really demanded is a new asymmetrical relationship between an existing large federations and one or more of its component parts. When Rene Levesque and his colleagues in the 'party quebecais' called their proposed relationship between Quebec and Canada "Sovereignty association", they meant political sovereignty and economic association.[22]

Daniel Elazen has suggested a term of cover the asymmetrical relationship between a large state and entity that is much smaller : "Federacy". The example he has given is the relationship between the United States and the Commonwealth of Puerto Rico. But the "Federacy" might well apply to some new asymmetrical relationship between Canada and Quebec, or India and Kashmir. He distinguishes federacy from "associate statehood", a relationship which can be terminated if one of the parties decides to secede.[23]

It may be re-emphasised that whatever be the structure and stability of a federal constitution depends on the manner in which it is worked. While modern technologies breaking barries and the world economy getting globalised, federalism is poised for acquiring new dimensions. While for many functions national governments are found to be too large, and decentralization is considered the key to efficient ordering of the public sector, nation states are in turning out to be too small for certain others. Hence, the emergence of supernational agencies like the WTO to coordinate and harmonise policies bearing on commerce among nations. Old ideas of sovereignty are in fact facing obsolescence as nations agree on their own to abide by internationally accepted conventions and standard whether that opens up a new era of three or four fair governments with a confederation of sovereign nations at the top and compound republics down below, only future can tell. Thinking on federalism must take into account of the changing contexts and explore show best the objectives sought to be achieved. Through the federal form can be served without compromising the independence and right to self-determination of nation states.

Federal System in Indian Context

The idea of federalism in the governance of countries was introduced almost all over the world as a matter of expediency. Each country adopts the federal formula which is most expedient to solve its own problems. It is, therefore, found that none of the two federal systems are identical. As early as in 1952, Professor W.S. Livingstone, an authority on federalism, argued that every nation and every society is, more or less, closely integrated, is determined by its own cultural, historical, political and economical peculiarities. Such diversities differ in nature from one federation to another.[24] In such countries, as for instance the United States, where social, religious, cultural and linguistic groups do not happen to be concentrated in geographically demarcated and homogeneous areas, the concept of federalism generally assumes a political form. On the other hand in societies (like Canada) where the population is horizontally divided on the basis of language and other similar factors (between Anglophonic and Fracophonic communities), language has been the main determinants of federalism. A situation, somewhat similar to that of Canada, prevails in India, where certain cultural diversities are regionally concentrated and, therefore, have federal implications. The regionally organized diversities such as linguistic (Punjab, Tamilnadu), cultural (Tamilnadu, Assam) and religious (Kashmir, Meghalaya etc.) make the Indian case quite appropriate for a federal government.

The founding fathers of the Indian constitution also did not adhere to any theory or dogma about federalism. Gaining from any experience of functioning of the United States, Australia, Canada and Swiss, they adopted the policy of pick and choose what was in the best interest of our country. Thus the constitution of India modifies the traditional principal of federalism to make a working formula to solve the peculiar problems of the country. In this way it becomes clear that the nature of federalism differs from country to country according to the prevailing circumstances and peculiar social, economic, linguistic and cultural conditions of a country to which it has to serve.

The choice of founding fathers to deal with sui-generis Indian problems were bound to opt for a sui-generis federation. "The case of indian Federalism" says Professor Alexandrowich, "is certainly sui generis". He further observes about Indian federation that "thus was happened to be superimposed (in contract to contractual) initially, was later subject to a thorough federal re-arrangement. That is why I submit that India is not simply an administrative federation of quasi-federal character such as Ex U.S.S.R., Mexico or Brazil, but a sui-generis voluntary association of linguistic communities which took proper shape after the adoption of the constitution. Thus to put India together with the U.S.S.R., Maxico or Brazil into a vaguely defined category of quasi-federalism does not meet the requirements of a systematic classification.[25] Similarly Dr. L.M. Singhvi also gives an appropriate account of Indian federalism when he says that "Indian federalism is sui-generis, but the federal distribution and balance of powers, the existence of states, their legislatures and governments, and the exercise by them of district competence in geographically defined areas within a constitutionally allotted fields are basic and unmistakable federal facts of Indian policy. The dynamics of Indian federalism has its main springs in the essential cultural unity, wide spread social diversity, constitutional education, economic leverages and the judicial and political processes. Federalism in India is not a mere superstructural contrivances; facets of Indian federalism and its sources go deep down into the foundations of Indian Life.[26]

Some scholars of governments, Indian and foreign describe India as a "quasi federal" state, and some even regard it as "a more unitary than federal". K.C. Wheare classified India as "a unitary state with subsidiary federal principle rather than a federal state with subsidiary unitary principles".[27] Sir Ivor Jenning feels that India has a federation with strong centralizing tendency, W.H. Morris Jons held the view that Indian federation was a kind of "corporative federalism" where bargaining took place between the centre and the states but ultimately a situation came out, both agreed to cooperate.

Thus, numerous scholars reflecting on the vast power left with the Government of India and subordinate role of the states and also the crucial powers of the union to partially annihilate an existing state, doubt whether India is a federalism at all. Some have call it a "pseudo federation" other feels that it would be more appropriate to call it a "quasi-federation". However, many political thinkers have suggested that their is no such thing as a quasi federation and that a system is either a federation or it is not a federation and that of India should be grouped among the federation by virtue of its constitution.

According to Dr. Ambedkar, India is a true federation but it could be federal or unitary. In normal times it could work as federal constitution and in the times of war or crisis as a unitary one. No other constitution possesses this flexibility. This has been done so on account of the situation peculiar in India. First, The British India was administrated on a unitary basis. A complete break with the past was not possible. So, the movement was from unitarian, the 'union' (Federalism) with a strong centre. Secondly, the message that has come down through the history is that whenever the centre has been weak, the country soon disintegrated. Hence, the necessity for a strong centre. Thirdly, ours is an underdeveloped country. So, a mighty effort at development was called for, which could not be possible without mobilising all the national resources under the central guidance and leadership. Forthly, in all the modern federations the accent is on the centre. Therefore, learning from their experiences, the founding fathers wisely opted for a strong centre.

The seeds of federal idea in India can be traced as far back as to the decentralisation policy of Lord Mayo in 1870. However, the authors of *Montford reform* declared themselves formally first of all in favour of federalism. They announced, "our conception of the eventual future of India is a sisterhood of states, self governing in all matters of purely local and provincial interest.[28] The interaction of dyarchy further encouraged the growth of federal idea in India. Sir Fredrick Whyte, Sir Malcolm Haily and Simon Commission conceived the future set up of India on federal lines, the Simon Commission openly declared "Apart together from any question of an ultimate federal union between the Indian states and British India, there are, we think, very strong reasons for the reconstruction of the Indian constitution in a federal basis. It is only in a federal structure that sufficient elasticity can be obtained for the union of elements of diverse internal conditions and the communities at very different stage of development and culture". At the first Indian National Congress suspected the motives of the British Government. They thought that the Indian states were being joined with the British provinces only to retard the growth of nationalism in India. The attitude of the congress leaders can be gauged from the Nehru report which unmistakably declared, "It would be a most one-sided arrangement, if the Indian states desire to join the federalism, so as to influence by their votes and, otherwise the policy and legislation of Indian legislation passed by it. It would be travesity of the federal idea. At first round table conference, however, most of the Indian political leaders and the Indian states agreed to join the federation. It was widely believed at the time that the Indian states had agreed to join the federation because of the pressure of the British. The federal idea was given a concrete shape in the Government of India Act, 1935. The Congress was not against the federal system but it was readily opposed to the federal idea as conceived in the Government of India Act, 1935.

The British wanted to bring the Indian states together with the British provinces at the centre in order to stem the rising tide of nationalism in the country.[29] The Indian states were to be a reactionary force and to act as a brake in the wheels of progress and democracy of the tough gave up the federal idea and continued the administration of the centre according to Act of 1919 but gave autonomy to the provinces. When India achieved independence it was considered prudent not to introduce the unitary government but only the federal government which was widely welcomed by the shades of opinion. The Indian states also agreed to join the federation.

Adapting Federalism to India : Multilevel and Asymmetrical Innovations*

The constitution adopted by India after attaining independence with the objective of establishing a "Sovereign, socialist, secular, democratic, republic" is federal in form, providing as it does for multi-level governance, each with their own legislature, executive and specified function and powers, initially the government levels recognised in the constitution, were two the union and the state, by amending carried out in 1992, local government and villages and town the panchayat and municipalities have also been accorded constitution status although the exact demarcation of their powers and function is left to states to specify their own legislation.[30] It is

* Balbir Arora and Douglas V. Verney (eds). Multiple indentities in a single state– Indian federalism in comparative perspective, Konark Publication, (New Delhi, 1995) p 71-95

a truism that the Indian constitution of 1950 was not a federal documents in the sense in which the Canadian (1867) and Australian (1900) constitutions established federations. The process of adapting federalism to Indian conditions began when the constituent assembly set aside the classical models then in vogue and opted for an unorthodox distribution of powers that made persists wince. However it must be recognized that loosening the centralists straitjacket of a unitary colonial regime required exceptional courage in the post-partition context, when many feared that too federal a constitution might encourage other fissiparous tendencies.[31] Viewed as further fragmentation and even vivisection, the simple demand for recognization of state on linguistic line was rejected as inopportune. In the 'strong centre' perspective, the second level of government was justified primarily in functional terms, rather than as a means of deepening the roots of democracy.

While the unitary bias of the original design was unmistakable a remarkable degree of flexibility and pragmatism was also worked it. It recognised the virtues of asymmetry in bringing about and maintaining union, particularly when it came to integrating states and people who had enjoyed considerable autonomy under the previous regime of central (British) paramountcy. It also took cognizance of the layering of social political realities and the importance of local self governments. In a social system characterized by what Francine Franket describes as "asymmetrical obligations among equals", special status and multilevel arrangement encountered no conceptual obligations.[32] In the ongoing search for new modes of adaptation to the pressures generated by democratic development, these elements of flexibility were significant. They were designed to make the federal system more responsive, but their true potential was obscured by the inter-governmental relations agenda that moulded thinking on federal reform once the first major treat of Congress party dominance arose in the late sixties.

Though there has been a widespread consensus that the 1967 general elections were a watershed for the federal system, many of the problems and issues thrown up at the time no longer appear as crucial today. Dissatisfaction with the distribution of powers between the centre and the states constituted the core of the reform agenda of the 1970s, and the terms of reference of the Sarkaria Commission (1983) reflected these concerns.[33] However, it can be argued that, since then, these concerns have been gradually overshadowed by demands for a more basic reform of the federal structure from this point of view, the political crisis of 1984 mark perhaps a second watershade in the evaluation of India's federal experiment.[34] Moving beyond the search for institutional refinements of cooperative federalism, the debate has shifted towards more fundamental restructuring at multiple levels.

In the section that follows, we shall present an overview of the centre-state relations debate in term of the search for a new equilibrium between central stability and states right we shall then turn our attention to the asymmetrical relations that have been worked into the constitutional design to meet specific needs and situations of people on the periphery. In the third section, we propose to examine the gradual increase in the number of structured levels and the development of a multilayered system of federal governance. The recent reforms tending towards establishing a set of self government institutions as a constitutionally recognised third tier of a federal structure will be assessed before attempting to delineate a perspective on the further adaptation of federalism to the changing needs and demands of India's diversity.

1. Flexible Federation with Strong Union

The centralist legacy of the colonial state was interwined with a significant streak of pragmatic decentralisation. Anxious to derise a durable system sufficiently responsive to the distinctive needs of specific units, and to processes of change, the constituent assembly retained the assence of what Danial Elazer has termed "decentralised imperialism" but sought to combine it with a tolerance of diversity of far reaching proportions.[35] Apart from carrying forward the special arrangements devised for a loosely integrated periphery, the difficult transition from decentralisation to non centralisation was timidly initiated at the structural level.

Federal Structure and Democratic Development

The democratisation of political processes had a profound impact on the original design, especially as a rapidly growing electorate discovered the multiple meaning of democracy. Demands of states for more power and greater participation in national policy processes were voiced with increasing insistence, as regional identities sharpened through electoral competition. The response of the central leadership for almost fifteen years (1969-85) was largely oriented towards further strengthening the system of controls devised for situations of exceptional danger. Central intervention in the governance of states increased significantly, reaching unprecedented levels due to the collapse of democratic functioning within the Congress party.[36] The Lacunae and shortcoming of the arrangements for cooperative federalism became apparent quite early and the reforms proposed by different commissions and states were remarkably convergent. Apart from deploring excessive central interference, they all stressed the need for more effective inter-governmental concertation at the political level through institutionalised 'executive federalism'.[37] However, government-opposition relations in central Parliament have always had a direct bearing on positions regarding institutionalised power sharing in a federal framework. After the sharp deterioration in these relations in the mid-seventies, the prospects of even a limited reform in the direction of executive federalism receded rapidly. In the surcharged political climate of the early Eighties, polarisation and confrontation gave rise to a qualitatively different type of conflicts in three key states; Assam, Kashmir and Punjab.

Extending Federalism : New Dimensions ?

Federal reform took on a new urgency in the 1980,s when the centre felt increasingly constrained to intervene directly in one state after another. The gradual erosion of the capabilities of state to cope with internal challanges through indiscriminate central interference led to the growth of extra constitutional forces and arenas of conflicts. It also become painfully clear that it was easier to intervene than to withdraw and restart the political process. Thus, further exploration of other options available has thus become more attractive all round. Referring to demands for greater autonomy for Punjab, Kashmir and elsewhere Prime Minister Narasimha Rao is reported to have said : If some people think that within the Indian constitution an amount of autonomy which meets with their aspirations is possible, then that is what we have to explore.

The persistence of militant, extremists and terrorist movements during the Eighties prompted a renewed search for acceptable levels of autonomy in order to make the democratic option more attractive to the people. Rajiv Gandhi attempted to resolve outstanding problems through a series of high level 'accords.' Despite their uneven success, they did mark a new approach that he termed "nation above party". At another level his efforts at evolving a more responsive district administration led him towards democratic decentralisation and revitalisation of local self-government institutions.[38] Finally, significant changes were taking place in other spheres: the phenomenal development of telecommunication, intensive economic liberalisation and the lowering of the voting age of eighteen, all contributed to new levels of awareness and expectations. Pressures emanating from resurgent identities at the sub-state level also had to be accommodated without compromising the territorial integrity of the states. A clear shift in orientation is discernible in the direction of an increased willingness rediscover and explore flexible federalism.

2. Unity and Uniformity: Asymmetrical Variations

Special status and unique relationship to meet specific needs and requirements were a part of the original design right from the beginning.

Special Status for Jammu and Kashmir

The accession of Jammu and Kashmir to the Indian union was based on a commitment to the safeguard of its autonomy under Article 370 of the Indian Constitution. It was to be governed by its own constitution, the only state accorded this possibility. Responding to a specific historical situation, the jurisdiction of the union Parliament was restricted initially to foreign affairs, defence and communications, with the state legislature supreme in all other matters and also vested with residuary powers. But the special status of the state of Jammu and Kashmir has been a matter of dispute between New Delhi government and the government of Jammu and Kashmir. The special status of this state itself a main issues in Indian Federal System.[39] Ever its creation the leaders of Jammu and Kashmir have toyed with idea of 'Kashmir Autonomy' and some other states of the Indian Union are struggling for the same status and autonomy.

Special Status in North-East States

The concept of special status was extended and given a permanent constitutional niche by the thirteenth amendment (1962) which formally introduced "Special Status" for the North eastern state of Nagaland under article 371A[40]. The main feature of this provision was the protection of local identity. Some of the areas located in India, which are inhabited by aboriginals, who are sccially and economically more backward, are treated as autonomous districts. These are administrated under the provisions of the sixth scheduled of the constitution and special efforts and case is needed for their uplift, for which the Central Government has assumed somewhat greater responsibilities. These are located in the state of Assam, Tripura, Meghalaya and the Union Territory of Mizoram. The reasons for such special arrangement are due to the fact that these areas are located in a very sensitive regions, right on the border of India with China, where the problem of security of India is involved, and have thus a strategic importance.[41]

3. Experimenting with New Levels

In many large federal systems, there are concurrent pressures of integration and differentiation, resulting in a multiple layering of structures. Though most studies on Indian federalism have been primarily concerned with intergovernmental relations between centre and the state, the significance of the other levels need to be stressed. The new agenda of federal reform is oriented towards greater autonomy and decentralisation of initiative within states. As economic liberalisation policies reduce restrictive central controls, these structures are likely to assume greater significance, provided they receive adequate administrative and financial support.

Multi-State Cooperation

What is noteworthy about multi-state cooperation is the relative failure of the Zonal Council established by Delhi under its control. This can be contrasted with the success of initiatives taken by the states themselves, on the few occasions that they have decided to work in concert. Immediately after the linguistic reorgnisation of states, an intermediate level was created to counter- balance the perceived disadvantages of dispersal. The country was divided into five multi-state zones, and councils were created under the tutelage of the union home ministry for better coordination of policy and implementation. These councils did not achieve much and gradually stopped functioning. The Sarkaria Commission made a detailed analysis of the reason for their failure, and recommended that they may be given a new lease of life. This ignored past experience which points clearly to the inherent limitation of centrally established and controlled institutions for multi state executive federalism. It is significant that whenever states have felt the need to come together for concerted action, they have understandably avoided the zonal council route, since their initiatives were generally directed by seeking changes in central policies. Such issues as common memoranda to the finance commissions and joint initiatives in the National Development Council could be discussed away from the gaze of central representatives. The zonal concept has been less successful in acquiring a political significance, even though it is still frequently used for administrative decentralisation by organisations having a nation wide spread. The primary reason of its lack of appeal is that it has developed no roots in the processes of electoral democracy. Designed to prome unity in an integrated framework, centrally sponsored multi-state regionalism has not been able to develop a popular constituency. On the other hand, the demands of diversity within states have found a more favourable response in recent years. The multilayered complexities of theses sub-polities are slowly being reflected in the structuring of democracy below the state level.

Levels Within States

What we shall call "Sub state political structures", i.e., between the state and the district structures, have a long but undistinguished history in Independent India, initially there was considerable resistance to even genuine decentralization of politico administrative structures, the possibilities appeared by the constitution. One such provision was Article 244 which inserts two distinct charters of decentralisation, one for the tribal areas of North East India (The Sixth Schedule) and other for specified areas elsewhere (The Fifth Schedule). The latter has had limited impact because it merely provides for : (a) Special responsibilities of the Governor and the union with regard to backward classes or areas; and (b) advisory councils for tribal areas, compromising mainly the elected representatives of these constituencies in the state assembly.[42]

Apart from the fifth and sixth schedules, the constitution envisages sub-state structure under 371(2) for Maharashtra and Gujrat. This provision for separate development boards for Vidarbha, Marathwada, Saurashtra and Kutch has had little practical significance because of the reluctance of state leaders to relinquish control over such important responsibilities and functions.[43]

While the reform of State-Centre relations has been extremely slow, there have been major breakthroughs in state local relations in last few years. These institutional innovations within the framework of existing states represent important step in the general direction of building a more responsive democracy.

4. Towards a Third Tier of Government

The term 'third tier' requires some explanation because it is commonly assumed that already there are three tiers of government in federal systems – Federal/Central, state and local. What is different about third tier federalism is that sub state structures are no longer simply creatures of the various states but enjoy constitutional recognition as a level of government.

The promotion of local self government was enshrined in the constitution as a goal to be pursued : the directive principles of state policy were quite categoric in their assertation of this Gandhian ideals.[44] Initial efforts at organising Panchayati Raj Institutions (PRIs) as adjuncts to the community development programme floundered on the rocks of an excessively bureaucratic system of planned development. Intended primarily to promote popular involvement in development activities, they sought to maintain a dividing line between democratic politics and the promotion of welfare. The distinction proved untenable, and this first generation of PRIs gradually ceased to function. The first major experiments at reviving the Punchayats was launched in West Bengal in late seventies, with a deliberate strategic of politicisation "aimed at a purposive penetration of the countrywide" accompanied by extensive land reform, they empowered hitherto marginalised sections of rural society. Their social welfare activities gained them the confidence of the people and consolidated the support base of the left parties. This success story was followed by after initiatives, and Panchayats began the slow journey to becoming units of self-government.

The second state to launch a similar experiment in political Panchayats was Karnataka. Karnataka's example was followed by other non Congress states, and new Panchayat enactments came into force in Andhra and Orissa.[45]

Finally the central government began a series of consultations to work out a national initiative in what was termed a transfer of 'power to the people'. After five workshops with district magistrates, PM Rajiv Gandhi convened a conference of state chief secretaries to discuss a reform package aimed at revitalising district planning through the Panchayat System. His proposal to amend the constitution for this purpose was initially viewed with suspicion, since the Congress party had done very little for punchayats in the states in controlled. The proposed centre-state-local relationship had never been established constitutionally, and the centralist record of the Congress party gave rise to misgivings regarding the real intentions behind to move. The perspective that appeared to dominate was one of political management rather than self government. Direct funding on Panchayat by centre was seen as a political play to contain opposition run state governments and reduce their importance. Always apprehensive of intrusive initiatives coming from New Delhi, the opposition parties rallied to denounce the bill as a 'nefarious design' to undermine the autonomy of the states.[46]

In a multi level system, the interface between the various levels of government a obviously to crucial importance. State level political leaders are anxious to retain their hold on local political processes while asserting their autonomy vis-a-vis central politicians. This relationship is one of the imponderables in the new third tier which the 73rd Amendment Act (1992) seeks to establish.

The seventy-third and seventy-fourth constitutional amendments in 1992 heralded a new phase of revival and reorganisation in local self government in rural and urban area in India.[47] The recent amendments required the states to streamline the post 1947 statutes to reinstitute the local bodies on a more regular and financially viable basis as the third tier of Indian federalism.[48] This is clear that progress along the path of constituting this 'third stratum' of democratic institution will be uneven, with each state free to give it the degree of autonomous existence it wishes. The relationship with state level politicians and the bureaucracy remains to be refined, and provision for ex-officio membership could considerably dilute its significance as a forum of local initiative.

5. An Evolving Federative System

It is universally recognised that major rethinking lies ahead on the adaptation of existing structures to the rapidly changing needs of the time. The pace of socio-economic changes in India has accelerated considerably, giving rise to none strains and testing the capacity of the federal system to organise and promote incremental reforms.

The two more notable changes of the 1990's in India have been the growing federalization of the polity and the reform of the economy with accent on liberalization and marketization.[49] Regional and ethnic identities, party system, transformation from one party dominance and multi-partisan coalitional and/or minority governance, and judicial activism have also contributed to a greater federalization of the Indian polity in the last two decades.[50] The process of federalization of Indian polity is likely to continue and grow.

The Demand of State Autonomy in Indian Federalism

Dr. Ambedkar said "the chief marks of federalism lies in the partition of the legislative and executive authority between the centre and the units by constitution".[51] The above statement shows that the founding fathers have adopted the federal ideas in the Indian constitution, but the framers of the Indian constitution were in favour of a strong and united India. Since the adoption of the constitution of the trend has been relentlessly, mindlessly toward amassing the power by the centre, creppling the autonomy of the state. This process of centralization has brought two inter-related phenomenon to the fore—

1. Tensions in centre-state relation and
2. Demand of autonomy for the state.

I. Major Tension Areas in Indian Federal System

Major areas of tension in Indian federalism are :

(A) Role of Governor : Since 1967, when the monopoly of the Congress party was, shattered the role of Governor assumed great significance. This has been aggravated because of nature of multi-party system and prevalence of the phenomenon of defections. The ruling party at the centre found in the office of governor as effective instrument to recapture power for itself. As Soli Sorabjee puts it, "It will not be exaggeration to say that no institution or constitutional office has suffered greater-erosion or degradation than the office of Governor. The public today generally regard the Governor as an employee of the central government and in some cases as a spy of the centre. The unfortunate fact is that few incumbents of this high office have any clear conception of their role in our constitutional scheme and in fact regard themselves as the lackeys of employees of the central government and readily act according to its behest."[52]

The office of Governor was used to topple down the state Government on one pretext or the other during seventies and eighties. As early as in 1953 Gian Singh Rarewala led coalition ministry in PEPSU was dismissed on the ground of law and order. Then again in 1959 Namboodripad led Communist government enjoying majority support in Kerala was dismissed likewise. Thereafter it has been done more than 100 times in various states. During Mrs. Gandhi's regime the trend of appointing government after consulting state Chief Ministers was relegated. Rajiv Gandhi followed the same pattern. The practice of sacking of Governors for partisan reason has also been followed.

(B) Misuse of President's Rule—The provision for imposition of President's Rule in the state under Art 356 was made to deal serious situations as a life saving device to be used as a measure of last resort. However in practice, this article has been frequently used for purely partisan interests.

1. Imposition of President's Rule—The use of Article 356 rests on the subjective satisfaction of the Presidedent. President's Rule can be imposed either on the recommendations of Governor or even without that, purely for the satisfaction of President himself. The Prime Minister can also make use of Article 356 to ensure that the administration in state carried on in accordance with the provisions of the constitution, and otherwise, dissolve the state Government on the basis of his own assessment of the representative character or otherwise.[53] In practice these provisions have been misused by:[54]

- Dismissing the state government and on partisan consideration.
- Suspending and dissolving the Assemblies on partisan consideration.
- Not giving a chance to the opposition to form government when electoral verdict was indecisive.
- Denying opportunity to the opposition to form government when ministry resigned in anticipation of the defeat on the floor of the House.
- Not allowing the opposition to form government even after the defeat of the ministry on the floor of the House.

Drawing attention to the repeated abuse of Article 356 the Sarkaria Commission has pointed out that during the period 1951 to 1987, of the 75 occasions when the President's Rule was imposed, only in 26 cases was it inevitable. Soon after coming to power in 1977, the Janata government dismissed Congress Government in nine states at one go. In 1980 on turning back to power Mrs. Gandhi repeated the performance in nine states governments by the Janata party. The use of Art 356 was made so frequently during Mr. Gandhi's tenure that is showed an intolerant attitude of the Central Government towards the Non-Congress (I) state governments. Presidents rule continued for almost five years (May 1987 – Feb. 1992) in Punjab at a search.

2. Deployment of Central Forces—The deployment of central forces in the state to maintain law and order has been many times without consulting the state Governments. "Public order" is exclusively a state subject. Neither the centre's legislative nor its executive power can transgress into this sphere of state authority. Only if "public order" in flouted on such a large scale in the state as to constitute "internal disturbance" does the centre's duty get activated as defined in Art 355, Ramakrishan Hedge points out that read together, the provision means that it is necessary to invoke the services of any central forces "in aid of the civil war", if the situation gets out of the exclusive control of state, though its primary responsibilities for "Public order" remains. In the exceptional situation, however, the centre shares the responsibilities, since its forces are being used besides the state police.

Deployment of any central force "in aid of the civil power" is exclusively a union subject. The 42nd Amendment (1976) had inserted in the constitution Article 257-A which empowered the union to deploy a central forces "for dealing with any grave situation of law and order in any state". During Janata rule this provision was deleted in 1979 by the 44th Amendment, "A grave situation of law and order" is basically different from the "internal disturbance" envisaged in Article 355.

However, in recent years, after any disturbance of law and order, central minister have felt free to roam in any state for sheer partisan ends, barking orders directly to state officials, ignoring the state ministers, and at times insulting them as well. For instance, on July 25, 1988, the union minister of state for home, Mrs. Ram Dulari Sinha, declared after a visit to Andhra Pradesh, "If such incidents continue the centre will have to intervene".[55]

The obvious meaning of centre's intervention is imposition of President's rule. Hedge points out that far graver incidents have occured in Congress (I) ruled states without either of these steps in redress. A situation in which the state government exist and function at the sweet will of the centres reflects a total negation of federalism. The provision for imposition of President's rule is not in conformity with federal as well as democratic principles. Frequently used for parton ends, it has become an irritating contention between centre-state relations. Hence, there has been a persistent demand for the deletion of the Art 356 from the constitution.

(C) Reservation of Bills—The power of the Governor to reserve a bill, passed by the state legislature, for the Presiden's assent is another cause of tension between the centre and the state. This has especially been so in case where, presumably under the direction of the Central Government the Governor has reserved a Bill against the advise of the state ministry.

Through this provision, contained in Articles 200 and 201, the centre wants to keep watch on the activities of the state. However, Governors have used articles in most of the cases to serve the interests of the rulling party at the centre which led to a good deal of controversy. The opposition ruled states have from time to time raised their voice against the misuse of Articles 200 and 201. In its memorandum to Sarkaria Commission, the Bhartiya Janata Party alleged that the bills have been reserved for consideration of the President in order to create difficulties for the statement governments. In its reply to Sarkaria Commission questionnaire, the West Bengal felt that Articles 200 and 201 have to be deleted or a constitutional amendment should clarify that the Governor would not act in his discretion but only on the advice of the state council of ministers. At the opposition conclave held at Srinagar in 1983, all the opposition parties demanded the removal of the power of the centre to vote through the President the laws passed by the state legislature. In 1983 the four chief ministers from southern states demanded legislatures to enact laws on subjects for which constitutionally they have executive responsibilities without having to seek the President's assent.

(D) Fiscal Matters—The most controversial and ticklish problem between the centre and the state in a federal system is that of financial relations. The demand of the states for greater fiscal autonomy has become one of the most debated issue of the Indian federalism. The tension between centre and states with regard to fiscal relation arises because of comparative powers of taxation, statutory versus discretionary grants, and economic planning.[56]

(i) Comparative Power of Taxation— As against those of states, sources of revenue of the centre are relatively elastic and expansive. The centre also controls vast resources generated through deficit financial, loans from organised money market in the country as well as huge funds of foreign aid. The residuary powers of taxation are also vested with the Central Government. The constitution also authorizes the centre to collect surcharges of taxes to raise additional funds in times of emergency. In practice surcharges has become a permanent feature of income tax structure. The corporate tax, which keeps on expanding in its exclusive preview of the centre. Giving the taxation powers the states do not have sufficient resources of their own to discharge their responsibilities. The gap between state revenues and their expenditure has been increasing, party due to state's own inability to mobilise even their resources which they can, as also incurring wasteful expenses in populism. The states are therefore dependent on central assistance.

(ii) Statutory vs. Discretionary Grants—There are four methods of devolution of funds from the centre to the states (a) obligatory sharing of union taxes on income (b) permissive sharing of union excise duties; (c) assignment of certain union duties and taxes wholly to the states; and (d) provision for giving financial assistance to the state in the form of grants and loans. Articles 280 and 281 provide for the appointment of an independent statutory Finance Commission every fifth year or earlier as the President of India desire.[57] With regard to sharing of resources and assignment of certain resources entirely to the states, Finance Commission was to regulate, co-ordinate and integrate the finance of the Government of India and the states

Governments. Originally, it was intended to cover all the financial transfer of from the centre to the state. However, slowly Planning Commission has been brought in for the purpose and now it plays a more important part in devaluation of resources from the centre to the state. As a completely central institution the Planning Commission is politically influenced and the states have a sense of discrimination in allocation of grants. The Planning Commission's authority to determine the scope and pattern of a major portion of central assistance to states has relegated the role of Finance Commission to a subsidiary one. The centre does not seem to be much serious even about the reduced role of Finance Commission. In addition provision for grants in aid by the centre is purely a political and arbitrary means of devolution. The centre has been making use of this more and that too a controversial manner.

(iii) Economic Planning—The process of planning in India has tended to push the political system to greater centralization due to the central control over resources for development and the preponderance of the centralised planning machinery. The gravest and most harmful consequence of the atrophy of the state's domain in the economic field is in regard to industries and economic planning. For example, according to the constitution, industries are essentially a state subject. Only those industries are to be regulated by the centre, the control of which by the union is declared as expedient in the public interest by Parliament. But industries have been virtually transferred into a union subject without an amendment to the constitution. More than 90 per cent of the organised industries in terms of value output have been brought under the bailiwick of the union. The regulation of industrial activities by the Union Government has several occasions inhibited the setting up of new industries.

In the name of national planning, the centre has been inordinately delaying for political consideration viable and important state projects. On the other hand, centre has been super-imposing its schemes on the states which were deemed by state government to be irrelevant to the conditions prevailing in the states. Hence, the opposition conclave held at Srinagar in 1983, said in a consensus statement that the present authority of the Planning Commission and union Ministry of Finance offering discretionary grants to the states must be drastically reduced.

II. Demand for State Autonomy

The demand for more state autonomy is one of the most controversial issue of the Indian federalism.[58] In the last four decades all consensus and cooperation has been eroded and replaced by a growing politics of confrontation. The states have been developing a sense of deprivation on the ground that the centre has denied them the autonomy that has been granted under the constitution.[59] Frustrated with slow economic progress and regional problems, the leader of regional parties in the state have consistently clamoured for more and more autonomy for the state. There has been much talk for and against autonomy.

Under the Indian constitution it is clear that Indian States are not like the "Indestructible state of an Indestructive union" in the U.S.A. and the constitution of Soviet Union.[60] In Indian federal system, the demand for state autonomy has often become a cover for ideological strategic against the centre. Notably by the communist dominated United Front in Kerala and West Bengal after 4th general election or an expression of aggressive cultural separation as in the case of DMK in Tamil Nadu and Akali Dal in Punjab. Thus the demand for autonomy has assumed the character of state right, which has been the bone of Indian federalism. Immediately after 1967 election there emerged a general criticism on the issue of centre-state relations in view of Congress losing power in eight states and office of Governors becoming controversial.

The state of Jammu and Kashmir is probably the only state in Indian federal system which only enjoy a special status. Punjab's Akali Dal, DMK government of Tamil Nadu, West Bengal, Asom Gana Parishad of Assam are struggling for the same status and autonomy which are given to the state of Jammu and Kashmir under the Indian Constitution of 1950.[61]

In 1969, the Tamil Nadu government took an initiative and appointed Rajamannar committee, to go into the question of centre-state relation and autonomy. The committee submitted its report in 1971. The recommendations made by its included readjustment in schedule VII of the constitution to transfer residuary powers to the states; repeal of the constitution's Article 249 and modification of Art. 252; repeal of Art. 200 and 201 and recognisation of Finance Commission and Planning Commission.

In 1977, the West Bengal Government published a memorandum on centre state relations, according to which in a country like India, with such diversities in race, religion, language and culture, national integration could be achieved through conscious voluntary efforts and devolution of powers to ward off fissiparous indencies. The West Bengal memorandum inter alia demanded that the word 'Federal' should be replace by the word 'union' in the preamble of constitution.

It also suggested the repeal of Articles 356, 357 and 360. According to it, the states consent should be made mandatory for the formation of new state and alteration of areas, boundaries or names of existing states.

In Punjab in 1978, Akali Dal released the revised version of Anandpur Sahib resolution, originally adopted in 1973. This resolution demanded greater state autonomy and wanted to leave very little with the centre. According to it, centre's authority should be confined only to defence, foreign relation, communication, railways and currently and the entire residuary powers be rested in the state.

In the post 1980 period, the opposition increasingly became regional in its orientation, it put forth the demand of state autonomy. Some prominent leaders including Farooq Abdullah, Barnala, Hegde, Rama Rao, Mahanta attended the conclaves arranged for discussion in autonomy at Vijayawada, Srinagar and Delhi.[62]

In the period of 90's the autonomy debate has became "Fight or die" matter. The time has arrived for change in both philosophy and administration in Indian Federal System. The latest and very controversial report of state autonomy is that the Jammu and Kashmir government constituted a committee to examine the issue of state autonomy in a federal way, but on 4 July, 2000 the union cabinet has rejected the resolution of Jammu and Kashmir Assembly demanding autonomy and restoration of the status of to the pre-1953 situation.

Thus, we find the autonomy committee report is a very comprehensive exercise on the subject of centre-state relations with a specific purpose to demand more autonomy within the constitution of India for the state.

Jammu and Kashmir is part of an extremely strategic frontier. This is the only state which enjoys an explict over all special status under Art. 370. But the special status of Jammu and Kashmir itself a main prop of Indian federal structure. Ever since its creation the leaders of Jammu and Kashmir have toyed with idea of "autonomy", recently after rejection the Jammu and Kashmir autonomy resolution, the demand continuous to be a debating point. My work attempts an enquiry into various aspects of the problem of autonomy of the state of Jammu and Kashmir.

References

1. Narang, A.S., *Ethnic identities and federalism*, (Shimla, 1995), p. 71.
2. Quoted in Dr. Chanderpal, *State autonomy in Indian Federation*, Deep and Deep Pub (Delhi, 1984) p. 39.

3. *Ibid.*, p. 18.
4. *Ibid.*, p. 39.
5. Wheare, K.C., *Federal Government*, Oxford University Press, (Oxford, 1967), p. 10.
6. *Ibid.*, p. 123.
7. *Ibid.*, p. 2.
8. Balbir Arora and Douglas. V. Verney (eds.), *Multiple identities in a Single state – Indian Federalism in comparative perspective*, Konark Pub (Delhi, 1995), p. 52.
9. Dr. Chanderpal, *State autonomy in Indian Federal System*. Deep and Deep Pub (New Delhi, 1984) p. 20.
10. Bernard, Schwarts, *American constitution law*, 1995, pp. 163-164.
11. Watts, Ronald, *New Federalism – Experiment in the Commonwealth*, Oxford University Press (Oxford, 1966) p. 20.
12. Livingstone, W.S., *Federalism and constitutional change*, Oxford University Press, (Oxford 1956), p. 25.
13. *Ibid*, p. 2.
14. W.H. Ricker's view cited in Chanderpal, *State autonomy in Indian Federal system*, Deep and Deep Pub, (New Delhi, 1984) p. 20.
15. *Ibid.*, p. 21.
16. Balbir Arora and Douglas V. Verney (edt), *Multiple identities in a Single State – Indian federalism in comparative perspective*, Konark Pub (New Delhi, 1995) p. 18.
17. A.V. Dicey's view cited in Chanderpal, *State autonomy in Indian Federal System*, Deep and Deep Pub (New Delhi, 1984), p. 23.
18. Wheare, K.C., *Federal government*, Oxford University Press, (Oxford, 1967), p. 56.
19. *Ibid.*, p. 56.
20. Balbir Arora and Douglas V. Verney (eds.), *Multiple identities in a Single State – Indian Federalism in Comparative perspective*, Konark Publication (New Delhi, 1995), p. 53.
21. Wheare K.C., *Federal government*, Oxford University Press, (Oxford, 1967) p. 21.
22. Balbir Arora and Douglas V. Verney, *op.cit...* p. 56.
23. *Ibid.*, p. 57.
24. Livingstone, W.S., *Federalism and constitutional change*, Oxford University Press (Oxford, 1956), p. 15.

25. Alexandrowich's View cited in Chanderpal, *State autonomy in Indian Federal System*, Deep and Deep Pub, (New Delhi, 1984), p. 36.
26. Singhvi, L.M., *Preface to union states relation in India*, I.C.P.S., (Delhi, 1969), p. 16.
27. Wheare, K.C., *Federal government*, Oxford University Press, (Oxford, 1967), p. 27.
28. Tiwari, O.P., *Federalism in centre-state relation in India–Toward a New era of Mutual Co-ordination*, Deep and Deep Pub, (New Delhi, 1996), p. 47.
29. *Ibid.*, p. 48.
30. Bagchi, Amaresh, Rethinking Federalism: an overview of current debate with some reflection in Indian Context, *Economic and Political Weekly*, 19.8.2000, p. 3032.
31. Balbir Arora and Douglas V. Verny (eds.), *Multiple identities in a single state, Indian federalism in comparative perspective*, Konark Publication, (Delhi, 1979), p. 71.
32. *Ibid.*, p. 72.
33. *Ibid.*, p. 72.
34. *Ibid.*, p. 73.
35. *Ibid.*, p. 73.
36. *Ibid.*, p. 73.
37. *Ibid.*, p. 74.
38. *Ibid.*, p. 78.
39. Dr Sharma, R.N., *Kashmir autonomy – an exercise in centre state relation*, Subhi Pub, (New Delhi, 2000) pp. 106-107.
40. Balbir Arora and Dauglas V. Verney, *Op. cit*, p. 80.
41. Hariram, *Special status in Indian federalism*, Seema Pub, (Delhi, 1983) p. 31.
42. Balbir Arora and Douglas V. Verney (eds.), *Multiple identities in a single state-Indian Federalism in comparative perspective*, Konark Pub (New Delhi, 1995) p. 85.
43. *Ibid.*, p. 86.
44. Article 40 directs the state to organise village punchayats and endow them with such powers, and authority as may be necessary to enable them to function as units of self government. In the distribution of legislative powers, local government has been entrusted to the state.
45. Balbir Arora and Douglas V. Verney (eds.), *op. cit.* p. 91.

46. Balbir Arora and Douglas V. Verney (eds.), *op. cit*, p. 92.
47. Singh M.P., "Toward a more federalized parliamentary system in India: Explaining functional change", *Pacific Affairs* Vol. 74, No. 4, University of British Colombia, Canada, 2001-2002, p. 560.
48. *Ibid.*, p. 560
49. Singh M.P., *op. cit*, p. 554.
50. *Ibid.*, p. 568.
51. Dr. Chanderpal, *State autonomy in Indian Federal System*, Deep and Deep Pub, (New Delhi, 1984), p. 24.
52. Soli Sorabjee's view cited in R.N. Sharma, *Kashmir autonomy an exercise in centre-state relation*, Subhi Pub, (New Delhi, 2000), p. 98.
53. *Ibid.*, p. 99.
54. *Ibid.*, p. 99.
55. Ibid, p. 101.
56. *Ibid.*, p. 102.
57. Basu, D.D., *The constitution of India*, Prentice Hall of India (New Delhi, 1999), p. 34.
58. Dr. Chanderpal, *State autonomy in Indian Federalism*, Deep and Deep Pub (New Delhi, 1984), p. 38.
59. Dr. Sharma, R.N., *Kashmir autonomy an exercise in centre-state relation*, Subhi Pub, (New Delhi, 2000), p. 103.
60. Dr. Chanderpal, *op. cit*, p. 38.
61. Puri, Balraj, "Emerging contours of peace in Jammu and Kashmir", *Mainstream*, Jan 27, 2001. p. 17.
62. Dr. Sharma, R.N., *Kashmir autonomy – an exercise in centre-state relation*, Subhi Pub, (Delhi, 2000) p. 106.

2

Jammu and Kashmir : An Introduction

Jammu and Kashmir, which occupies an extremely strategic position on the Indian frontiers, is the only state in the Indian union with a Muslim majority. The credit for founding and consolidating the state of Jammu and Kashmir, goes to Maharaja Gulab Singh. According to Sisir Gupta, it was he who "laid the foundation for a strong personal rule is a difficult area of the country"[1] . He gave this state a "separate political entity" in the year 1846 by concluding the treaty of Amritsar with the British Government.[2] Under Gulab Singh, the condition of the people on the whole improved and they began to breathe an atmosphere of relative freedom and security. But culturally, the state presented three isolated peculiarities, since the population of Jammu is predominantly Hindus, that of Kashmir valley predominantly Muslim and the Ladakhis are mainly Buddhist. Consequently, mutual incongruencies and dissimilarities "had great potentiality for conflicts". In addition to these internal conditions, externally the location of this state, in the words of Hayek, is "in a strategic position which makes it the centre of several intense international rivalries"[3] Jammu and Kashmir covers an area of 222,236 sq. km. one of the largest states of India, including 76,114 sq. km. under Pak occupation, 5130 sq. km handed over by Pakistan to China, and 39,605 sq. km. illegally occupied by China. The net area with India is 101,387 sq. km[4]. The population of the state in 2001 was 10,069,917, which included 5,300,574 males and 4,769,343 females[5]. These figures exclude Pak and Chinese occupied areas. The density of population, at 99 persons per sq. km., is one of the lowest in India.

The State Flag (Red in Colour with white strip)

Source: Stuart Notholt and Jorge Candeias, 11 December, 1998.

Area of Jammu and Kashmir

1.	Total Area of Jammu and Kashmir State	2,22,236 sq.km.
2.	Area under illegal occupation of Pakistan	78,114 sq. km.
3.	Area illegally handed over by Pakistan to China	5,180 sq. km.
4.	Area under illegal occupation of China	37,555 sq. km.
5.	Area under effective control of India	101387 sq. km.

Population Distribution, Percentage, Decadal Growth, Sex Ratio, Population Density and Literacy Rate; 2001[6].

Population 2001	*Decadal Growth*	*Sex Ratio*	*Population density*	*Literacy rate*
10,069,917 (No Census conducted in 1991)	29.04	900 (Female per 1000 Male)	99	65.75 (M) 41.85 (F)

Jammu and Kashmir

Administrative Divisions			
Number of District	14	Number of town	75
Number of Sub District[1]	59	Number of villages	6,652

Population 2001	*Decadal Growth*	*Sex Ratio*	*Population density*	*Literacy rate*
10,069,917 (No Census conducted in 1991)	29.04	900 (Female per 1000 Male)	99	65.75 (M) 41.85 (F)

Jammu and Kashmir

Administrative Divisions			
Number of District	14	Number of town	75
Number of Sub District[1]	59	Number of villages	6,652
Area (in Square Km)	101,387	Population density (per sq km)	100
Number of Households	1,568,519	Household size	6.5
Population		*Population (0-6 years)*	
Persons	10,143,700	Persons	1,485,803
Males	5,360,926	Males	765,394
Females	4,782,774	Females	720,409
Sex Ratio[2]	892	Percentage of Population in the age group of 0-6 years	14.6
Rural	7,627,062	Sex Ratio (0-6 years)[3]	941
Urban	2,516,638		
Percentage of urban population	24.8		

Scheduled Caste (SC) Population[4]		*Scheduled Tribe(ST) Population*[4]	
Persons	770,155	Persons	1,105,979
Males	403,256	Males	578,949
Females	366,899	Females	527,030
Percentage of SC	7.6	Percentage of ST	10.9
Literates		*Literacy rate (age 7+)*[5]	
Persons	4,807,286	Persons	55.5
Males	3,060,628	Males	66.6
Females	1,746,658	Females	43.0

Economic activity		*Category of Workers*	
Number of Workers		Cultivators	1,591,514
Persons	3,753,815	Agricultural Labourers	246,421
Males	2,679,941	In household industries	234,472
Female	1,073,874	Other Workers	1,681,408
Work participation rate (in %)[6]	37.0	Cultivators (in %)[7]	42.4
Number of main workers	2,608,668	Agricultural Labourers (in %)[7]	6.6
Number of marginal workers	1,145,147	In household industries (in %)[7]	6.2
Number of Non-workers	6,389,885	Other workers (in %)	44.8

Source : Census of India 2001.

District-wise Distribution of Area, Population Scheduled Castes and Scheduled Tribles-2001

S. No.	*District*	*Area (Sq Km.)*	*Population*	*Scheduled Castes*	*Scheduled Tribibes*
Total	14		10,143,700	7,70,155	1,105,979
1	Anantnag	3984	11,72,434	541	1,01,143
2	Badgam	1371	6,29,309	474	14,550
3	Baramulla	4588	11,69,780	377	83,896
4	Doda	11691	6,91,929	62,962	79,751
5	Jammu	3097	15,88,772	3,94,904	53,304
6	Kargil	14036	1,19,307	139	1,05,377
7	Kupwara	2379	6,50,393	75	51,753
8	Kathua	2651	5,50,084	1,27,369	34,174
9	Leh	82665	1,17,232	618	96,174
10	Pulwama	1398	6,52,607	97	21,496
11	Srinagar	2228	12,02,447	1,065	45,427
12	Punch	1674	3,72,613	952	1,49,018
13	Rajouri	2630	4,83,284	38,526	1,60,049
14	Udhampur	4550	7,43,509	1,42,061	1,09,867

Source : Census of India, 2001

Principal Languages of the State Persons Speaking Principal Language

Language	*Kashmir*	*Jammu*	*Ladakh*	*Total*
Kashmiri	21,75,810	1,95,114	769	23,71,693
Dogri	8,161	1,30,845		11,39,006
Gojri	95,096	2,23,194		3,18,289
Pahari	51,065	1,95,377		2,46,442
Punjabi	45,890	1,12,005	523	1,58,418
Hindi	11,954	28,458		40,412
Urdu	4,521	7,057		11,578

Source : Census of India, 1981

Religious Composition of Population

Year	*Hindu*	*Muslim*	*Sikhs*	*Buddhists*
1891	27.20	70.51	-	1.17
1901	23.71	74.16	-	1.10
1911	21.83	75.94	1.00	1.24
1921	20.16	76.75	-	1.18
1931	20.19	77.28	1.38	1.06
(Total Pop.)1931	*Hindu*	*Muslim*	*Sikhs*	*Buddhists*
3646243	736222	2817636	50662	38724

1961–1981

Year	*Division*	*Total Population*	*Hindus*	*Proportion Muslims*	*Sikhs*	*Buddhists*
1961	Kashmir	1988089	4.51	92.22	0.84	—
	Jammu	1572887	58.71	38.05	2.94	—
	Ladakh	88651	0.64	45.43	2.04	53.81
	J & K	3649627	28.45	68.29	1.77	1.36
1971	Kashmir	2435701	4.57	92.03	1.16	—
	Jammu	2075640	62.05	33.79	3.67	—
	Ladakh	105291	1.09	46.66	0.34	51.82
	J & K	4616632	30.41	65.85	2.29	1.25
1981	Kashmir	3134904	3.95	94.96	1.05	.06
	Jammu	2718113	66.32	29.60	3.68	0.04
	Ladakh	134372	2.63	46.05	0.24	50.88
	J & K	5987389	32.24	64.19	2.23	1.16

2001

	Hindu	*Muslim*	*Christian*	*Sikh*	*Buddhists*	*Jains*
Population	30,05,349	6,793,240	20,299	207,154	113,787	2518
Percentage	29.6	67.0	0.2	2.0	1.1	0.0
Literacy rate	71.2	47.3	74.8	84.4	59.7	86.5

Source : Census of India, 1981, 2001.

The State of Jammu and Kashmir geographically is the most important state in Indian Union, with Afghanistan, Pakistan, Soviet Union and China as its neighbours. The state is situated between 32°17' and 36°17' north latitude and 73°26' and 83°30' east longitude. Geographically, the state can be divided into four zones. First, the mountainous and semi mountainous plain commonly known as Kandi Belt, the Second, hills including Siwalike ranges, the third, mountain of Kashmir Valley and Pir Panchal range and the fourth Tibetan tract of Ladhakh and Kargil[7] .

The state of Jammu and Kashmir, which had earlier been under Hindu rules and Muslim Sultans became part of the Mogul Empire under Akbar from 1586. After a period of Afghan rule from 1756, it was annexed by the Sikh Rules of Punjab in 1819. In 1820 Ranjeet Singh handed over the territory of Jammu to Gulab Singh[8] .

Kashmir was the creation of the first half of 19th century of a Dogra Chieftain Gulab Singh, who had won the favour of Ranjeet Singh the builder of the great Sikh Empire. After the Battle of Sabraon in 1846, Kashmir was handed over to Gulab Singh[9] .

By the year 1497, the population of valley of Kashmir had been struggling against alien rulers for about 370 years[10]. Their struggle, according to Balraj Puri, had achieved "a genuine non-communal nationalism" which was not even accommodated in the mainstream of Muslim politics of India before independence." This reasoning seems to be sound, for the Kashmiris have their well recorded history and rich culture, wherein they have shown least signs of losing their nationality and rich cultural identity. In this behalf Walter Lawrence had rightly observed: "It is a matter of surprise that under rapid transitions of Government, varying in race, religion and language, the people of valley should have retained their peculiar nationality unimpaired". Lawrence refers to the times when the Kashmiris were under the yoke of alien rulers. After having seen centuries of servitude, the Kashmiris in 1947 saw a new hope in some sort of special status which was to be the net result of the demand of National Conference for "freedom before accession". This demand, when it acquired a place in Indian constitution, became one of the most debated and controversial issue of the Indian federal system.

The state of Jammu and Kashmir is probably the only state in Indian federal structure, which only enjoy a special status. Punjab's Akali Dal, DMK government of Tamilnadu, West Bengal and Assam are struggling for the same status and autonomy, which are given to the state of Jammu and Kashmir under the constitution of India[13]

Demand for State Autonomy of Jammu and Kashmir

The demand for more state autonomy is one of the most controversial issues of Indian federation. There has been much talk for and against autonomy. The first fact about state autonomy that has to be accepted is that it is not independence under the Indian constitution it is clear that the Indian states do not enjoy the right to secede as the republics in the Soviet Union, with their theoritical right to secede when we talk of state autonomy now, we are not thinking of the provincial autonomy of the Government of India Act or university autonomy, of attenuated autonomous institutions with no financial powers, or of the imagined autonomy of a broadcasting corporation of which any government is afraid under the state list of the seventh schedule of the constitution, it means that the state enjoy vast legislative and thereby executive powers. Thus by state autonomy we mean that these powers should be real, if not enlarged.

The question arises how far the state–legislatures and the state governments enjoy in practice the autonomy, which they enjoy in theory. This depends on how effectively the constitution of our country is working, instead of being reduced to ritualism. Next to the constitution, the most important factors that affect autonomy is the impact which the political system, more specifically the party system, makes on our constitutional system. It is not so much the text of the constitution as the working of the parties that makes a difference of the working of the autonomy of the states with one party in control throughout our country for several years, autonomy of states almost ceased to exist in practice. With different parties at the centre and in the states in power, autonomy is asserted and is necessary. The either case, autonomy should be real, but in present practice this fact is being completely forgotten. State legislative parties are subjected to long rolling, and almost all state ministers are nominated by the centre. This itself detracts from autonomy and discourages it.

The compulsion of planning have made the state more dependent than they are required to be under the constitution. Thus, unless the states are given more sources of revenue, instead of being allocated shares in divisible or indivisible pools, they would be best to the mercies of finance commission and the vagaries of party politics.

However, autonomy has gained further relevance and importance recently in the context of state of Jammu and Kashmir.

Let us talk about the question of autonomy in the context of Jammu and Kashmir. It is of two types. One demanded by the committee appointed by the government of Dr. Abdullah, but it has been rejected by centre on the plea that the state already been enjoying sufficient autonomy as compared to other states in the Indian union and this approach will lead to imbalance and disequilibrium. The Azadi that is being demanded by the militants is not within the constitution and under the influence of Pakistan. The scope for both the demands are different but one thing is clear, i.e., non-interference of the Central Government in its day-today administration is essential.

Autonomy Vr Azadi Vr Self-determination–Autonomy Needs to be Defined

The people of Kashmir talk about Azadi, people talk about self-determination, they talk about autonomy. But it is not clear what is exactly meant by Azadi and self-determination and what is the content of the autonomy.

So, what does Azadi in Kashmir mean? Or what does for that matter self-determination mean? What is the kind of autonomy that is feasible, given our own desire to give Kashmir maximum autonomy.

What is self determination? As a general term, it is on expression of the aspiration to rule one self and not to be ruled by others. The right of self-determination means the right of the people to shape their own political economic and cultural destines[14]. The Indian state of Jammu and Kashmir is one of the areas of the world besides Tibet, East Timor, Palestine etc. with respect to which the demand for the right of self determination has been raised from time to time. Leaders of the secessionist groups like All India Hurriyat Conference (AIHC) and the Jammu Kashmir Liberation Front (JKLF) have been airing the demand of Azadi or Independence from the India. They argue that their demand is based on self-determination of the people of Jammu and Kashmir that is neither an Indian colony nor a self-governing territory in any sense. It is an internal part of India like any other state so, the question of the right to self determination in the context of Jammu and Kashmir is a misnomer[15]. Those who are demanding the right to self-determination for the people of Jammu and Kashmir either do not understand the proper meaning of the term self- determination or knowingly misuse it for ulterior motives.

Let us talk about Azadi. This is not the first time that a state has demanded autonomy in its administration. States in India have always demanded more and more authority for their internal administration. But the demand of Kashmir is totally different from any other state of the Indian Union. Many leaders of the state of Jammu and Kashmir are demanding for Azadi from the Indian Union, and many people of the state wanted "Azadi" and not autonomy. It is easy to demand Azadi, but how will the state sustain itself? Where will the money for development come from? Who will defend the border from China, Pakistan and even India, if Azadi become reality, then only the rules of guns would prevail. The Chief Minister of Jammu and Kashmir (Dr. Farooq Abdullah) also said that "they are not demanding Azadi from India, they are fighting a battle for survival, Delhi must realise that and make an all out effort to tell the people that they are an integral part of India"[16]. He also said that "The people, in their part, must decide whether they want to be a part of India or not"[17].

The Autonomy demand has now become a debate. The current controversy and the debate around the issue of Autonomy and passed in State Assembly by an overwhelming majority, it is a very major issue before the country and shall continue to occupy centre stage for the conference colleague have so far referred only very briefly to that musky.

It is essential that the full story of five decades long episode recaited and responsible for all the mistake and wrong politics be fully allotted to where they belong. Such grave errors and crimes against the people cannot be allowed to remain hidden under the carpet as it were. It is essential to recall briefly all the significant stages in this awful history.

Historical Background of Autonomy*

The state of Jammu and Kashmir came into being as a single political entity in 1846 under what is called the treaty of Amritsar. (Till 1846, Jammu, Kashmir and Ladakh were separate and distinct areas different rulers)[18]. The British government, vide this treaty concluded on 16th May of that year, transferred and made over, "for ever, in independent possession, to Maharaja Gulab Singh, and the *heir male of his body*, all the hilly or mountainous country, which its

---

* Balraj Pori * Jammu and Kashmir – Triumph and tragedy of Indian federalization, 1981.

dependencies, situated to the eastward of the river Indus, and westward of the river Ravi"[19]. In consideration of this transfer, Gulab Singh paid "to the British government the sum of seventy five lacs of rupees"[20].

While Jammu and Ladakh were already being ruled by Gulab Singh, the valley of Kashmir, which the Lahore Durbar had sold to the British government was transferred by the latter to the Dogra ruler who acquired it after stiff local resistance. The boundaries of the new state were further extended but its ruler through a number of military expeditions, of course, with the concurrence of the British Government. Ranbir Singh, son of Gulab Singh added Gilgit in the life time of his father of his dominion. Later during the role of Maharaja Pratap Singh, grandson of Gulab Singh, his forces defeated the rulers of Chitral in 1891 and of Hunza and Nagar in 1875 who accepted the suzerainty of the Dogra Darbar[21].

While the treaty transferred the state to Gulab Singh "in independent possession", it unambiguously specified British supremacy over his rule. Its Art 4, for instance, committed the Maharaja not to change the limits of his territories "without the concurrence of British government." He undertook, vide the next article, to refer to "the arbitration of the British government any dispute or question they may arise between himself and the government of Lahore or any other neighbouring state and to abide by the decision of any British Government."

According to Article 6, Maharaja engaged "for himself and heirs to join, with the whole of his military force, the British troops, when employed waiting the hills or on the territories adjoining his possessions". He further engaged, in Article 7, "never to take or retain, in his service any British subject, nor the subject of any European or American state, without the consent of the British Government." Under Article 9, the British government undertook the responsibility of protecting the territories of Maharaja Gulab Singh from external enemies. Finally and more specifically the Maharaja acknowledged, vide Art. 10, "the Supremacy of the British government"and in token of such supremacy, agreed to "present annually to the British government one horse, twelve perfect shawl goats of approved breed and three pairs of Kashmiri shawls"[22].

Special Status Under British Raj

However, a distinct feature of state relationship with the paramount power was absence of any provision for stationing British resident in the state which was the practice in other princely states of the country.

The residents were representatives of the central government in the states under British Raj as the governors are in independent India; except that they had far greater powers-undefined are arbitrary– than the latter now have, which is bound by the letter of the constitution, albeit without a similar ceremonial status. The state thus enjoyed a sort of special status within the British India Empire.

The Ango-Afghan war of 1878 and the gradual extension of the Russian empire almost upto the borders of the state increased its strategic value for British empire. After consolidating their hold over the rest of India, directly or through Loyal princes, and in particular entrenching their administration in the neighbouring Punjab, the British were now anxious to extend their sway over Jammu and Kashmir state as well.

While Gulab Singh and his son and successor Maharaja Ranbir Singh resisted proposal to station a British Resident in the state, the British government succeeded in doing so after the latter's death in 1885.

Lord Kimberley, British Secretary of state for India, in a communication to Lord Rippon, the Viceroy of India, dated 23 May 1884, confirmed that no Resident was appointed in the state in 1846, nor was suggestion of his appointment pressed in 1873, because it did not justify ' disregarding objections which were expressed by authorities entitled to respect" (referring to Kashmir Darbar). But he added that in the interval circumstances had greatly changed, inter alia, due to " the course of events beyond the border, which have materially increased the political importance of Kashmir". He, accordingly, adviced the viceroy, "to proceed in the matter at any time after the death of Maharaja Ranbir Singh"[23].

End of Autonomy

The new Maharaja Pratap Singh like his father and grandfather, resisted this encroachment of his power, but gave way in the end. The decision of British government to appoint a resident in the State "evoked a remonstrance from the Maharaja." They expected "some opposition in this matter on the part of the Durbar." 'The Maharaja did not want any interference from any quarter or any, the smallest, diminution of the long enjoyed right and dignity of this state"[24]. In the reply to the objections of the Maharaja it was 'properly pointed case of other great princes and chiefs of India, cannot be regarded either as derogatory to the dignity of the Kashmir state, or as indicating a desire on the part of the paramount power to interfere unnecessarily in its internal affairs"[25]

The British fully exploited rivalry in the royal family between the Maharaja and his brother Raja Amar Singh, to increase their hold on the states. As the Maharaja resisted further British attempts on the autonomy of the state, a plan was prepared to deprive him of power.

It was alleged that he was in league with Russia and Dalip Singh (the dethroned ruler of the Punjab), and that he had conspired to get Sir Trevor Chinchale Plowden, the British residents in the state (who had been transferred by the time) his own brother Ram Singh and Amar Singh and one of the Maharanis murdered.

The Maharaja, in utter frustration, declared that, if his own brothers were determined to ruin him with false accusations, he would submit to his fate. He gave his consent to such arrangements, as were proposed to him. He signed, or as is more correct, was made to sign an Irshad, which amounted to an addict of resignation on 8 March 1889. According to it, he relieved himself of all part in the administration and placed it in the hands of a five member council of regency for a period of five years. In a letter to the viceroy dated 14 May, 1889, he said, he "was obliged to write what was desired, rather, demanded" by the Resident. The Foreign Secretary, in his letter of 1 April, 1889, conveyed the decision of the British government to the Resident in Kashmir which inter alia stated that "full power of (the state) government will be vested in a council consisting of Maharaja's brothers and three or four officials selected by the Government of India". The president of the council, he added, will be Raja Amar Singh (younger brother of the Maharaja and a willing and trusted British instrument in his abdication whom Pratap Singh referred to as his "chief enemy"). "I am further to request you", the letter continued, "to make the Maharaja and the members of council thoroughly understand that although the council will have full power of administration, they will be expected to exercise those powers under the guidance of the resident. They will take no step of importance without consulting him, and they will follow his advice whenever it may be offered."

In its very first meeting held on 18 April 1889 the council dutifully declared: "the Resident shall be the final referee in all matters and may veto any resolution passed by the council or suspend action may veto any resolution passed by the council or suspend action thereon pending further explanation."

Maharaja Pratap Singh's "Voluntary abidication" aroused suspicion and also earned him considerable sympathy in Indian and British political circle; particularly after the *Amrit Bazar Patrika*, Culcutta, published in October 1889 secret officials papers which established that 'His Highness was not deposed because he resigned, or oppressed his people, but because Gilgit was wanted for strategical purposes by the British Government". British M.P., Brandlaugh asked why the government of India "virtually annexed the state of Kashmir to British India, and subjected its ruler to great indignities". His adjournment motion in the house of common on 3 July was supported by 88 members while 226 members opposed it.

Restoration of Maharaja

Maharaja's powers were then nominally restored. In 1891 he was appointed the president of the council. But Raja Amar Singh was made the vice-president, who with British blessings was more effective. Otherwise too, the resident remained the virtual ruler.

Meanwhile Gilgit Agency had been set-up in 1889, which the Maharaja had resisted till his abdication. It consisted of the Gilgit Wazarat , the Chiefship of Hunza and Nagar, the Chials district in Indus Valley and the Government of Punjab, Yasin and Ashokoman. It was under the overall charge of a political agent who was to be British.

In Sept. 1891, the Resident informed His Highness and the President of the council that it had been decided, in view of Russian movements in the Pamirs and the attitude of Hunza, to re-inforce the Gilgit Agency, by troops of the British Government "who will cooperate with the Kashmir forces in case of trouble"[26]. His Highness, who had learnt his lesson from her earlier experience after his resistance to the British proposal regarding Gilgit submitted in reply as under:-

"From my childhood I had been continuously taught by my late lamented father to spend my life even if necessary in loyalty to the crown ... It is Government of India great kindness to aid the state by their own troops in the frontier"[27].

The gesture of Maharaja was appreciated. In 1905, the Viceroy Lord Curzon abolished the council and partially restored his powers. Raja Amar Singh, who remained the Prime Minister and the commander-in-chief of the states forces, of course, wielded the real power and could be trusted to took after the British interest.

The Maharaja, too, missed no opportunity to lag behind in proclaiming his loyalty to the British and his willingness to honour the wishes of the British Government. He, for instance, issued strong warning to and look prompt action against his subjects suspected of any affinity or sympathy with the national freedom movement. He indicated the legal and other measures he was contemplating "to meet the dangers (of sedition) which, any day it might become my duty to face, specially Kashmir being restored (sic.) to be men of different nationalities and ideas".

The Government of India pleased with such protestation of loyalty decided in 1914 to release the central that the Resident exercised on the finances of the state. In Sept. 1920 the Maharaja made plea for restoration of further powers to him. In return, the Government of India demanded an assurance that "the Maharaja would accept the advice of the Resident in administrative matters, whenever it was offered and would also inform the Resident of any important changes in the existing rules and regulations and the frontier policy"[28]. The Maharaja accepted these conditions and thereupon all his powers were restored to him on 4 February 1921.

The Treaty of Amritsar, which according to many historians conferred a special status on the ruler of Jammu and Kashmir state in the princely order of India, thus, continued to be eroded. After three quarters of a century the state was reduced to a status of an illusory autonomy, which retained the Legal Skeleton intact but robbed it of political flesh and blood.

Reassertion of Autonomy

After the death of Pratap Singh in 1925, his Nephew Hari Singh ascended the throne. Pratap Singh, who had no son, was not allowed to nominate his adopted son as his heir. After his death in 1915, Raja Amar Singh's son, Hari Singh was recognized by the British government to be his successor. The new ruler was not as passive and docile a personality as his predecessor was and seemed imbued with a desire to restore the autonomy of the state. "The power of the Residency continued neither in the same form nor to the same extent as before"[29]. He won an important concession from British government which restored to the courts of His Highness full criminal jurisdiction over all Indian visitors and full civil jurisdiction over all persons in the state irrespective of their nationality. Earlier British or British Indian subjects were subject to the authority of the residuary courts[30].

During the reign of Maharaja Pratap Singh an agitation with the slogan 'state for state's people" had started, this agitation grew stronger as time went by, in 1927, the agitation was so strong that the Maharaja was forced to issue a degination of the term "State Subject"[31].

In January 1927, Maharaja Hari Singh issued an order that none who was not a '*hereditary state subject*'[32] should be appointed to posts under the government without his own express permission. The term hereditary state subject was held to mean and include all persons born and residing within the state before the commencement of reign of Maharaja Gulab Singh and those who settled therein before the Samvat 1984 (1885 A.D) and since then been permanently residing therein.

"In pursuance of the identical policy he had also instructed that grants of Lord for building and other purposes were to go only to the state subjects. Non-hereditary state subjects were debarred from acquiring immovable property in the state or selling or transferring it to other than hereditary state subjects."[33]

In regard to contracts also it was decreed that the claims of state subjects should have priority over those of non-subjects even if, "other things being equal, the bid of the latter is five per cent more favourable." Further, the Department of Civil Supplies was instructed that preference should be given to indigenous products.

These measures guaranteed the rights of the permanent citizens of the state in the same spirit and almost the same manner as they are being done now under Article 370 of the Indian constitution. But unlike the present position, the idea of autonomy and right of the state subjects at the time appealed mainly to Hindus of the state, whose sense of local patriotism was aroused to neutralise the impact of the freedom movement on them. Kashmiri Pandits take credit for initiating a movement known as 'Kashmir for Kashmiris', under the leadership of Shanker Lal Kaul, for inducting the Maharaja to enact the state subject law. The Dogra Sabha, the first organised party of the people of the state, had launched a similar movement in Jammu.

Muslim Apposition to Autonomy

But the Muslims of the state and outside, apposed the idea. They were afraid that if service opportunities were limited to the people of the state, Hindus, particularly the Kashmiri Pandits (all Kashmiri Hindus are Brahmins and are called Pandits) would be the main beneficiaries as the number of educated Muslim in the state was limited. Kashmiri Pandits, who were 1.7 per cent of the population of the state according to the census of 1921, "constituted 80 per cent of all those who had received or were receiving higher education"[33].

As early in April 1912, Khan Bahadur Yusuf Shah, MLC Punjab and president of the central standing committee, Muslim Kashmiri Conference, Lahore, in a letter to the Maharaja said that annual Muslim Kashmiri Conference held at Amritsar and attended by two thousand Kashmiris had in a resolution hoped that he would be pleased to devise means to enable Muslim subjects to participate in the benefit from the free education introduced by him. "For this larger number of Muslim teachers is appointed." The resolution pleaded that Muslims from Punjab be employed in the state if they were not available in the state[34]. Revenue Minister, Rai Bahadur Dr. A. Mitra, informed the chief minister in a letter dated 13 January 1913 that there were only 40 Mohammadan teachers. More could not be appointed also qualified applicant were few. R.B. Pandit Radha Kant, Judge High Court, expressed the view, in a communication to the chief minister, on 7 February 1913, 'I do not think it is necessary to import Punjabi Mohammadans simply because they were Mohammadans."[35]

The Revenue Minister agreed that ordinary posts outsiders should not be appointed. But there should be exception for Education Department. He said, "It would benefit H.H.'s Mohammadans subjects if Mohammadans teacher were to be appointed in as schools as possible. The only effective way to make education popular among the Mohammadans is to approach the ignorant masses through teachers professing their own religion in whom they will naturally have greater confidence."

The Maharaja closed the controversy with the following remarks: "I do not wish to draw a line of demarcation between my Hindu and Mohammadans subjects what I wish to lay stress on is fitness for service. Mohammadans or Hindus not belonging to the state, have no claim on the state, in preference to state subjects."

The Muslim Kashmiri Conference put on the record its sense of disappointment at the answer of the Maharaja and considered "it a clear manifestation of the gross indifference of the state towards claims of its Muslim subjects". Notwithstanding continuous protests from Muslim leaders of Kashmir and their sympathizers in Punjab, the state subject law was formally enforced in 1927.

The issue was again raised before the Dalal Commission which enquired into the disturbances in Kashmir on 13 July 1931. It recommended modification in the state subject law[36]. All India Muslim Conference also pressed the right of 'Mussalmans of British India, especially of the Punjab, to be taken in state service so long, at least, as the local Mussalmans themselves remained unqualified."[37]

"It has been seen that Maharaja Hari Singh is an intense and uncompromising pro Kashmiri"[38], concluded G.S. Raghwan in the *warning of Kashmir*, "The effort made by His Highness", he writes "with a considerable degree of success to reverse the virtually mitigated internal autonomy of the state were part of a well thought scheme."[39] But the Maharaja's urge for more autonomy for the state and special safeguards for its citizens lacked support of its Kashmiri Muslim intelligentsia.

In this context the choice of a Hindu ruler for a Muslim majority Kashmir, by the British under the treaty of Amritsar. seems deliberate. The secretary of state for India, the Earl of Kimberley admitted it in so many words in his letter to the Government of India dated 23 May 1884, according to which transfer to Sovereignty of Kashmir to Hindu ruling family implied justification for "the intervention of the British Government on behalf of the Mohammadan population." Thus the Hindu ruler and his Muslim subject could act as a check on the aspiration of each other. While the ruler prevented emotional and political links between Muslims of the state with Muslim countries like Afghanistan and intervening Muslim areas. Muslim discontent within the state could always be used by the central government as an excuse to interfere in its affairs and to bring on assertive ruler to book.

The Muslim of the state also tended to took to the Resident and the viceroy for the readdress of their grievances against their own ruler. The list of demands submitted by a delegation of Kashmiri Muslims to the viceroy Lord Reading during his visit to state in 1924, for instance, included a demand for restoring the power of the Maharaja to the Resident[40].

Centre-State Tension

Maharaja Hari Singh seemed to suspect British hand in forment discontent in the state. In a proclamation to his subjects on 9 July 1931, he demanded of the outside people "not to interfere in any way in matters concerning my state and my people, as I do not interfere in matters concerning British India and British Indians". "The whole basic of political action", he warned, "is impaired if one political unit interferes in the domestic concerns of another"[41]. These comments imply assertion of an almost equal status and a protest against the attitude of the British governments, with which Maharaja's relations were far from cordial.

There were two specific reasons which are believed to have strained their mutual relations. First was Maharaja Hari Singh's oft quoted statement in the First Round table conference in London in November 1930 which was not viewed with favour by the British. He had said: "As Indians and loyal to the land whence they derived their birth and infact nurture, the princes stood as solidly as the rest of their countrymen for India's enjoyment of a position of honour and equality in the British Commonwealth of nations."[42] The other possible provocation was Maharaja's move for the return of administration of the Gilgit Agency which was taken over by the British political agent in 1889. The settled part of the area called the Gilgit Wazarat was still administrated by the Kashmir Durbar. The British were in no mood to loose the grip that they had acquired over the state during the lifetime of the late Maharaja Pratap Singh. They took a rather serious view of the assertive mood of Maharaja.

The Muslim discontent within the state supported by the Muslim leaders of British India, particularly of the Punjab, obviously facilitated the task of the British government to cut the ambitions of the young prices to size.

Instead of getting back the political Agency of Gilgit, the Maharaja was forced to further surrender to the British India Government the settled part of Gilgit Wazarat on 26 March 1935 on a sixty years lease. Earlier he had also yielded to the British pressure to appoint Lt. Col. E.J.D. Colvin of the Foreign and political department of the British India Government as the first British Prime Minister of his state in March 1933. What lends credence to the theory – that the Maharaja seemed to share–regarding British encouragement to the discontent within the state was the fact that its leading supporters outside the state were Loyal British subjects. But to discover a casual correlation between the British and Muslim attitudes towards the Maharaja would be or over simplification of the political phenomenon in Kashmir which had also autonomous causes and developed its own momentum which continued even after the contradictions surfaced between the growing radical urges of the political movement of the state and its sectarian Muslim supporters in British India.

Meanwhile Indian princes and the British government were getting closer against the common threat of the resurgent Indian nationalism.

Like his other counterparts, Hari Singh got an opportunity of demonstrating his loyalty to the British empire by his active campaign for its defence during the Second World War which began in 1939. Earlier, during the long debate over the formation of Federation of India, the assertion of their rights by the Indian princes, including that of Kashmir, far from scaring the British government, provided a useful handle to it to contain the demands of Indian National Conference.

By the time the war ended and negotiations on transfer of power started, Maharaja Hari Singh's ambitions were again revived. He not only remained indecisive about the affiliations of his state with either of the two dominations of India and Pakistan which came into being on 15 August 1947 but was also thinking "whether or not it was in the best interest of both of dominions" and his state "to stand independent". But his urge for 'independence' could not be fulfilled.

Kashmir at the Time of Indian Independence

On 15th August, 1947, the sub-continent was making grand preparation for the day of Indian Independence but Kashmir, was heading for a catastrophe. While transferring the power to two newly born Independent dominions the British followed the crude policy of 'cut and run' with the result that under the terms of the Indian independence Act of July, 1947, the rulers of the five hundred and odd Indian states assumed full sovereignty and competence to accede to, or federate with either Pakistan, or India or to remain independence[43]. The status of these states was already very well designed in the Cabinet Mission's Memorandum of May, 1946, that "His Majesty's government will cease to exercise powers of paramount. This means that the rights of the state which flow from their relationship with the crown, will no longer exit and that all the rights surrendered by the state to the paramount power will return to the states. Political arrangement between the states on the one side, and the British crown and British India, on the other will thus be brought to an end. The void will have to be filled either by the states entering into a federal relationship with the successor Government or Governments in British India or failing this, entering into particular political arrangements with it or them"[44].

Sisir Gupta rightly emphasize this "explosive character of the issue of Indian states"[45].Their transfer from a highly intricate system of paramountcy to simplified political structure in India and Pakistan was sure to follow communal lines on the other hand, the rulers of these states were governed by the principle of accession, the instrument of which also recognized their sovereignty. But it was silent about the communal issue involved therein as is rightly highlighted by Alistair Lamb: " It can fairly be said that in deciding accede to India the Maharaja of Kashmir was well within his rights according to the 1947 Act, which had nothing to say about communal issues in this respect"[46]. But Jinnah and his colleagues in the Muslim League purely thinking on communal lines, had always considered that the state of Kashmir, at least, would form a part of Pakistan[47]. On the same basis, the Muslim Conference in Kashmir, a vital force from within, also held the view that the best future of Kashmir lay in or in close association with Pakistan.

On account of its strategic location, Britain and United States wanted to turn Kashmir into an 'Imperialist' base and it would have fulfilled their purpose if Kashmir had gone to Pakistan, which to all intents and purposes was prone to toe the western line. The Government of India had put no pressure upon the Kashmir ruler to accede to India, Sardar Patel suggested to Kashmiri ruler to decide in any way he liked, but to do it before partition took place. But Sardar Patel wishes Kashmiri to join India on the basic of her culture, history and tradition.

Maharaja Hari Singh found himself in a tight corner. "He dislike the idea of becoming a part of India, which was being democratized, or of Pakistan, which was Muslim ... He thought of independence"[48]. He offered to sign a standstill agreement with both India and Pakistan aimed at continuing the existing relationship pending his final decision regarding the future of the state. He sent two identical telegrams to both India and Pakistan on August 12, 1947 in the following words:

"Jammu and Kashmir Government would welcome standstill Agreement with India/Pakistan on all matters on which there exit at the present movement with outgoing British India government. It is suggested that existing arrangements should continue pending self lement of details and formal execution of fresh orders".[49]

The Foreign Secretary to the government of Pakistan replied on 15 August 1947:

"The Government of Pakistan agree to have a standstill Agreement with the Government of Jammu and Kashmir for the continuance of the existing arrangements pending settlement of details and formal execution of fresh agreement"[50]. The Government of India replied to the Prime Minister of Kashmir.

"Government of India would be glad if you and some other ministers duly authorized in this behalf could fly to Delhi for Negotiating standstill agreement between Kashmir Government and Indian

Dominion. Early action desirable to maintain intact existing agreements and administrative arrangements.[51]"

For a variety of reason, no stand still agreement was concluded between Kashmir and India. According to Mr. Mahajan, the former Chief Justice of India, Mr. Nehru, the Prime Minister of India was interested not so much in the accession of the state to India as in the power being given to the popular leaders. Whatever the reason, "The absence of a formal agreement between India and the Maharaja was interpreted by the Pakistanis to meant that ultimately Kashmir would become a part of Pakistan[52]. And in fact Pakistan started putting pressure on the Maharaja to join Pakistan. On October 20, 1947, a large column of several thousand tribesmen armed with bren guns Mortars and flame throwers[53], attacked the frontier of the state. It was alleged that the tribesman were being aided by Pakistan. The state was at this time in imminent peril and the Maharaja saw his dream of independence shattered like a 'house of cards'. He thought of accession of save his state.

To save his life, Maharaja Hari Singh left Srinagar, on 25th October, and went to Jammu, the winter capital of Kashmir. He left his 'beloved people' to face the crisis. He appointed Sheikh Mohammed Abdullah, the emergency administrator before leaving the summer capital. Sheikh Abdullah advised the Maharaja that if the state was to be saved, he must accede to India and ask for immediate military helps. Faced with such a serious crises, Maharaja Hari Singh at last with great reluctance wrote to Lord Mountbatten, the Governor- General of India.

Kashmir's Accession with the Indian Union

Maharaja Hari Singh's letter to Lord Mountbatten read:

"I have to inform you excellency that a grave emergency has arisen in my state and request the immediate assistance of your government. As your excellency is aware, the state of Jammu and Kashmir has not acceded to either the dominion of India or Pakistan. Geographically my state is contiguous with both of them. Besides, my state has a common boundary with the Union of Soviet Socialist Republic and with China. In their external relations the dominions of India and Pakistan cannot ignore this fact. I wanted to take time to decide to which dominion I should accede or whether it is not in the best interests of both dominions and my state to stand independent, of course with friendly relations with both"[54]. After the paragraph followed an account of the tribal invasion and then His Highness wrote:

"With the condition obtaining at present in my state and the great emergency of the situation as it exists, I have no option but to ask for help from the Indian Dominion. Naturally they can not send the help asked for by me without my state acceding to the dominion of Indian. I have accordingly decided to do so and I attach the Instrument of Accession for acceptance by your government"[55].

Attached to the letter was the Instrument of Accession duly signed by the rulers, Maharaja Hari Singh. The operative part of the same read.

"I Shriman Indar Mahander Rajrajeshwar Maharajadhiraj Shri Hari Singh Ji Jammu Kashmir Naresh Tatha Tibet Adi Deshadhipathi Rules of Jammu and Kashmir state in the exercise of my sovereignty in and over my said state to hereby execute this my instrument of accession..."[56].

Lord Mountbatten, the Governor–General of India indicated his acceptance in the following words:

"I do hereby accept this Instrument of Accession. Dated this twenty seventh day of October Nineteen hundred and forty seven"[57].

This Instrument of Accession was in no way different from that executed by some 500 other states. It was unconditional, voluntary and absolute. It was not subject to any exceptions. As such, it bound the state of Jammu and Kashmir and India together legally and constitutionally. And so, regarding the legality of the accession in the Judicial sense of the word there is no doubt.

There is no doubt the Government of India had no authority to question the right of Maharaja to sign the Instrument of Accession, as he alone had the right and power to take a decision for his state. To have asked the ruler to establish his right to sign the Instrument of Accession would have meant that the Government of India was going to meddle with the internal politics of the state. Law does not permit any such intervention in the affairs of another state. India had no claim to Kashmir before the state acceded to it. It can not be denied that the Maharaja of Kashmir offered to accede to the Indian Dominion after assaults and raids had started on the state, when at his meeting with Lord Mountbatten on November 1, Mr. Jinnah claimed that the Accession Kashmir to India was based on violence, Lord Mountbatten replied, " the accession had indeed been brought about by violence, but the violence came from tribemen, for whom Pakistan, and not India was responsible"[58].

Let us now consider whether the Maharaja had the right to sign the Instrument of Accession[59] for his state or not. During the

British administration in India, the crown dealt with the Maharaja alone. It recognized him only. Also, when the Government of India concluded a standstill agreement with the Maharaja, it did so on the basis that the Maharaja was the sole representative of the state. These association were perfectly justified for, in a monarchical form of government, it is the monarch who personifies and represents the state. And the Government of India, in its relations with the Maharaja, acted in accordance with law and recognized international practice. The accession of the state to India cannot be called in question on any legal grounds. After accession, the Indian Government became responsible for the defence of this state.

It is a notable point that there was no reference to the "will of the people" in the instrument of accession and there was no dispute about the accession between the leading and popular party of the state and the ruler. If there was any vigorous tussle it was for power and power alone.

One thing is certain that the circumstances leading to the accession were quite complex due to the internal and external complications. Especially, the accession took place when the state was in imminent danger of being overseen by the tribal raiders acting under the instigation of Pakistani authorities. The result was that the state leadership desired the issue of accession to remain open, at least to enable them, to acquire sufficient safeguards and greater amount of internal autonomy. The ultimate result was the special status of this state in the Indian Union.

References

1. Gupta, Sisir, *A Study of India-Pakistan Relation*, Asia Publication House, (New Delhi, 1976) p. 22.
2. Rao, H.S. Gururaj, *Legal Aspects of Kashmir Problem*, Asia Publication House (New York, 1967), p. 1.
3. Hayek, Loiis.D., *Impact of the U.S. Policy on the Kashmir Conflict*, University of Arizona Press (Tucon, 1971), p. 11.
4. Sharma, S.D., *Kashmir Autonomy - An exercise in centre-state relation*, Subhi Pub (New Delhi, 2000), p. 1.
5. *Census of India*, Series 2, Jammu and Kashmir and Kashmir provision population total, series 2 of 2001, Published by Controller of Publication (Delhi, 2001), p. XV.
6. *Ibid*., p. XV.

7. Sharma, S.D., *Kashmir Autonomy-An exercise in centre-state relation*, Sushil Pub (New Delhi, 2000), p. 3.
8. Dr. Barry, Turner, *Stateman Year Book*, Pub by Sara Loyed, (London, 2001) p. 808.
9. Till 1846, Jammu Kashmir and Ladakh were separate and district areas under different rules.
10. Puri, Balraj, "*Jammu and Kashmir*" in Weiner, Myron (eds.) *State Politics in India*, Princeton University Press (Princeton, 1986), p. 216.
13. Puri, Balraj, "Emerging contours of peace in Jammu and Kashmir" *Mainstream*, Jan 27, 2000, p. 17.
14. *Indian Quarterly – A Journal of International Affairs*. Vol. LVII, No. 2., April-June 2001, p. 57.
15. *Ibid*., p. 72.
16. Dr. Sharma, S.D., *Kashmir Autonomy – An exercise in Centre-State relation*, Subhi Pub, (New Delhi, 2000), p. 76.
17. *Ibid*., p. 76.
18. Anand, A.S., *The Constitution of Jammu and Kashmir,* University Pub, (New Delhi, 1994), p. 8.
19. Puri, Balraj, *Jammu and Kashmir: Triumph and Tragedy of Indian Federalism*. 1981, p. 22.
20. *Ibid*., p. 22.
21. *Ibid*., p.22.
22. *Treaty of Amritsar*, See Appendix I,
23. Quoted by Balraj Puri, *Jammu and Kashmir – Triumph and Tragedy of Indian Federalism*, 1981, p. 24.
24. Letter of Maharaja Pratap Singh to the Viceroy Lord Dufferin, Quoted by Puri, Balraj, *Jammu and Kashmir-Triumph and Tragedy of Indian Federalism*, 1981, p. 24.
25. Letter to Lord Randolph Churchil, the secretary of state for India to the Viceroy of India, dated 27.TM.1885, Quoted by Puri, Balraj, *Jammu and Kashmir: Triumph and Tragedy of Indian Federalization*, 1981, p. 24
26. Puri, Balraj, *Jammu and Kashmir – Triumph and Tragedy of Indian Federalization*, 1981, p. 26.
27. Letter of Maharaja to the Resident dated 15.09.1891, Quoted in "Balraj Puri, *Jammu and Kashmir – Triumph and Tragedy of Indian federalization*. 1981, p. 26.
28. Puri, Balraj, *Jammu and Kashmir – Triumph and Tragedy in Indian Federalization*. 1981, p. 31.

29. Raghwan, G.S., *The Warning of Kashmir*, (Allahabad, 1931), p. 35.
30. *Ibid.*, p. 40.
31. Anand, A.S., *The Constitution of Jammu and Kashmir - Its development and comments*, Universal Pub, (New Delhi, 1944) p. 30.
32. *The state subject definition*, See Appendix II.
33. Puri, Balraj, *Jammu and Kashmir Triumph and Tragedy in Indian Federation*, 1981, p. 29.
34. *Ibid.*, p. 29.
35. *Ibid.*, p. 29.
36. Raghwan, G.S., *The Warning of Kashmir*, (Allahabad, 1931), p. 38.
37. *Ibid.*, p. 62.
38. *Ibid.*, p. 54.
39. *Ibid.*, p. 36.
40. Puri, Balraj, *Jammu and Kashmir : Triumph and Tragedy in Indian Federalisation*, 1981, p. 31.
41. Raghwan, G.S., *The Warning of Kashmir*, (Allahabad, 1931), p. 83.
42. Quoted by Puri, Balraj, *Jammu and Kashmir: Triumph and Tragedy in Indian Federalization*, 1981, p. 32.
43. Sharma, B.M. and Chaudhary, L.P., *Federal Polity*, Asia Publishing House (New Delhi, 1967) p. 129.
44. Hari Ram, *Special status in Indian Federalism: Jammu and Kashmir*, Seema Publication (New Delhi, 1983), p. 41.
45. Gupta, Sisir, *Kashmir: A Study of India – Pakistan Relations*, Asia Publishing House (New Delhi, 1976), p. 90.
46. Lamb, Alistair, *Crisis in Kashmir* : 1946-66, (London, 1966), p. 89.
47. *Ibid.*, p. 38.
48. Anand, A.S., *The development of the Constitution of Jammu and Kashmir*, Light and Life Publishers (New Delhi, 1980), p. 83.
49. Lakhan Pal, P.L., *Essential Document and Notes on Kashmir Dispute*, (Delhi, 1958), p. 45.
50. *Ibid.*, p. 45.
51. *Ibid.*, p. 45.
52. Maharaja, M.C., *Accession of Kashmir to India – The inside story*, (Sholapur, 1967), p. 2.
53. Anand, A.S., *The development of the Constitution of Jammu and Kashmir*, Light and Life Publication, (Delhi, 1980), p. 88.

54. Quoted in Anand, A.S., *The Development of the Constitution of Jammu and Kashmir*, Light and Life Publication (New Delhi, 1980), p. 90.
55. *Ibid.*, p. 91.
56. *Ibid.*, p. 92.
57. *Ibid.*, p. 92.
58. *Ibid.*, p. 96
59. *The Instrument of Accession*, See Appendix III.

3
Accession and Integration of the State of Jammu and Kashmir with the Indian Union—Politics in Jammu and Kashmir since 1947-1975

The state of Jammu and Kashmir acceded to the dominion of India on October 26, 1947 when its ruler Maharaja Hari Singh, signed an Instrument of Accession and the Governor General of India, Lord Mountbatten, accepted the Instrument.[1]

With the accession of the state of Jammu and Kashmir to India, Jurisdiction in matter of External Affairs, Defence and Communications was transferred to the Government of India and the Union Parliament was given power to make laws for the purpose of those three matters only. Sovereignty, in so far as the internal administration of the state was concerned, remained with the ruler. The retention by the states of their sovereignty even after executing the Instrument of Accession and ascending to the dominion concerned caused a lot of problems and confused thinking. It was argued that by accending to a dominion, the states lost their independence completely. The supporters of this view maintained that the states could not remain sovereign after their accession even in the limited sense of word.

The special problems were definitely created by those who, even after having understood the legality of the accession wanted it to be modify to suit their further designs. The Sheikh Abdullah, for instance, declared just after the Accession that "he did not feel that the Kashmir people could possibly to bound by the decision of Maharaja to accede India."[2]

After the Accession, an emergency administration headed by Sheikh Abdullah, was set up in the state. The Maharaja desired that the emergency administration operated with the authority of the Council of Ministers responsible to the Maharaja. This arrangement could not work. The National Conference leader demanded that Ministerial establishment of the Maharaja should be abolished and all powers to be transfer to the National Conference. The Government of India advised to Maharaja institute an interim government in the state with Sheikh Abdullah as the Prime Minister. This arrangement could not work and finally the Maharaja was asked by Sardar Patel to leave the state and on his own departure, he appointed his son Karan Singh as a Regent. Dr. Karan Singh became the head of the state, in absence of his father. This development took place in April-May 1949. Thus, Sheikh Abdullah became a truly constitutional Prime-Minister of the state.

After having assumed political as well as the administrative powers, the Sheikh dominated the National Conference and fully controlled the political string of Jammu and Kashmir states on its Indian side. Politically he moved fast towards the establishment of self rule and abolished monarchy in the state. The Sheikh was in favour of limited union powers for this state, for he thought the people of Kashmir would themselves finally determine the political future of this state. He therefore wanted a special position to be accorded to this state in the federal constitution of India.

After the Maharaja left the state, his son Dr. Karan Singh as Regent, initiated the consideration of the relation between the centre and the state. At this stage constitution of India was in the final phase of the its making and hence the constitutional relationship between the state of Jammu and Kashmir and Indian union also come up for its incorporation in the constitution. The principles adopted in integration of other states. However, were not followed in case of Kashmir. The issue, therefore, were discussed in a meeting held in Delhi in May 1949, between the Indian leaders and leaders of Jammu and Kashmir. The meeting resulted in deciding certain principles which could govern the relations between India and the state of Jammu and Kashmir, these included.[3]

- The constitution of Jammu and Kashmir, would be framed by the people of state through their representatives in the constituent assembly.
- Maharaja Hari Singh's future would be determined by the same constituent assembly.
- The division of power between centre and the state of Jammu and Kashmir would be governed by the provision of Instrument of Accession.

- The constituent assembly would decide the grant of further powers to the central government.
- The power relating to citizenship, fundamental rights directive principles would be uniformly applicable to the state of Jammu and Kashmir.
- The Government of India would take over the operational and administrative control of the state army. As a result of these agreed principles, when the draft Artical-306A was placed before the Constituent Assembly of India, the relations between the Central Government and state of Jammu and Kashmir were placed as under.[4]
- The provisions of the constitution of India with regard to the government in the other Indian state, which had acceded to dominion of India, were not to apply to Jammu and Kashmir, which was reserved the power to draft a constitution for its government.
- The state was empowered to establish a constituent assembly representing the people of the state of draft the constitution of the state;
- The government was empowered to legislate in regard to the state on the subjects enumerated in the union list, which were declared by the President of India to correspond to the matters specified in the Instrument of Accession and such other matters which the concurrence of the Government of the state, the President would by order specify;
- The provisions of the constitution of India pertaining to citizenship, fundamental rights and directive principle of the state polity, embodied in the constitution of India were to apply to the state.
- The other provision of the constitution of India were to apply to the state by an order of the President, which he was empowered to issue with concurrence of the government of the state except in case of the matters incidental to the constitutional provision for the government of the state and the subject transferred to the Government of India under the Instrument of Accession where the President was only required to consult the government of state.
- The President was empowered to amend or repeat the special provisions for the state on recommendations of the Constituent Assembly of the state.

After the above mentioned provisions were agreed, the Sheikh wrote the Gopala Swami Ayangar that the working committee of the National Conference did not agree with the Draft Article of Indian Constitution. They were fearful about the application of the provisions of the constitution of India with regard to citizenship and fundamental rights. They feared that once Fundamental Rights were applicable to the state, the people from outside could acquire the land and prejudice the land reforms in the state. Consequently Ayangar redrafted the Article but the revised draft was again rejected by National Conference. Finally, a revised draft was agreed upon between the two representatives one from central and other from state leadership. The revised draft was prepared by Ayangar in consultation with Mirza Mohd Afjal Beg and Art 306 A became Art 370 in the Final constitution.

Special Status of the Slate in the Indian Union

The constitution of India came into force on 26th of January 1950. After India had become an independent republic, hardly any scope for survival of the 'Maharaja' and 'Nawabs' was left. No question of singling out any state or any Maharaja or Nawab had to arise, neither for any discrimination or hostile treatment, nor for granting any extraordinary concessions or "special position" or "status" universal application of the democratic principles and norms and agreed patterns had to be applied to each and every state that had acceded of India.[5] But the special status granted to the state of Jammu and Kashmir under Article 370 of the Indian Constitution is one of the most controversial and highly debatable topic on the Indian Federal System.

One thing on which most of the people in the Kashmir Valley, at least Ninety per cent, are united in the preservation of the autonomy of Jammu and Kashmir as guaranteed by the constitution. The Accessionists and the secessionists may violently differ with each other on most other issues, but they are unanimous in their strong, unshakable faith in the state's right to shape its internal affairs itself and seem to be sentimentally attached to it. Naturally, therefore, when any Indian leader favoured and talked of gradual abolition of Art 370 of the constitution of India which, as is commonly and universally accepted, grants a special status to Jammu and Kashmir as part of India Union, many in the valley were hurt and found paised against attempts at bringing about abrogation of the Article.

Article 370 was specially meant to be a temporary provision as the constitution makers were confident that the Indo-Kashmir link would convince the people of Kashmir of their bright future by the close Association with India.[6] Art 370 is Mentioned in part XXI the last but one part of the Indian Constitution under the heading (TEMPORARY, TRANSTITIONAL AND SPECIAL PROVISION), covered the case of Jammu and Kashmir alone. Its meant that the state was not covered by the Liberal provisions of the Indian constitution. Such as the Section on Fundamental Rights, nor aid the autonomous union, institution like Supreme Court, the Election Commission, the Union Public Service Commission and Auditor General had any jurisdiction in the state. Constitutionally, therefore, Kashmir was without a system of checks and balance.

Art 370[7] – Special Constitutional

Art 370 gives special status to the state of Jammu and Kashmir, "Its an issue which involve not only historical, constitutional, political, social and economic consideration of far reaching consequence but also psychological and emotional one".[8] It is fact that Instrument of Accession was similar to that executed by each one of the rulers of other Indian states, yet entirely separate provisions for Jammu and Kashmir state were made through Art. 370.[9] The future state Assembly was given the right to spell out such provisions of the Indian Constitution as would apply to this state and whether these the special circumstances prevailing in the states. The abrogation or modification of Art 370 was also to be recommended by the state Assembly to the President of India in due course of time. The President of India otherwise not empowered to abrogate and amend any of the provisions enshrined in this Article. Possesing such special privileges, the state leaders began to seek an honourable place for their state in Indian federal structure on the basis of a rigid "balance of power" their aim was to obtain special safe guards for the Muslims of Kashmir, who feared that they would be lost in the vastness of India, if speical status was not given to this state. There is no doubt that these leaders had a constant apprehension regarding the future of this state. Even at present the state enjoys a greater amount of autonomy and power as compared to other Indian states and the centre's jurisdiction within the state is more limited. These arrangements have various dimensions which are detailed below.

1. Special Status to State Boundaries

The state of Jammu and Kashmir forms a part of the Territory of 'India-that is Bharat – a union of states'.[12] The Indian Government, from the very start includes those territories in the union which immediately before 26th November, 1949, were included in the Indian side of Jammu and Kashmir.[13] The state constitution on the other hand includes all territories including those illegally occupied by Pakistan in its fold, on the basic of the fact that these were on the 15th day of August 1947 under the sovereignty and suzerainty of the ruler of the state. The state constitution also makes these territories an integral part of the union of India by its own force.[14]

The Parliament of India by law and proper procedure, can form new states and alter the areas, boundaries or names of existing states. But no bill providing for increasing and diminishing the areas of Jammu and Kashmir state or altering its name and boundaries can be introduced in Parliament without the consent of the state legislature.

This is unique status given to the boundaries of this state. The result is that even the central government, in India, is not authorised to delimit the boundaries of the state lest the existing relation between the various communities of the state should be effected and certain portions of the lower plains of this state should be combined with any of adjoining territories of the Indian union in any future delimitation of boundaries.

2. Special Status to Permanent Residents

Citizenship of India was granted to the "Permanent Residents" of this state with effect from 26th January, 1950.[15] The Central Government of India wholly left the definition of the expression "Permanent Resident" to the state legislature, which is fully empowered to make laws defining the classes of persons who are or who shall be permanent residents.[16]

3. Curtailed Fundamental Rights and Constitutional Remedies

The provisions of Fundamental Rights of Indian Constitution were applied to Jammu and Kashmir state with effect from 14th May 1954, meaning there by that no retrospective effects so as to affect the rights and liabilities accured before that date. The State Government is fully empowered to impose reasonable restrictions on freedom of assembly, association, movement, residence and property, on an additional ground of security of the state, which cannot be put to judicial review.[17]

The state legislature is fully empowered to legislate in respect of preventive detention to the detriment of Fundamental Rights of Indian Constitution. The Parliament of India is quite helpless in this matter. Even the President of India has no power to make an order in respect of persons under preventive detention, in the state.[18] The state also enjoys absolute freedom in enacting laws for declared evacuee properly in the state. It is worthy of note that no courts in the country has any jurisdiction to entertain any suit, proceeding or application or grant of stay or injunction in respect of anything done or proposed to be done in this state regarding the declared evacuee property.[19] The Fundamental duties enshrined in part IV-A of the Indian constitution are not applicable to the state of Jammu and Kashmir.[20] The result seems that the permanent residents of this state are free from the liabilities of these obligations.

4. Directive Principle of State Policy

Directive principle of state policy in Indian constitution are not applicable to Jammu and Kashmir state. The state constitution includes its own "Directive Principles of state policy".[21] The brightest aspects of these principles in this state is the right of free and compulsory education in certain cases. The state, provides to every permanent resident of the right to free education upto the university standard.[22]

5. Curtailed Jurisdiction of Indian Parliament

The Jurisdiction of Parliament in relation to Jammu and Kashmir is confined to the matters enumerated in union and concurrent lists, subject to certain modifications. In the concurrent list most of the matters are out of its jurisdiction.[23] The reason is again the special constitutional status granted to this state under the Indian Constitution. Another important feature of this arrangement is that in the case of all other states of India, the residuary power of legislation belong to the Parliament,[24] but in the case of Jammu and Kashmir, these are vested in state itself. The Jammu and Kashmir legislature is the only such Legislature in India which functions under its own constitution and does not enjoy merely enumerated powers like other states.

Clearly, therefore this state enjoys a considerable quantum of autonomy as compared with other states of the Indian Union. The executive and the legislative powers of the state extend to all matters except those with respect of which Indian Parliament has power to make laws for the state under the provision of the Constitution of India.

6. Governor's Rule in Centre-State Relation

The constitution of Jammu and Kashmir enjoys the Governor with special power in matter of his role to give assent to a bill passed by the House of the state legislature. The Governor of the state in the country, except the state of Jammu and Kashmir, may reserve any Bill for consideration of the President which in their opinion would so derogate from the powers of High Court as to endanger the position which that court is designed to fill. What the Governor of Jammu and Kashmir does when he is constitutionally inhibited to reserve the bill for the consideration of the President of India with regard to those matters which may appear to be controversial or unconstitutional, or opposed to directive principles of state policy or against national interest and integrity? In these circumstances the governor of Jammu and Kashmir ought have to step into the shoes of President. That is, be ought have to act as the President of India will act such as he may declare assent, or without assent (i.e., pocket veto) or send for reconsideration.

7. Special Status in Union State Relation

The Parliament of India cannot legislate for the state of Jammu and Kashmir even in national interests. Parliament also cannot take a decision affecting the disposition of the state of Jammu and Kashmir without the consent of state government.[25] The result seems that the Government of India shall have to consult the Kashmir Government while giving effect to international agreement. In the light of this provision it seems strong enough as to why the consent of the state Government was not obtained when the Central Government of India, handed over Hajipur and Chhamb areas to Pakistan in early 196. The Sheikh, later on, expressed his grievance against this attitude of Central Government of India, which acted independently without consulting the state leadership in this behalf. This is a unique privilege enjoyed by the state.

The Government of India cannot deploy any armed force of the union or any other force subject to the Central of the union for dealing with any grave situation of law and order in Jammu and Kashmir state.[26] Similar letters have been imposed upon the executive power of the union to safeguard the autonomy of the state; A unique privilege, which is only enjoyed by this state, is that a proclamation of Emergency under Art 352 (1) cannot have any effect in the state (Except in regard to distribution of Revenues) unless it has been made at the request of or with the concurrence of the State Government.[27] Thus the President of India could extend the provisions of the Emergency (Made by him on 25th of June, 1975, for entire India) after obtaining the concurrence of the state government. The proclamation of Emergency was, therefore made applicable to this state on 29th June, 1975. Financial emergency cannot be declared by the President in this state.[28]

The Central Government cannot suspend the state constitution the ground of failure to comply with the direction to the state Government by the union Government of India under Art. 350.[29] In the case of failure of constitutional machinery in this state, it is Governor of the state who shall, according to the Jammu and Kashmir constitution have the power, with the concurrence of the President of India, to assume to himself or any of the powers of the Governments of the state, except those of the High Court of the state.[30] The Parliament has no power under Art 368 to amend the constitution of this state.[31] An amendment made to the constitution of India under this Article does not apply to this state unless applied by an order of the President under abuse (i) of Article 370.[32]

While an Act of Parliament required for the amendment of any of the provisions of the constitution of India, the provisions of the state constitution of Jammu and Kashmir are amended by an Act of its own legislature passed by a majority of, not less than two third of its membership.[33]

The constitution position of the state referred to above Art 370, made the state of Jammu and Kashmir distinct as compared to all other states of India. The constitution does not only give special place to the State of Jammu and Kashmir, but also creates temporary, traditional, special provisions, with respect of the states of Maharashtra and Gujrat, Nagaland and Manipur, Assam, Andhra Pradesh and Sikkim. Thus, we find that Art. 370 which contains temporary provision with respect of Jammu and Kashmir. Part XXI also includes certain other provisions, which in a singular way regulate certain situation pertaining to certain matters as a special case in respect of certain other states under Art. 371, but the position of this state differ from other states in following respect.

The provisions of dealing with governmental machinery in the state of India do not apply to the state of Jammu and Kashmir.

The Legislative Authority of the union Parliament, in respect of this state is limited to other matters in the union and concurrent list, which are declared by the President in consultation with the government of the state, to conform to terms of the Instrument of the Accession.

Only such of other provisions of the constitution shall apply to this state as the President may be order specify.

Thus, we find that this state enjoys a considerable quantum of autonomy as compared with other states of Indian union, further if we examine the working of Jammu and Kashmir, we find that first 40 years of its working, it has never stood in the way of smooth functioning for a united India. We have been quite successful in achieving the step-by-step integration of the state with rest of India. The first major step in this direction was taken by means of a Presidential order issued in 1954. This order has been amended many a time, and what has been happening in the state for the last 10 years has nothing to do with special status provided under 370. This noise of autonomy seems to be major political in nature and international in this character, which is beyond the radius of Art. 370.

After examine the scope of Art 370 of the constitution which enables the state of Jammu and Kashmir to enjoy special benefits. Now let us examine why the state of Jammu and Kashmir demanding special treatment (Autonomy) to solve their problem.

The Demand for Special Treatment

The National Conference which in its earlier phase of struggle against the ruler had always demanded "Some special safeguards in every sphere for Muslims", had also a future vision and plan for Kashmir. Afzal Beg, an important leader of National Conference, had opined in early 1952:

Jammu and Kashmir state will be an autonomous republic within the Indian Union. And as far as the constitution of the state is concerned, we aim at making its framework such that the state will be an autonomous unit within the said union.[34]

Their point of view of special position was accepted by Indian leaders and Kashmir was promised what was called a special status in Indian union. All these promises further bound the Government of India. Which declared, after all, that "It was people of the state of Jammu and Kashmir acting through their Constituent Assembly, who were to finally determine the constitution of state and the Jurisdiction of the union of India over this state".[35] The Sheikh was now led to believe that the constitution of India had provided for a federal union and in the distribution of sovereign powers, Kashmir was treated differently from other constituent of India. He therefore, told the state Assembly that 'our struggle for power has now reached its successful climax".[36] He began to believe also that this power was going to be sovereign one. On the basis of this sovereign power the Sheikh was inspired to ask the representative of the Assembly to translate the vision of 'New Kashmir' in reality through self-determination.[37] The National Conference leadership therefore, rightly began to think of self-determination and internal autonomy.

In 1951, the Kashmir Assembly under Sheikh's Prime Ministership affirmed internal autonomy over all matters except Defence, Foreign Affairs and Communication. This attitude of Sheikh Abdullah not only gave the birth of Kashmir problems but also creates major differences between centre and the state.

In 1951, election were held to create an assembly to evoke a constitution for Jammu and Kashmir, even as this Assembly was underway, New Delhi decided to clarify its relation with Kashmir. A delegation headed by Mirza Afzal Beg, including D.P. Dhar, Syed Mir Quasim arrived in Delhi and had intense talks with the Indian Government. Later Sheikh Abdullah joined his team and Pt. Nehru envied members of the opposition to participate in the talks, the result was the Delhi Agreement of July 14, 1952.

Delhi Agreement of July 1952[38]

The Constituent Assembly, convened on 31st October, 1951, thus was not only to frame the constitution for the state but was to give certain more important decisions regarding the future relationship of the state with the union. It started its work in the right earnest and as days passed by, need for decision on certain important matters relating to framing of the constitution and any further application of the union constitution to the state was felt. Besides, questions arising out of the need to settle the future of the ruling dynasty and of arriving at a concrete solution about the fundamentals of the constitutions of the state as an integral part of India had also to be considered.

1952 proved a very important year in the state's constitutional evaluation. It witnessed the conclusion of the historic Agreement between Pt. Jawahar Lal Nehru and Sheikh Saheb which was announced at a press conference in Delhi on July 24, 1952.[39]

The terms of the agreement were explained to the Constituent Assembly of Jammu and Kashmir by the state's Prime Minister, Sheikh Abdullah on August 11, 1952. Both the leaders provided the background and highlighted the significance of the Agreement. Pt. Nehru told the Lok Sabha.[40]

"The position since the constitution was framed is thus contained in the Article 370 and in the President's order following it. Article 370 was obviously of transitional nature and it allowed the President to make any additions to it, any variation to it, later on, the object being that if any change or addition was required, we need not have to go through the cumbrous process of amending our constitution, but the President was given the authority to amend it in the sense of adding a subject, part of a subject, whatever, it was to the other subjects, in regard to Kashmir. But in Art 370 the old principle was repeated and emphasized that all these changes and any change, required the approval of the Constituent Assembly and Kashmir state.

When this was put down in our constitution, there was no Constituent Assembly of Jammu and Kashmir State, but we envisaged it. We had envisaged it for a long time. And if the Constituent Assembly was not there, then it required the consent of the Jammu and Kashmir Government. So that was the position".[40]

The implication is plain, additional subject could be acquired by the centre only with the approval of the state's Constituent Assembly.

The Delhi Agreement covered ten points, namely (a) Residuary Powers (b) Citizenship (c) Fundamental Rights (d) Supreme Court (e) National Flag (f) The President of India (g) The Headship of the State (h) Financial Integration (i) Emergency provisions (j) Conduct of Election to Houses of Parliament.

The Main Features of Delhi Agreement

A. Residuary Powers [41]

It was agreed that while under the present constitution, the Residuary powers vested in with the centre in respect of all states other than Jammu and Kashmir, in the case of Jammu and Kashmir state they vested in the state itself and should continue as such. In this regard Sheikh Abdullah observed as follows :

"We have always held that the ultimate source of sovereignty resides in the people. It, is, therefore, from the people that all powers can flow under these circumstances, it is upto the people of Kashmir through this Assembly to transfer more powers for mutual advantage to the custody of the union/centre".[42]

B. Citizenship [43]

It was agreed between the two Governments that in accordance with Article 5 of the Indian Constitution, person who have their domicile in Jammu and Kashmir shall be regarded as citizens of India, but the state legislature was given power to make laws for conferring special rights and privileges on the 'State Subjects' in view of the "States subject notifications of 1927 and 1932, the state legislature was also empowered to make laws for the 'state subjects' who had gone to Pakistan on account of the communal disturbances of 1947, in the event of their return to Kashmir.

C. Fundamental Rights [44]

With regard to the Fundamental Rights, some basic principles between the parties were enunciated: it was accepted that the people of state were to have Fundamental Rights. But in view of the peculiar position in which the state was placed, the whole chapter relating to 'Fundamental Rights' of the Indian Constitution could not be made applicable to the state, the question which remained to be determined was whether the chapter on fundamental rights should form a part of the state constitution or of the constitution of India as applicable to the state:

D. Supreme Court [45]

With regard to the jurisdiction of the Supreme Court of India, it was accepted that for the time being, owing to the existence of the Board of Judicial Advisers in the state, which was the highest judicial authority in the state, the Supreme Court should have only appellate jurisdiction.

E. National Flag [46]

For historical and other reasons connected with the freedom struggle in the state, the need for the continuance of the state flag was recognized. It was agreed by the state Government that the state flag would not be a rival of the Union flag. It was also recognised that the Union flag should have the same status and position in Jammu and Kashmir as in the rest of India.

F. The President of India[47]

It was decided that powers to grant reprieves and compute death sentences etc. should also belong to the President of the Union.

G. Headship of State [48]

The Government of India appreciated the principle proposed by the basic principles committee as adopted by the Assembly in regard to the abolition of the hereditary rulership of the state. The following arrangements were mutually agreed upon this regard :-

(i) "The Head of the state shall be the person recognised by the President of union on the recommendation of the legislature of the state.

(ii) He shall hold office during the pleasure of the President.

(iii) He may, by writing under his hand addressed to the President, resign his office.

(iv) Subject to the foregoing provisions, the Head of the state hold office for a term of five years from the date he enters upon his office".

H. Financial Integration [49]

It was recognized that while it would be necessary to evolve some sort of Financial arrangement between the state and the union in view of far reaching consequence involved therein, it was agreed that a detailed examination of the subject would be necessary before during that.

I. Emergency Provision [50]

On behalf of the Government of India, it was stated that Art. 352 of the constitution was necessary as it related to vital matters affecting the security of the state. The Government of India did not press for application of Article 356 or even Article 360. Item 1 in the Seventh Schedule relating to the defence of India applied and the Government of India would have full authority to take any steps in connection with defence etc. The state representatives indicated that they were averse to internal disturbance being referred to in this connection as even petty internal disorder might be considered sufficient for application of Article 352. To meet the state's point of view it was therefore decided that Article 352 might be accepted with addition of the following words at the end of the first paragraph :-

"But in regard to internal disturbance at the request or with the concurrence of the Government of the State". It was also agreed that the whole matter of application of Art 353, 354, 358 and 359 will be further examined the Delhi Agreement recognised special right. But the Agreement soon came under attack.[51] The Praja Parishad launched a massive campaign in Jammu. The movement desired and aimed at states full accession with India without any reservation. They opposed the 'Special status: Their slogan of complete integration of state with India in the rallying çry "Ek Vidan, Ek Nishan, Ek Pradhan – One constitution, one flag and one President." The constitution of India and latter Delhi Agreement had conceded to the people of Kashmir a special status with distinction that its Chief Minister was termed as Prime Minister of Jammu and Kashmir. Further the Flag of National Conference hoisting along with Indian flag on all government offices in particular on secretariats with regard to the head of the state, in the beginning of the state, head was the Maharaja, and later Dr. Karan Singh, as elected the head of the state, his office in Jammu and Kashmir initial constitution was named as Sadar-e-Reyasat (State's President) consequently. The Jammu people under the leadership of the Praja Parishad fought to abolish all the three distinction of the state. One of the main reason for it was that Dogra's had lost power over Kashmiris after a century rule and they could not reconcile with the idea that yesterdays stave was today's master, that too over his own earlier masters.

Sheikh's Dismissal as C.M.

The Praja Parishad movement caused the tragic event of 1953, when Sheikh Abdullah was dismissed from Prime Ministership and arrested on 6th August. Dr. Karan Singh gave order for Abdullah's arrest.[52] After the dismissal of the Sheikh, Bakshi Gulam Mohd. was sworn in as the Prime Minister of Jammu and Kashmir, he was a strewed politician. He was not averse of blackmailing the centre, thus he would get more central assistance.

The Constitution of the State of Jammu and Kashmir

The constitution of Jammu and Kashmir finalished and came into effect on January 26th 1957.[53] The constitution of the state is written document constituting of 158 section (Articles) divided into 13 parts. There are 6 schedules attached to it.

Preamble : The Premble of the constitution confirms the Accession of the state with the Union of India. It reads:[54] "We the people of the state of Jammu and Kashmir, having solemnly resolved, in pursuance of the Accession of this state to India which took place on 26th day of October, 1947, to further define the existing relationship of the state with the Union of India as an intergal part therefo, and to secure to ourselves.

Justice; social, economic and political;

Liberty of thought, expression, belief, faith and worship;

Equality of state and opportunity, and to promote among us all;

Fraternity assuring the dignity of the individual and the unity of Nation:

In our constitutional Assembly this 17th day of November 1956, do hereby adopt, enact and give to ourselves this constitution".

The phraseology used in preamble has been liberally borrowed from the constitution of the country. The salient features of the constitution of Jammu and Kashmir may be summarised in the following manners.[55]

Separate Flag

Very important and significant exception has been made in case of only this state. The constitution of Jammu and Kashmir (under see 144) provided a separate flag of the state.

Dual Citizenship

Generally, in a federal setup a person is a citizen not only of the state in which he resides but also of the federation, under different conditions; and both the federal and State Governments, each independent of the others, operating direct upon the citizen who is thus subject to the two governments and owe allegiance to both, but the Indian Constitution like Canadian, does not introduce any dual citizenship, only one citizenship, viz-–The citizen of India (Art 5), and birth or residence in a particular state does not confer any separate status as citizen of that state. Here an important but controversial exception has been made through the constitution of India for the permanent residents of Jammu and Kashmir. The state of Jammu and Kashmir grants dual citizenship to its permanent residents.

Separate Directive Principles–Part IV of the Jammu and Kashmir's Constitution (Section 11 to 25) enlists a few principles which are treated as fundamental in the governance of the state.

Fundamental Rights and Duties–The provisions of Fundamental rights of Indian constitution were applied to Jammu and Kashmir. State government is fully empowered to impose reasonable restriction on freedom of assembly, association, movements, residence etc. on an additional ground of the security of the state.

State Boundaries–The Parliament of India empowered to form new states and alter the areas, boundaries and names of the existing states (Art 3), But no bill seeking to increase of diminish the area or altering the name of boundaries of Jammu and Kashmir can be introduce in Parliament without the consent of the State Legislature.

Emergency Provisions–No modern federation can ignore to provide for the assumption of large powers by the federal Government whenever united action is necessary by reason of emergent circumstances, external and internal. In India there are three different kind of Emergency situation which call for a departure from the normal government machinery set-up by the constitution viz. –

(a) An Emergency due to war, external aggression, an armed rebellions. (Art 352)

(b) Failure of the constitutional machinery in the state. (Art 356).

(c) Financial emergency (Art 360).

If at any time the Governor is satisfied that a situation has arisen in which the Government of India state cannot be carried on in accordance with the provisions of the constitution of the state he has the power to assume to himself all or any of the powers of the Government of the state with the concurrence of the President of India. Hence in case of other states it is calles Presidents role but in case of this it is Governor's rule.The constitution of this state provides emergency provisions limited to only breakdown of constitutional machinery.

Bicameral Legislature—Part VI of the constitution of the state explain the composition and function of the state Legislature. Sec 46 says "There should be Legislature for the state which shall consists of the two governments. Legislative Assembly and Legislative Council are the two houses of State Legislature. The Legislative Assembly shall consists of one hundred and 11 members chosen by direct election from territorial constitution of the state. And in legislative council eleven members are elected by members of Legislative Assembly from amongst persons who are resident of the provision of Kashmir and are not member of Assembly. 11 members are elected from the provision of Jammu, six members by Municipal Corporation and Panchayat in the state, eight members are nominated by governor.

Legislation Autonomy—In the sphere of Law making of the State Legislature enjoys a considerable amount of autonomy as compared to other States. The constitution of India enumerates elaborately the Legislative powers of the union and states in part XI of the constitution. It is further qualified by providing three lists. The union list with 97 subjects, the concurrent list with 47 subject and the state list with 66 subjects. In this division of powers an exception has been made in the case of state of Jammu and Kashmir. At the time of Accession of the state of Jammu and Kashmir the Union Government was given the authority only in respect of three spheres, i.e. Defence, Foreign relation and communication. With the passage of time and Necessity the Union Government can make laws from the union list for the state of Jammu and Kashmir only in consultation with the Government of the state. So far as the concurrent list it concerned only 17 subjects are common and the rest are with the state. The state has absolute control over state list and all residuary laws making power, further the jurisdiction of Parliament can not be extended in the national interest (Art 249), or for giving effect of international agreement (Art. 253), will respect to a matter in the state list in the case of this state. Thus, we find that the scope of law making powers to the union is on true federal principle recognised in this word in respect of Jammu and Kashmir in the Indian constitution. Though it is not true in case of other federal units of the country. This situation is definitely enviable for the rest of units of the state of Indian union.

The constitution of Jammu and Kashmir is a constitution within the Indian constitution. The political system of Jammu and Kashmir is a sub-system with a sub-constitutional system. Jammu and Kashmir is the only state in India which has its own constitution. It is the creation of Instrument of Accession read through the Art 370 of the Indian constitution. The title of the constitution as provided by the constitution itself is "Constitution of Jammu and Kashmir". However, the provisions of this constitution were applicable to the state on 20th day of January 1947.

To sum-up, after examining the scope of constitutional autonomy being enjoyed by the state of Jammu and Kashmir, we find that the state enjoys a sufficient amount of autonomy and freedom in internal administration. Moreover, according to one study, 25 per cent of the constitution of India is not at all applicable to this state till today. The detail of this study is as follows:-

- Total Articles in the constitution of India – 395. (without amendenent)
- Articles not applicable to the state of Jammu and Kashmir-87.
- Articles applicable with amendments-32.

In such circumstances of the case of more autonomy in respect of the state of Jammu and Kashmir appears to be weak.

The constitution of Jammu and Kashmir was amended in 1965 and the office of Prime-Minister was replaced by the office of Chief Minister. The Chief Minister actually assumed the power and prerogation which P.M. enjoyed before the constitution was amended.

General Election of 1967 and State Autonomy

Till 1967, when the Congress party was both in the centre and almost all the states, the relationship between centre and the state by and large were smooth and there were only few tensions. But this picture entirely changed in 1967 when non-Congress government came into power in some states. These states challenged the dominant rule of central government. They wanted greater independence of action. The state which were most vocal of criticizing the growing power of centre and have put forward demand for greater autonomy include West Bengal, Punjab, Karnataka, Tamil Nadu. Later on Andhra Pradesh, Kerala and Jammu and Kashmir also joined this category.

Indira Gandhi's Era and State Autonomy

Under Pt. Nehru, the Indian federal structure had worked through federalism within the Congress party rather than through constitutional channels. The dominance of the Congress at the centre and in almost all the states had ensured homogeneity of power between the two, purity within Congress made it more representative and flexibility by internalizing political dissent and creating a competitive mechanism within the consensual framework of the party. The state level leaders enjoyed considerable political autonomy from the centre. Mrs. Indira Gandhi, on the other hand, sought to create a highly personalized and centralized political system trying to make those responsible for Parliament, the court, the civil services and the federal system answerable to her. She was keen to co-opt Sheikh Abdullah and National Conference into Congress fold.

Indira Gandhi's Government in India was very keen to find out some workable solution with the Sheikh to achieve political harmony in the state of Jammu and Kashmir. Ultimately an agreement called Indira-Abdullah accord was eventually reached to avoid an era of confrontation.[56] Since Sheikh had failed to secure the right of self-determination for the people of Jammu and Kashmir, which he had been advocating for more than two decades, the event of 1975 provided him with an opportunity to give up the demand and make efforts to undo the erosion of the state's autonomy during his absence from active political life. (The Sheikh was released for a short period in 1958 and then in 1964) but went back to prison on both occasions. In 1974 Sheikh Abdullah's and Indira Gandhi's representatives began negotiation. By February 1975, an accord was hammered out.

Kashmir Accord–1975[57]

In the 1972 elections, Jammat won five seats in the legislature. The Congress won 57 of the 74 seats. Negotiations with Sheikh Abdullah and his leutenants led to the Kashmir accord, under which the Sheikh was brought back to power in February 1975. Mir Qusim stepped down and made way for him. Opposed to the merger of the National Conference and the congress, the Sheikh had began to work for their separation. The Congress's refusal to join the cabinet suited him. As Indira Gandhi did not trust the National conference, she was in favour of strong Congress presence in the state. The Kashmir Accord was a negotiation between the representatives of the centre and the state.[58] The Accord brought the real leadership of the state back into mainstream of National life.[59] Its main points were:-[60]

1. Jammu and Kashmir in its relation with the Union of India continue to be governed by the Art 370.
2. The residuary powers of Legislation will continue to be with the state. However, Parliament will continue to have powers to make laws relating to the prevention of activities relating to disclaiming, questioning or disrupting the sovereignty and territorial integrity of India, secessionist activities, insult to the constitution of the National Flag.
3. Where any provision of the constitution of India has been applied to the state, with adaptation and modification such be altered or repeated by an order of the President under art 370, but provisions of the constitution of India already applied to the state of Jammu and Kashmir. Without adaptation or modification are unalterable.
4. The state of Jammu and Kashmir have its own legislation on many matters.
5. No question was possible on the question of nomenclature of Government and Chief Minister.

But the Accord did not offer any autonomy, the accord did not give any extra power to the state of Jammu and Kashmir. The Accord affirmed the constitutional relevance of Art 370. Nevertheless, it stopped short of reviving the nomenclature of Saddar-e-Riyasat and Wazir-e-Azam, which has been abolished a decade earlier. It also rejected Sheikh's demand of the Jurisdiction of the Supreme Court and Election Commission.

The retention of autonomy of Jammu and Kashmir, under Art 370 since its inclusion in the Indian constitution, was a continuous passion of Sheikh particularly upto the accord of 1975. However, all along the years 1952-74, the Government of India tried to erode the article. The process continued uptill 1974, when the Sheikh-Indira. Accord was concluded. By the time most of the central laws were operated in the state of Jammu and Kashmir, there was hardly anything left in Art 370, which had not been accomplished in accordance with the wishes of the central leaders.

References

1. Government of Jammu and Kashmir, *Report of the State Autonomy Committee,* (Srinagar/Jammu), July 2002, p. 16.
2. Lamb, Alistair, *Crisis in Kashmir* : 1946-66, (London, 1966), p. 58.
3. Anand, AS, *The constitution of Jammu and Kashmir*, Universal Publication, (New Delhi, 1994) p. 26.
4. Ibid, p. 27.
5. Kaul, Pyarelal, *Crisis in Kashmir*, Suman Publication, (Delhi, 1991) p. 47.
6. Kak, B.L., *Kashmir-Problem and Polities*, Seema Publication (New Delhi, 1981) p. 121.
7. For Article 370, See *Appendix IV.*
8. Jagmohan, *My Frogen Turbulance in Kashmir*, Allied Publication. (Delhi, 1991), p. 230
9. Gupta, U.N., *Indian Federalism and Unity of Nation.* Vohra Publication, (Allahabad 1988), p. 63.
10. Gupta, U.N., *Indian Federalism and Unity of Nation.* Vohra Publication, (Allahabad 1988), p. 63.
11. Hari Ram, *Special Status in Indian Federalism : Jammu and Kashmir.* Seema Publication (Delhi 1983) p. 16.
12. *Constitution of India*, 1977, Art 1(2), p. 2.
13. Gupta, U.N., *Indian Federalism and Unity of Nation*, Vohra Publication, (Allahabad, 1988), p. 64.
14. *Ibid.*, p. 64.
15. Hari Ram, Special Status in Indian Federalism – Jammu and Kashmir. Seema Publication, (Delhi, 1983,) p. 64.
16. *Ibid.*, p. 64.
17. Gupta, U.N., *Indian Federalism and National Unity*, Vohra Publication, (Allahabad, 1988), p. 64.
18. *Ibid,* p. 65.
19. Hari Ram, *Special Status in Indian Federalism*, Seema Publication (New Delhi, 1983) p. 73.
20. *Ibid,* p. 74.
21. Gupta, U.N., *Indian Federalism and National Unity*, Vohra Publication, (Allahabad, 1998) p. 65.
22. *Ibid.*, p. 65.

23. *Ibid.*, p. 65.
24. Basu, D.D., *Introduction to the Constitution of India*, Pub by Prentice hall of India, 1977, p. 234.
25. Hari Ram, *Special Status in Indian Federalism* – Jammu and Kashmir, Seema Publication (New Delhi, 1983) p. 79.
26. *Ibid.*, p. 80.
27. Gupta, U.N., *Indian Federalism and National Unity*, Vohra Publication, (Allahabad, 1988), p. 66.
28. Basu, D.D., *Introduction to the Constitution of India,* 7th Edition, Prentice Hall of India (New Delhi, 1978) p. 235.
29. *Ibid.*, p. 235.
30. *Ibid.*, p. 235.
31. *Ibid.*, p. 235.
32. *Ibid.*, p. 235-36.
33. Ibid., p. 236.
34. Puri, Balraj, "*Jammu and Kashmir,*" in Weiner, Myron, (eds.) *State Politics in India*, Princeton University Press, (Preston, 1968) p. 227.
35. Basu, D.D., *Introduction to the Constitution of India*, Published by Prentice Hall of India (New Delhi, 1978) pp. 228-29.
36. Hari Ram; *Special Status in Indian Federalism – Jammu and Kashmir*, Seema Publication (New Delhi, 1983) p. 57.
37. *Ibid.*, p. 57.
38. For Delhi Agreement of July 1952 – See *Appendix V IV.*
39. Government of Jammu and Kashmir, *Report of the State Autonomy Committee* (Srinagar / Jammu) July 2000, p. 47.
40. Pt. Jawahar Lal Nehru's speech in the Lok Sabha on July 24, 1952 Quoted in the Report of the State Autonomy Committee, (Srinagar/ Jammu, 2000 July) p. 49.
41. Anand, A.S., *The Constitution of India; Its Development and Comments*, Universal Publication (New Delhi, 1994) p. 149.
42. Government of Jammu and Kashmir, Report of the State Autonomy Committee, (Srinagar/Jammu, July 2000), p. 51.
43. Anand, A.S., *The Constitution of India – Its Development and Comments*, Universal Publication, (New Delhi, 1994), p. 150.
44. *Ibid.*, p. 151.
45. Government of Jammu and Kashmir, *Report on the State Autonomy Committee* (Srinagar/Jammu, July 2000) p. 53.

46. Ibid., p. 54.
47. *Ibid.*, p. 54.
48. *Ibid.*, p. 54.
49. *Ibid.*, p. 54.
50. Ibid., p. 54.
51. Bhattacharjea, Ajit, *Kashmir - The Wounded Valley*, USBPD, (Delhi, 1994) p. 194.
52. Twist with desting, *India Today*, July 10, 2000. p. 26.
53. *Ibid.*, p. 26.
54. Anand, A.S., *The constitution of India. Its Development and Comments*, Seema Publication (New Delhi, 1994) p. 246.
55. Fazili, Mansoor; *The Constitution of Jammu and Kashmir*, Astair Pub (Islamabad, 1984) p. 61.
56. Kashmir Accord 1975, *A Political Analysis* by G.R. Nagar, Gulshan Publication (Srinagar, 1988) p. 88.
57. For Kashmir Accord of 1975, *See Appendix.*
58. Ali, Ashgar, *Can Autonomy be a Solution, EPW*, July 2000, p. 2359.
59. *Kashmir Accord-1975, A Political analysis* by G.R. Nagar, Gulshan Publication, (Islamabad, 1988), p. 89.
60. Dr. Sharma, R.N., *Jammu and Kashmir Autonomy – An exercise in centre-state relation,* Subhi Pub (New Delhi, 2000) p. 108.

4

Politics in Jammu and Kashmir after Kashmir Accord (1975-1989)

There are no two opinions about the fact that the problem of Kashmir partially owes to the mishandling and misgovernment by the various governments of the state and the centre.[1] The central leadership from the very beginning tried to make the state governments on the line of the centre. The policy of the Indian leadership in respect of Kashmir has been to keep it within the Indian union, no matter whether this can always be done through fair and democratic means or not. "It has been the policy of state becomes essentially, it should support the government function".[2]

The tradition of Government of India of not tolerating any government in Kashmir if it is likely to turn against the authority in New Delhi was taken a step further by Indira Gandhi. She not only wanted to ensure that those in power in Srinagar were pro-India but that they were also ready to work with Congress party.[3] In fact with Sheikh rising to power in 1975, the Accord brought the real leadership of the state back to the mainstream of national life.[4] Since Sheikh had failed to secure the right of self-determination for the people of Kashmir which he had been advocating for more than two decades. The event of 1975 provided him with an opportunity go give up the demand and make effect to undo the erosion of the state's autonomy during his absence from active political life.

After this Accord the Sheikh declared that the accession of Jammu and Kashmir into Indian union was final. He underlined the Instrument of Accession as the basic for centre-state relations thereby claiming more and more powers for the centre and reducing the central interference is the internal autonomy of the state. The Sheikh aptly clarified the reality that Act. 370 forms the basis of centre-state relationship by stating:

While the states, Accession to India in 1947, removed the apprehensions of the non-Muslim minority in Jammu and Kashmir, the incorporation of this Article was meant to allay the fears of Muslim majority by the provision of internal autonomy of the state.[5] About a month earlier, the Union Home Minister had already declared that "the differences during the elections will not be allowed to come in the way of cordial and harmonizing relations between the centre and the state".[6] After a few days the Chief Minister also reciprocated by declaring Kashmir is keen on cordial ties with the centre for secularism and democracy, and added:

"Any attempt to erode the internal autonomy of the state being enjoyed on the basis of the special status under Article 370 would not be tolerated our relations with the centre will be based on the unity of hearts, it cannot be forced or brought about any pressure".[7]

Indira Gandhi's Government in India, was very keen to find out some workable solution with the Sheikh to achieve political harmony in the state of Jammu and Kashmir. The Kashmir accord of 1975 will be regarded of democracy and secularism on which the Indian Unions established.

1977's Assembly Election—Preservation of the Special Status

One of the most important factors in the politics of the valley was the re-emergence of the National Conference headed by the chief minister, Sheikh Abdullah at the time of Lok Sabha election in Jammu and Kashmir, early in 1977. In the State Assembly elections, the same year, the National Conference decided to contest all the 76 seats in the state alone, without an electoral alliance with any other party. The most important feature of this election was that the special status of Kashmir was used as a devise to mobilize public opinion, at least in Kashmir division, by almost all political parties. The Sheikh maintained that his party would consider no sacrifice too great for the attainment of its goal to achieving a place of honour and dignity for the people of the state in the Indian Union through Art. 370. It is noteworthy that in the earlier stages of the election campaign, the Sheikh himself had re-opened this sore spat of the Indian constitution. He appealed to the masses in the valley from his sick bed to vote in "large number for the National Conference candidates and thus, defeat the design of unworthy politicians out to be little Kashmir nationalism for the shake of capturing power".[8] It is noteworthy that over the years Kashmir sub-nationalism has been asserting itself and itself and its biggest votary has been the Sheikh himself. He applead to voters in the following terms: "By casting your vote for National

Conference, you have to prove that Kashmir Nationalism cannot be undermined by conspiracy only the people of Kashmir can decide about its future there can be no compromise on the internal autonomy of Kashmir".[9] Thus, the landslide victory of the National Conference in the Jammu and Kashmir Assembly elections was seen by political observers in the valley as a clear mandate for preservation of the state's special status. In a very real sense, the Sheikh was himself the candidate in the 42 constituencies of the valley. Those who voted for National Conference decidedly voted for Sheikh Abdullah and special status of Kashmir. The Sheikh Abdullah went a step further and described the poll of 1977 as an extraordinary device to preserve the identity of Kashmir. He warned "Kashmir was a part of India and Kashmiris were Indian, but they wanted to live in India with dignity and honour. If they were not assured this, they would not hesitate to separate from the Indian Union".[10]

It appears strange that the National Conference and its leaders politicalised this Art. 370, in spite of the standing assurance in the Kashmir Accord as under "the state of Jammu and Kashmir, which is a constituent unit of the Union of India, shall in its relation with the Union, continue to be governed by Article 370 of the constitution".[11] After having emerged victorious in the first ever free election in the state held under Governors rule, the Sheikh had become a champion of State's right in India, demanding more and more powers for other state. In this he had found an ally in the CPI(M) Chief Minister of West Bengal, Jyoti Basu, who strongly supported special status of Kashmir this:

The special status of Kashmir within Indian union as laid down in Art 370 of the constitution should be retained. The way this Article had been worked by the Congress government at the centre, had raised grave doubts and suspicion among the people of the state these must be removed now, particularly in view of the fact that the leaders of the state government have underlined the Instrument of Accession to India.[12]

The Sheikh had taken the fresh stand that he was never opposed to accession of Kashmir to India as such but only to the increasing quantum of accession. He asked forcefully, "Why not have Article 370 in respect of other states also?" The National Conference won the General Election in 1977 and Janta Party "not only reconciled itself to its defeat in the state but also forget the bitterness". The Union Government, understanding fully that the Sheikh is identified with the campaign for the greater state autonomy, accorded him unfailing understanding and respect and the Union President himself described him not Shere-i-Kashmir but Sher-e-Bharat. In 1977 the state held its first free and fair elections, barring incidents of violence, and consequently there is now a strong realisation that "Indian democracy which in the past stopped at Pathankot, had for the first time crossed the Pir Panjal Ranje"[13]. Moreover, the major factor which paved the path for normal relations between the state and the centre is the massive dose of central help for this state without which it would be difficult to achieve anything, as the states own income, for instance during 1976-77 was Rs. 56.90 crores which in turn is insufficient even to pay the wages to the state administration. Central grants in the same year were Rs. 95.21 crores.[14] Pointing toward the centre-state relations, the Sheikh declared "Jammu and Kashmir had to be on the right side of whatever party was in power, the state could not have a policy of confrontation with the Centre which would be disastrous not only for Jammu and Kashmir but also for the whole country". Special status of Kashmir is, therefore, one of the major stables factors in centre-state relation. For the same reason the Janta Party, at the centre, retraced its steps very quickly, stopped dealing with Kashmir in a causal manner and formulated a policy based on the constitutional position of the state in the Union. Every important Janta leader assued the state leadership that centre-state relations on the basis of Kashmir's special status would be maintained.

Sheikh Abdullah remained undisputed leader of the state upto the time when he died in 1982. This period of 5 years of Sheikh's rule was one of the great important at is allied the anti-national elements in the state. He was never secular, he was a valley Muslim who cared little for Buddhists and Hindus or of Jammu and Ladakh. He was only concern for the Muslims of the Valley. He opted for accession to India because hated by Jinnah and others leaders to had no place in Pakistan.[15] He accepted accession with India but centre-state relation after Sheikh Abdullah took over as chief minister of the state became a controversial issue.

Sheikh's Stand on Laws Applicable to Jammu and Kashmir State

A federation is a structure as well as a process. As a structure a federation has various starts ranging from dangerously loose to extremely tight ones. As a process a federation includes operation relations between the centre and the state governments.[16] But Indian constitution according to Amal Ray, " provides a cooperative federal system with its slant toward a powerful centre"[17]. In this cooperative federal structure there is a division of functions between the centre and the state on the basis of territory and the subject matter,[18] from the territorial point of view. Indian Parliament, subject to the provisions of Indian constitution, may make laws for the whole or any part of Indian territory. A law thus made cannot be valid merely because it has an extra territorial operation. But this is not entirely true in the case of Jammu and Kashmir since the total Legislative sphere has been divided between the state Legislative and the Parliament – the former exercise only enumerated powers in regard to the state while the latter enjoys the residuary powers. The powers of the Indian Parliament are further limited in the union and concurrent lists to legislate in consultation with the state government, after getting a declaration from the President of India that the matter corresponds to those specified in the Instrument of Accession by which the state acceded to Indian Union further the Indian Parliament with the concurrence of state legislature, is also authorized to make laws in these lists when the same are specified by order of the President of the Union.

The State Assembly (No doubt without Sheikh as Prime Minister) decided finally to make Kashmir as an integral part of India.[19] Consequently, the constitutional position of the state could not remain rigid and static.[20] However, due to these special features all the provisions of the Indian constitution do not apply to the state of Jammu and Kashmir some of these apply, some do not apply at all, while others apply with specific modifications.

By the end of 1972, the central laws, which had been extended to the state, numbered 243.[21] Out of these laws, 46 relate to matters enumerated in the concurrent list.[22] These laws became a controversial issue after Sheikh Abdullah took over as Chief Minister of the State after having won the state election in 1977. His government desired to review these laws since these were "accepted" according to his point of views "by those state governments which were not truly representative of the people".[23] He himself emphasized that he returned to power in 1975, after making it unambiguously clear that he could assume office only on the basis of the position, as it existed on August 8, 1953, when he was arrested and deposed. He further held that the elected representatives had the right to reject all such laws, which tend to restrict the state's autonomy.

The Sheikh's stand, according to Gundevia, is that "Kashmir's accession to India stands but it was based on the Instrument of Accession which limited the powers of the government of India to three subjects. Defence, external affairs and communication".[24] There was, however, a strong reaction against the very idea of reviving these laws by the state government and the move was assailed in Indian political quarters and inside the state itself, holding the view that these laws were very beneficial to the people of the state and had cemented the state's relation with the union. State government changed its attitude, fearing a phase of centre-state confrontation which Sheikh was keen to avoid. His Finance Minister remarked that "the would modify or repeal the laws only when the constitution allowed to do so".[25] Beg declared that "whenever we feel that a change in any Act is needed to suit the local conditions, we shall consult the centre in a cordial atmosphere and nothing would be done in regard to the proposed review without consulting the Central Government".[26] Thus, the attitude of the National Conference leadership towards this issue appears to have undergone a constructive change. Viewed legally and constitutionally, the state legislature or the Chief Minister of the State is not authorised to set up committee for revision of the central laws already applied to the state. There is absolutely no provision in the constitution of India or that of the state, which can empower the state government to recommend revocation or make amendments to central laws.

The Indian Dilemma in the State of Jammu and Kashmir After Sheikh Abdullah's Death

Sheikh Abdullah died a hero's death on Sept 1982 and vacated the seat of Chief Minister for his son Farooq Abdullah. During these years of Sheikh's rule, the demand of two region Jammu and Ladakh for more autonomy against discriminatory of state resettlement act evoked much problem to him. Thus, Sheikh Abudullah who ruled at the hearts of millions of the people of the state for more than fifty years left on indelible impact on the state with the rest of the country.

It can be argued that Indian dilemma in the state of Jammu and Kashmir after Abdullah's death derives from three major factors:[27]

First, the increasing instability of the regime in the state of Jammu and Kashmir which become apparent after the death of Sheikh Abdullah obliged India to revise its own policy toward that state; and each modification of policy only served to unsettle an already precarious balance of forces. The fact that there emerged no adequate substatute for Sheikh Abdullah was a serious blow for India. Sheikh Abdullah may not, to put it mildly, have always seen to eye to eye with the power that be in New Delhi; but he was strong. What came in his place had many of the qualities of a vacuum.

Second, the effectiveness of the central government of India was at the time of Sheikh Abdullah's death visibly in decline, not least because of the growing crisis of Sheikh radicalism in the Punjab (in which Pakistan was to be accsued by some Indians of playing a mischievous part). What seemed initially to be sign of strength, the storming in June 1984 of the main Sikh shrine the Golden Temple in Amritsar, soon turned into disaster; its direct consequences was the assassination of Indira Gandhi on 31 Oct. 1984. With her went we can see, much of the political will at the heart of the Indian republic. There was no immediate replacement of her caliber (her son Rajiv Gandhi was certainly not such a one); and it may be that her place will not be taken at the helm of Indian affairs for a long time to come. At all events this dramatic weaking at the centre, combined with the lessons suggested by the rise of Sikh separation, undoubtedly both encouraged dissent in the state of Jammu and Kashmir and made it infinitely more difficult for New Delhi to cope with it, all this, of course; developed at a period when Pakistan, too, was showing sign to internal regional discord.

Third, by the time of Sheikh Abdullah's death, following the onset of the Iranian Revolution and reaction of the Soviet invention of Afghanistan. Muslim sentiment in South Asia was beginning to undergo a profound transformation. A new Islamic Military, even among people were traditionally regarded as being as docile as the Kashmiris were once though to be, emerged. Such an altered patterns of attitudes posed security problems of extreme difficulty, a discovery which Indian and Israel were not alone in sharing with Soviet Union. Repression, it now seemed, could only palliate: it could never cure. The counterviling rise of Hindu extremism in Indian. Moreover, certainly was done nothing, to calm and reassure the Muslims of the subcontinent.

During 1977-82 period Sheikh Abdullah continued his no friendly stance toward the centre. He encouraged fundamental forces allows Friday prayers in offices banned cinema shows during Friday prayers and "Islamised' the administration as far as possible. He tried his best to undermine the authority of the centre on the state, discouraged appointment of I.A.S. officers from the centre and disallowed the work of Income Tax Authorities, he was encouraged opening more of them, and foreign money was now allowed to flow in liberally to fund fundamentalist organisations, ultimately it was "Resettlement Bill" which was introduced by Sheikh Abdullah in the Jammu and Kashmir Assembly on 30th March 1982, that raised real force. The

Bill sought the permanent return and settlement of Muslims who had migrated to Pakistan and area held by Pakistan. They were to be rehabilitate in Jammu under Muslim dominance, but the Sheikh made no such offer to people who had migrated to India. Governor B.K. Nehru, however, returned the bill and sought the opinion of the Attorney General of India. But after the demise of the Sheikh Abdullah his son as Chief Minister got the bill passed.[29] Rabi Ray, Janta Dal leader and former speaker of Lok Sabha, had described this bill as "dangerous for the security and integrity of India"[30] the implementation was, however stopped on a public interest appeal to the Supreme Court.

In short Sheikh Abdullah created most infavourable condition to cooperate with New Delhi, he mentioned his nationality as "Kashmiri" not Indian,[31] special status of Kashmir was one of the major stable factors in Abdullah's period,[32] the result was that the centre-state relation became strained.

1983's Election–Communal Polarization

The Sheikh died in 1982, but before his death, he made his son, Dr. Farooq Abdullah, the President of NC and asked the people of Kashmir to place their trust on him, for he said, his son would accomplish what he had not been able to.

1983 was a year for election in Indian states. Indira Gandhi had originally hoped that in the state of Jammu and Kashmir the National Conference, under Dr. Farooq Abdullah, would join with the Congress (I) to campaign as an alliance in which the Congress (I) would have been allotted twenty-three out of the total of the seventy-six elective seats. By April 1983 it had become apparent that this was but a dream. Relation between Dr. Abdullah and New Delhi were rapidly deteriorating; and the National Conference now announced that it had no option but to contest all seventy-six elective seats in the state. The congress (I) replied that it, too would fight all seats.[33] Hence, 1983's election which were held on 5th June, turned into a straight fight between the National Conference and the New Delhi.

It had been Indira Gandhi's intension to fight this election in alliance with Dr. Abdullah in hope that such a display of unity would permit the issue of the actual status of the state of Jammu and Kashmir within the Indian Union to be given the minimum publicity. In the event, this was the central issue of the campaign.[34]

Dr. Abdullah, while careful not to challenge explicitly the finality of the state of Jammu and Kashmir's accession to India, yet maintained that Art 370, despite the massive erosion it had suffered over the years, still had very real meaning; and he demanded that state should not be furcated exercising all its existing rights under that Article (and regaining lost once, too).

Indira Gandhi's Congress I, while it did not go out of its way to challenge in public the significance of Art 370, yet, because its only real strength lay in Jammu, found itself willy nilly the champion of adjusting "regional imbalance" by, it was certainly implied, strengthening the link between Jammu and the Indian Union the better to protect Jammus, largely non-Muslim inhabitants – from the oppressive politicians of the near in Srinagar.[35] Thus, in 1983 Indira Gandhi, who at the beginning had set out to conciliate Dr. Farooq Abdulla and bring about an effective National Conference–Congress I collaboration which would take-the spotlight off the problem of the constitutional status of the state of Jammu and Kashmir, now found that the whole issue had been so polarized that she and Dr. Abdullah stood facing each other like boxers in the ring after the first round of what promised to be a long and bloody contest. It was as if Sheikh Abdullah were still alive and this was a repeat of what had happened after the Delhi Agreement of 1952 and the Kashmir Accord of 1975.

In 1983, however, the Congress won two seats in the valley and 8 went to the National Conference. But in Jammu, the Congress won 23 seats of the 32 seats against six won by National Conference. By March 1984, Indira Gandhi concluded that something was happening in the state of Jammu and Kashmir which promised to replicate the Sikh crisis in Punjab, one such trouble spot was enough. On 26th March she dismissed her kinsman B.K. Nehru as Governor of Jammu and Kashmir and replaced him by Jagmohan Malhotra, a man of great determination whose abilities in suppressing communal disorders had been well displayed as lieutenant- Governor of Delhi. It was a step, which was certainly a relation of both the Kashmir accord of 1975 and Delhi Agreement of 1952. It put the very survival of Art 370 in doubt. It was prelude to a revolution in India's relation with the state of Jammu and Kashmir and the beginning of what can only be described as a disaster.[36]

Farooq Abdullah's Dismissal

In July, 1984, the Farooq Abdullah Ministry was toppled by the Congress by engineering a defection in the ranks of National Conference. The Congress put G.M. Shah on seat.[37] An elected government in Kashmir was dismissed by Delhi.

We have a federal constitution, but it's a federal constitution that concentrate political power and also economic power in Delhi. And this power has often been misused.[38] In 1984, it was misused in Kashmir when Farooq Abdullah's government was dismissed. It was a popularly elected government with tremendous support from the people in what was described as the only other fair election in Kashmir.

Farooq Abdullah's government, which had a massive majority in the assembly, was dismissed for reason that had nothing to do with the governance of the state, political or economic. He was dismissed for extraneous consideration. When Farooq Abdullah was dismissed every segment of Indian opposition at that time–that is, every political party in the country excluding the Congress party, be it regional or national – opposed that decision. And when Farooq decided to mobilize people to agitate against the dismissal, every opposition leader of any consequences from other parts of the country stood by Farooq Abdullah. Unfortunately, Farooq could not keep his movement going. And a situation came when Farooq decided that he should have an accord with Delhi.

The dismissal of Government sent signals to the people of Kashmir that any honest decision that they may take in regard to the governance of state could easily be set aside by the power that be in Delhi. Naturally the anger against Delhi built up. Farooq was the man who articulated that anger.[39]

When the Congress found that the law and order situation was progressively becoming worse and G.M. Shah, "failed to control the rising tide of violence". Shah resigned on 6th March 1986 and the Governor's rule was imposed the next day.[40] Jag Mohan took over as Governor. After a period of Abdullah accord, Farooq Abdullah returned as Chief Minister in 1986.[41]

Rajiv Gandhi's Era–New Beginning of Centre-State Relation

Rajiv Gandhi, Mrs. Gandhi's son took over the Prime Ministership after her assassination, won a sweeping victory in the General Election in late 1984 and retained the post in his own right. Indira Gandhi was assassinated in 1984 and with that came the end of an era in Kashmir and came Rajiv Gandhi-Farooq Abdullah Accord.

When Farooq signed an accord with the Congress, the Kashmiris experienced a tremendous sense of betrayal, a betrayal that was expected by them. They had given all the support and all the love they could to the man who had been dismissed, and when he went to sign an accord without caring to consult them, it was into acceptable.

The other reason for the opposition to the accord was that Kashmiri identity was being compromised by Farooq's agreement with a party that on its own could never come to power in the state and could not, through this accord, be brought into the ruling set up.

Farooq then ran his coalition government with the Congress party. The accord was also opposed in NC working committee, a senior cabinet minister had said to Farooq " you will become Chief Minister of state but you will no longer be leader of people of Jammu and Kashmir".

When National Conference joined hands with the Congress, people felt that they had surrendered, the Congress accord with Farooq not be misconstrued as an understanding with Kashmir; the reality is that in one stroke Farooq lost the people's faith.

1987's Assembly Election–A coalition between the centre and the State of Jammu and Kashmir

For the year 1987 elections, the Jamat-e-Islami, Awami Action Committee and other small parties believing in Islamic Fundamentalism, came together and made a Muslim United Front (MUF) they with a joint manifesto and a common election symbol, decided to take on the National Conference and its partner the Congress. But MUF won only 4 seats,[43] and Farooq was sworn as Chief Minister of the state. He joined hands with Congress. He had justified the decision in term of a "hard political reality', he had came to accept that "It , want to implement programme to fight poverty and run a grant I have to stay on the right side of the centre".[44] A decade earlier, Sheikh Abdullah to had reached a similar conclusion "Jammu and Kashmir had to be one of the right side whatever party in the power at the centre".[45] But the Sheikh jealously preserved the distinct position of Kashmir identity in Indian policies whereas Farooq's action was widely perceived as total capitalism to the centre.

Sarkaria Commission's Recommendation with Special Reference to Jammu and Kashmir

In the back ground of decade eighties in particular witnessed a struggle to get the federal issue on the Nations agenda. When the political challenged assumed new dimensions and tensions between centre and the state of Jammu and Kashmir grew in sharpness. In this context the Government of India announced on March 24th 1983, the appointment of a commission to examine and review the working of existing arrangement between the union and the state of Jammu and Kashmir and other states in regard to power functions and responsibilities in all sphere and recommended appropriate changes and measures. The commission came to be known as the sarkaria commission on centre state relation after the name of its chairman, justice (Retd.) R.S. Sarkaria, the Commission submitted its report in 1988. The main proposal of the Sarkaria Commission are, [46]

- It made strong suggestion that Article 370 was not a transitory provision, this appears to have been made specifically in response to 'in the interest of National integration".
- The Residuary power of Legislation in regard to taxation matters should remain exclusively in the competence of Parliament while the residuary field other than that of transaction should be place on concurrent list.
- The enforcement of Union laws, particularly those relating to the concurrent sphere, is secured through the machinery of the states.
- To ensure uniformity on the basic issue of National policy, with respect to the subject of a proposed legislation, consultation may be carried out with the state government individually and collectively at the forum of the proposed intergovernmental council. It was not recommended that the consultation be a constitutional obligation.
- Ordinarily, the union should occupy only that much field of a concurrent subject on which uniformity of policy and action is essential in the larger interest of the Nation, leaving the rest and details for state action.
- On administrative relations, Sarkaria made the following observation "Federalism is more a functional arrangement for cooperative action, than a static constitutional concept." Art 258 (power of Union to confer power etc. on state in certain cases) provides a tool by the liberal use of which cooperative federalism can be substantially realised in the working of the system. A more generous use of this tool should be made than has hitherto been made done, for progressive decentralization of power of the government of the state.
- Art 356, should be used 'sparingly in extreme case when all alternatives fail to prevent or rectify a breakdown of constitutional machinery in the state.

After the Sarkaria Commission, Union government and Jammu and Kashmir Chief Minister Farooq Abdullah agreed to restart a dialogue on autonomy by beginning discussions on devolution of more financial and administrative power to the state, but this agreement on Sarkaria Commission was not end the Kashmir's problem of autonomy. It only makes the beginning of new phase. Kashmir valley has started violence to secure this political goals.

Autonomy and Terrorism

In 1986 widespread anti-Hindu riots, emerged by Muslim Secessionist element, struck the southern district of the Kashmir provinces. The violence spreads to other parts of the provinces. The communal violence, the Muslim perpetrated against the Hindu, was the first expression of the organise armed resistance. The Hindu in Kashmir who had always put themselves in the vanguard of the forces, which opposed Muslim Secessionism and movement for the violence which unleashed in Kashmir.[47] In coming years violence had become regular factor in the state of Jammu and Kashmir. The situation has not improved during the Congress period. The National Congress also did not improve state's situation.

The National Conference had lost its appeal as representing Kashmir aspirations after its force association with the Congress.[48]

During the period of 1986-87, the militants started a 'Poster' war with a view of alienating the entire Muslim population of Jammu and Kashmir against the state and the Union Government and the local administration. Delhi's grave concern over the adverse situation was ignored on the courts; First, because most of the politicians and the Government officials had sympathy with the militant and their causes and second; because the situation was already out of the state Government's control and they found themselves in no position to curb the terrorist activities even if they cared to.[49]

These were further a qualitative change. The Sikh in abroad supporting and funding militancy in Punjab and Jammu and Kashmir respectively joined hands and helped in escalating the secessionists activities. During the first half of 1989 the violence in one form or the other and agitation and Bandhs (Strike) had become a regular factor.[50] The state Government, a coalition of Congress and the National Conference, took no action against the rapid fundamentalisation of the Muslim Secessionist movement and the Militarisation of Secessionist forces. A large number of Military training camps were organized in PoK and Jammu provinces in 1987. The military violence began to spread in Kashmir provinces towards the close of 1989. When "the violence continued unabated" the central government did nothing.[51] They should have dismissed the state government in early 1988, imposed the Governor's rule and given a free hand to Jagmohan to control the situation. This reaction encouraged Pakistan. The I.S.I. and all the militant organisations and secessionist movements continued to escalate rapidly. The aim obviously was to link up the Punjab separatist movement with that of Kashmir.

The party level, both Congress and National Conference, by and large, played a supine role, they frequently talked about common political fight of National Conference and Congress against the anti-National and Communal forces were now here in sight. The workers and leaders of these parties were conspicuous by their absence when fundamentalist and pro-Pakistan elements were all over Srinagar and other towns of the Valley. The administrative machinery was left high and dry, and its effectiveness in the political vacuum could not but be limited"[52]. In fact, the new coalition Government proved to be totally ineffective and yet Rajiv Gandhi and his government failed to see the "disconcerting trends".[56]

In November 1989, in spite of the total lawlessness in Jammu and Kashmir Rajiv Gandhi's Government thought it fit to hold Lok Sabha (Parliament) election in Kashmir. The National Conference nominees were elected unopposed because of the other boycotting the elections. Soon after they blamed the centre for its misdeed in Kashmir and held it responsible for the prevailing situation. They also balanced the centre for treating Jammu and Kashmir as its colony"[57] and for not fulfilling the "promise which it made to the people of Kashmir in 1947".

History had completed yet another circle in Kashmir alienation from the Indian states. Kashmiris would now resort to violence to secure their political goals. The National conference, which had crumbled with the onset of the military, proposed the restoration of autonomy of the state, which the state had in 1952,[58] the Congress leaders proposed the exclusion of Jammu and Kashmir state from the constitutional position, it had before the promulgation of the Presidential Order of 1954, by virtue of which provinces of the constitution of India in respect of citizenship, fundamental rights, jurisdiction of Supreme Court, emergency power of the President of India, and part of the 7th schedule, envisaging the division of powers between the union and the states were extended to Jammu and Kashmir. The Congress leader claimed that a separate political identity of the state based upon the Muslim character of its population would provide an alternative to the secessionist of the state from India for which the Muslim organisations were operating in the state.

Imposition of Governor's Rule and Dissolution of State Assembly

The return of the Janta Party to power at the centre in Dec. 1989, with its pro-Muslim vote bank politics, had the worst possible impact on the valley.[59] The Janta Party government depended heavily on its BJP supporters who were keen to curtail Kashmir's autonomy. The pressure of event in 1990 proved to be as momentous for Kashmir as in 1947. But now there was no Sheikh Abdullah to mobilize the valley against Pakistani intervention and stress its secular heritage; nor a Mahatma Gandhi or a Jawaharlal Nehru to create confidence in India.[60] The face of India that they would see was that of Jagmohan, who replaced General Krishna Rao and returned as Governor on 19 January 1990. Farooq promptly resigned, as expected, and Jagmohan was back in full control.

The appointment of Jagmohan was perhaps well meant but he could not have cleaned up the augean stable without the full support of the centre. Although V.P. Singh (Prime Minister) was supportive to begin with, Srinagar politicians were able to Polson of mind of the centre leaders once they know that Jagmohan meant business. They ultimately persuaded V.P. Singh to appoint George Fernandes as Minister of Kashmir affairs over the head of the Governor. Neither V.P. Singh nor George Fernandes was able to see the consequences of this action soon the Minister and the Governor were not on taking terms, while Jagmohan was promoting the pro-India elements in the valley. Kashmir was never witnessed such anarchy.

Jagmohan's appointment was made without the consultation of the state government and Farooq Abdullah, the then Chief Minister of the state, was informed after the appointment was made. Farooq Abdullah resigned in protest.[61] Jagmohan, the Governor, kept the Assembly in suspended animation and imposed the proclamation of constitutional breakdown under Section 92 of the constitution of Jammu and Kashmir. Later on, the Governor exercised crucial function by virtue of Art 356 of the constitution of India because of breakdown of law and order machinery due to insurgency.[62] The Kashmiri could not understand what was happening in their land, of course, the Indian leaders were in no way better informed.

Reference

1. Thakur, Harish, *Alienation and Integration in Jammu and Kashmir*, Aalekh Publication (Jaipur, 2001) p. 12.

2. Chander Prakash, *Functional Politics in Jammu and Kashmir*–An unpublished M.Phil dissertation submitted to JNU Quoted by Hari Ram–*Special status in Indian Federalism–Jammu and Kashmir*, Seema Publication (New Delhi, 1983), p. 135.
3. Gehlat, N.C., *Trends in Indian Politics,* Deep and Deep Pub, (New Delhi 1988) pp. 132-133
4. *Kashmir Accord 1975*, A Political analysis by G.R. Nagar, Gulshan Pub. (Srinagar, 1988). p. 89
5. Hari Ram, *Special Status in Indian Federalism–Jammu and Kashmir*, Seema Publication, (New Delhi, 1983) p. 137.
6. *Ibid.*, p. 138.
7. *Ibid.*, p. 138.
8. Sheikh Abdullah's sick-bed taped appeal to his voters quoted by Hari Ram, *Special Status in Indian Federalism–Jammu and Kashmir*, Seema Publication (New Delhi, 1983) p. 108
9. *Ibid.*, p. 109
10. *Ibid.*, p. 109.
11. Puri, Balraj, "Wasted year over Article 370", *Indian Express*.
12. Hari Ram, *Special Status in Indian Federalism Jammu and Kashmir*, Seema Publication. (New Delhi), p. 110.
13. *Ibid.*, p. 139
14. *Ibid.*, p.. 139.
15. Dr Sharma, R.D., Kashmir Autonomy–An Exercise in Centre-State Relation, Subhi Publication (New Delhi 2000).
16. Ray, Amal, *Tension Areas in Indian Federal system*, World Press (Calcutta, 1970) p. 134
17. *Ibid.*, p. 4.
18. Jain, M.p., *Indian constitutional law,* (Bombay, 1970) p. 271.
19. Hari Ram, *Special Status in Indian Federalism Jammu & Kashmir,* Seema Publication (New Delhi 1983), p. 141
20. Jain, M.P., *Op. cit.*, p. 39.
21. Singh, Balbir, *The Working of the Jammu and Kashmir Legislative Assembly; 1967-72* (Jammu, 1973). p. 39.
22. Ibid., p. 39.
23. Hari Ram – *Special status in Indian Federalism – Jammu and Kashmir,* Seema Publication (New Delhi, 1983), p. 141.

24. *Ibid.*, p. 142.
25. *Ibid.*, p. 142.
26. *Ibid.*, p. 142.
27. Lamb, Alastair, Kashmir-A disputed Legacy, oxford University press, oxford, 1991, P 322-23.
29. Dr. Sharma, R.D., *Kashmir Autonomy – An exercise in Centre State Relation,* Subhi Publication (New Delhi, 2000) , p. 93.
30. Jay Singh, Hari, Kashmir *A Tale of Shame,* UPSPD Ltd. (New Delhi 1996), p. 92.
31. Ibid., p. 95.
32. Hari Ram, *Special Status in Indian Federalism Jammu and Kashmir,* Seema Publication, (New Delhi, 1983), p. 139
33. Hari Jay Singh, *Kashmir–A Tale of Shame,* UPSPD Ltd, (New Delhi, 1996), p. 92.
34. Lamb, Alistair, *Kashmir–A Disputed Legacy 1946-1990,* Oxford Press, (London, 1991), p. 328.
35. *Ibid.,* p. 329.
36. Hari Jay Singh, *Kashmir–A Tale of Shame*, UPSPD Pub. (New Delhi, 1996), p. 108.
37. *Ibid.*, p. 108.
38. Fernandis, George, *India's policies in Kashmir cited in thmus, Raju, G.C. (eds.); Perspective on Kashmir: the roots of conflict in South Asia,* West View Press Publication, (Oxford, 1992) p. 287.
39. *Ibid.,* p. 287.
40. *Ibid.,* p. 287.
41. Gandhi, D.V., *Leaders of India- A profile of eminent Public figures of the country, Indraprastha Publication,* (New Delhi, 2000), p. 1.
43. Nanda, K.K., *Conquering Kashmir–A Pakistani Obsession,* Lancer Publication (New Delhi, 1994), p. 298.
44. Behera, Navnita Chadda–*State Identity and Violence,* Manohar Pub, (New Delhi, 2000), p. 155.
45. *Ibid.*, p. 155.
46. Narayan, T., A classic Batch-up, *Outlook*, July 17, 2000, p. 29.
47. Kaul Santosh, *Kashmir's Constitutional Status,* Annual Publication, (New Delhi, 1999), p. 1444.
48. Bhattacharjea, Ajit., *Kashmir the Wounded Valley* UPSPD Ltd, (New Delhi, 1994), p. 257

49. Nanda, K.K., *Conquering Kashmir – A Pakistani Obsession,* Lancer Publication, (New Delhi, 1944), p. 300
50. *Ibid.*, p. 303.
51. *Ibid.,* p. 303.
52. Jagmohan, *My Frozen Turbulence in Kashmir,* (New Delhi, 1991), P. 110.
56. Nanda, K.K., *Conquering Kashmir.*
57. *Ibid.,* p. 304.
58. Kaul, Santosh, *Kashmir's Constitutional Status*, Anmol Publication, (New Delhi, 1999), p. 145.
59. Jaysingh, Hari, *Kashmir–A tale of Shame,* UPSPD Publication (New Delhi, 1996), p. 110.
60. Nanda. K.K., *Conquering Kashmir–A Pakistani Obsession,* Lancer Publication, (New Delhi, 1994), p. 261
61. Kaul, M.N., *Encyclopedia of India,* Reema Publication (New Delhi 1992) p. 129.
62. *Ibid.*, p. 130.

5
Autonomy and Terrorism—Politics in Jammu and Kashmir

The decade of 90s was the decade of so many changes in Indian politics, in this decade not only in international scenario where a federalist nation like U.S.S.R. decomposed into thirteen separate nationalities, but Indian federalism also had to face some major challanges where on the one hand different regional parties like DMK, ADMK, Akali Dal, Telugu Desham party, Asam Gana Parishad and National Conference started airing strong voices for greater autonomy and, on the other hand, through 73rd and 74th amendments the state took some serious steps toward the decentralisation of Indian federalism. Those amendments are important dimension of the emerging scenario in nineties, although in a cumbersome manner, the possibility of local Government emerging as the third-tier of the Indian federal polity, the XIth and XIIth schedules indicate the extent of devolution of powers from the states to elected panchayats and municipalities, decentralised planning and economic development vis-a-vis social justice have been promised but are yet to be seriously implemented. This item remains an unfinished task in the agenda of building a federal polity.

The nature of politics in India during the 1990s definitely shows that the Indian politics has to be more federal in its structure as well as working in future, everybody from political parties to juries and academics agree that Indian political system needs to be more 'federal' and the states grievances have to be carefully listened to if political as well as social, economic progress of the nation is to be insured.[1]

Basically, the decade of 90s was the decade of growing federalism. The two most notable changes of the 90s in India have been the growing federalisation of the polity and reform of economy with accent on liberalisation and marketization. India's federal system of government – "Quasi federal" in K.C. Wheare's classic characterization in the early post World War II decades has in the 1990's become considerably more federalised than in the past.[2]

The 1990s witnessed a new federal favour in the Indian political system. The whole matrix of the constitutional head of the state. The President and the Governors and head of the governments – the Prime Minister and the Chief Minister are now compelled by the changed circumstances to function significantly differently from the way they did in the era of Congress dominance. The Presidents and Governors have come to be elected or appointed with diverse party background due to a variegated pattern of inter party composition of the presidential electoral college (consisting of elected members of the Parliament and the State Legislative Assemblies) and different sets of parties or coalition in power at the centre and in the states, and what is more important, they have shown greater autonomy and discretion. This has increased the autonomy of the state governments.[3]

But also in the Kashmiri politics the decade of 90's witnessed many changes. From 1990 onwards the sense of alienation grew stronger and a genuine desire to attain freedom was born in the Kashmir Valley. At the same time the secessionist movement in Kashmir did not contain itself to demanding autonomy but also started giving stress on liberation.

There are no two opinions about the fact that the problem of Kashmir partially races to mishandling and misgovernment by the various governments of the states and the centre. The central leadership has from very beginning tried to make the state governments toe the line of the centre. The policy of Indian leadership in respect of Kashmir has been to keep it within no matters whether this can always be done through fair and democratic means or not. "It has been the policy of the centre until and unless the official leadership of the state becomes essentially undesirable, it should support the Government function."[4] The tradition of the Government of not tolerating any government in Kashmir if it is likely to turn against the authorities in New Delhi, was always a major cause of the alienation of the valley.

Alienation of the people of the valley was the most serious problem in the relations between centre and the state. The politics of Abdullah family and the people of the valley never fully supported merger with India. But the active anti-Indian feelings were encouraged by our own mishandling of the people. We always dealt with them through Sheikh Abdullah and Farooq Abdullah, a bridge which were weak and most unreliable. From 1990 onwards the anti-Indian Sentiments grew stronger. At the same time the secessionist movement in Kashmir did not contain itself to demanding autonomy but also started giving stress on liberation. This insurgence was thought over but not in a concensus. One group put forward the argument that the Kashmir problem aggravated because Kashmir's autonomy was not given due respect. But the second group who was represented by people like Jagmohan and some likeness of him argued that Kashmir is not just a part of India, but is such a part which because of enjoying undue autonomy has went wayward. This group demanded not a political but military solution of Kashmir problem. This stream is the most orthodox of Indian nationalist trend, having a rationalist feeling for India does not mean that one should neglect of overlook the genuinety or Kashmiri national identity.

The mode in which the Kashmir problem has entered into this decade is given out of the bounds of Constitutions for insurgents. Article 370 is no longer the subject of contention for them, the only option was either independence or a accession with Pakistan. But Congress, National Conference, Janata Dal, and various Left parties are of the opinion that the way to keep Kashmir integrated to India, has only one way, and it passes through Article 370. If this link breaks-up then even the residual chances of relation between India and Kashmir to return back to normalcy will be aborted.

The Central Government give the impression that they know the answer best of Kashmir's problems, but they know so little.

Politics in Jammu and Kashmir in Governor's Rule

Mr. V.P. Singh, who was heading the National Front Government, after the general election held in 1989 for the Parliament in India, appointed Jagmohan as the Governor of Jammu and Kashmir again and he took over on the 19th January 1990, Farooq Abdullah did not relish the idea of heading the state administration with Jagmohan as the Governor and resigned.

The Governor's rule was imposed and the State Legislative Assembly dissolved. Even Chief Minister Farooq Abdullah himself admitted that "the failure of his Government in realising the promise of National Conference—Congress accord such as fair administrative and initiation of a new era of prosperity as also the economic aspects of the accord have done a great harm to the image of his government."[5] He lucidly remarked that he had nothing to address his people about except "his failure" so he returned to his old rhetoric of planning centre for not understanding his problems and the old Pakistani bogey.[6]

Jagmohan, by various innovative actions and firm handling, succeeded in a short-time span in wresting the initiative from the militants and re-establishing the authority of the state.[7] Jagmohan's success did not suit Farooq Abdullah and he pursuaded Rajiv Gandhi to work for his recall. The Congress party accused Jagmohan of being anti-Muslim and blamed him for his harsh measures against the insurgant. Jagmohan had to resign on May 25th 1990 following the mounting pressure on P.M. V.P. Singh from Left Front and Congress.

Mr. Girish Chander Saxena was appointed the Governor of Kashmir and he took over from Jagmohan. During the tenure of Girish Saxena which lasted till 10th March 1998, the situation in Kashmir valley never improved, it continued to deteriorate. Pakistan had also succeeded to "hitch Kashmir militancy on to Islamic fundamentalism".[8] The situation in the valley in March 1998 was worse than what it was in January 1990. The state administration was inefficient and the militants in the valley practically run a parallel government.

General K.V. Krishna Rao was sworn in as Governor of Jammu and Kashmir on 12th March 1993. Earlier the outgoing Governors, Girish Saxena had submitted his resignation on 10th March, passing the way for a new initiative in the troubled state. The Indian Prime Minister P.V. Narasimha Rao had also expressed his dissatisfaction with the situation in Kashmir in the Parliament on 4th March and emphasised that there was a "need for a new approach to solving the vexed problem".[9] He also indicated that "there would be major changes in the administrative set-up of the state in the near future."[10] Other than few cosmetic changes nothing much happened. It remained business as usual in Krishna Rao's tenure in the Kashmir Valley. The appointment of General K.V. Krishna Rao as the Governor indicated the centre desire to break from past and initiated a new era. But situation in the Kashmir never improved. The secessionist movement in Kashmir did not contain itself to demanding autonomy but also started giving stress on liberation.

The Promise of Anything Short of Azadi and Beginning of Erosion of State Autonomy

Autonomy has remained, since the days of accession, the heart beat of the people of the State, the demand for Azadi or freedom was raised by a section of the angry youth in 1995, the union leadership realised that what is needed for this unit of the union is autonomy and that "sky should be the limit" in terms of then Prime Minister of the Union Shri P.V. Narasimha Rao.[11] In 1995, Narasimha Rao announced that the Union Government would be prepared to consider autonomy "short of independence' for Jammu and Kashmir.

Rao decides to have Election–It was toward the end of the then Prime Minister P.V. Narasimha Rao's term of office that an announcement was made to have the Lok Sabha election in Jammu and Kashmir state, simultaneously with the general election in the country.[12] It was a major decision by the Narasimha Rao Government to have the elections in Jammu and Kashmir after long seven years, during which the state witnessed the most harrowing time of terrorism and insergency. The Chief Election Commissioner, T.N. Seshan, announced that the elections to the Lok Sabha would take place in time, before the term of President's rule was over on July 17 for the Assembly Elections, a further period of President's rule would be asked for in Parliament.[13]

P.V. Narasimha Rao declared that Article 370 of the Constitution which granted special status of Jammu and Kashmir "is an inseparable part of the Constitution", meaning it would be retained.[14]

The schedule for Lok Sabha poll fixed for Jammu and Kashmir was May 7, Ladakh and Jammu; May 23, Baramullah and Anantnag and May 30 Srinagar and Udhampur. The Kashmir electorate was also apparently keen to vote. Despite non-participation by some political parties, there was tremendous enthusiasm among the 44 lakh electorate in the six Lok Sabha Constituencies in Jammu and Kashmir, on the other hand, some political parties announced their non-participation in the polls. The most important party in the state, the National Conference, stated that ground realities were not conducive for the elections. It, however, did not link its demand for greater autonomy for the state with the elections, and said the two were separate issues.

The Congress party secured 26.16 per cent of the polled votes in the State, won four seats – Baramullah, Srinagar, Ladakh and Jammu, while the Bhartiya Janata Party secured 18.68 per cent of the total votes polled and bagged Udhampur seat, the Janata Dal got 16.77 per cent of the total votes and could win only the Anantnag seat.[15]

Political observers saw the large scale participation of the people, the polling percentage averaged 49 per cent in the state – conclusively proved that the people of Jammu and Kashmir have won the proxy war waged by Pakistan and opted for restoration of the Democratic Institutions such as Parliament and the State Assembly in the place of militancy that had during the past seven years completely weakened the functioning the State's Civil Administration and effected economic growth in Jammu and Kashmir.

Devegowda's Effect to Solve the Autonomy Problem

("The Sky is the Limit" to "Restoration of Maximum Autonomy")

After assuming Prime Ministership, H.D. Devegowda moved a statutory resolution on extension of President's Rule in the State for six months from July 18, 1996. On the question of autonomy, demanding which Dr. Farooq Abdullah, National Conference leader, had not participated in the Lok Sabha polls, Devegowda made it clear that this issue would be decided after holding discussions with an elected Government in the State – which meant after the Assembly polls and after all opposition parties have agreed to this. Devegowda pointed out that his United Front 'Common Minimum Programme' had already made this clear. However on June 11, the National Conference concluded a two-day meeting of its Executive Committee, saying that the party would not put any pre-condition for participation in the Assembly elections, declaring that "We will decide (about participation in the polls) only after the election dates are announced."

Dr. Farooq Abdullah welcomed the new United Front Government's assurance on restoration of maximum autonomy to the Striyetorn state and said the NC called for its speedy implementation.[16] Dr. Abdullah told reporters that his party would try to grant autonomy to all the three regions – Jammu, Ladakh and Kashmir and ensure fulfillment of cultural aspirations of the people belonging to different ethnic groups.

On June 16, Prime Minister Devegowda stated that the Election to Parliament from Jammu and Kashmir was a triumps for "our democratic polity and it showed the maturity of the people in rejecting militancy and militants, including those inspired from across the border." "Building up on those positive developments, we shall complete the task of restoration of normalcy and popular government in Jammu and Kashmir."

Centre's New Economic Pakage for Jammu and Kashmir

Soon after the announcement of the Assembly Elections, Prime Minister, Devegowda, unveiled in Parliament the New Economic Package for Jammu and Kashmir in the installments. On July 23, he said the Government would take up work on the 290 km. railway line from Udhampur to Baramullah as a National project. A special allocation of Rs. 50 crores was being made this year for the project which was estimated to cost Rs.2500 crores in total. The Prime Minister, emphasizing that terrorism has been reduced considerably in the valley, said that the package was important in view of the fact that massive unemployment of youth in the state had been contributory factor to the growth of militancy there. In addition to providing employment in the state, on completion, the rail communications would help the mobility of the people from the state to the rest of the country for employment, education, trade and other purposes. The survey work from Udhampur to Banihal had been completed and survey work upto Baramullah would be over by March 1997. The Government would provide Rs.200 crores for this phase of the work. With adequate funding, the entire line upto Baramullah could be completed in 8-10 years.

The Jammu and Kashmir national highway, the only surface link between the Kashmir valley and Jammu, is at present be set with problems of frequent blockade as a result of landslides and snow avalanches. To provide a dependable alternative link between the two regions of the state, the Government would take up the Bhugal Road Project under the centrally sponsored scheme of "roads of economic importance". The Project spread over a length of 85 km. is estimated to cost Rs.77.40 crore (1994-95 costs). The project cost would be shared between the centre and the state in the ratio of 50:50. The road would generate considerable employment potential along the entire stretch passing through backward areas of the state. When completed, the road, apart from generating economic activities, would help mitigate the scene of isolation of the people of Kashmir. Work on the Dulhasti Hydro Electric Project (3x130 MW) came to a halt in 1992 with the withdrawal of the French Civil Contractors, it was completed in July 1995. Another major Hydro-Electric Project, the Uri Hydro Electric Project (4x12 MW), is under construction in the State. The work on this is going on according to schedule and the first unit is likely to be commissioned this year to provide the much-needed relief to the power starved state.

Unveiling in Parliament the second economic package for the state on August 2, the Prime Minister said the Government had written off loans of thousand of small scale industrialists, sanctioned more money for migrant camps and given the state Rs.352 crore as special central plan assistance to balance its budget. The "second economic package", Gowda said, was not an attempt to carry favour of influenced voters. It was aimed at helping the "suffering masses" in Kashmir the package included waiving of outstanding loans given to people upto Rs.50,000 with interest, a special central plan assistance of Rs.352 crore and development of infrastructure for tourism.

The State Government identified 31,000 borrowers from small scale trade and industry, transport, hotel and transport business who had taken loans of Rs.181.87 crore. The interest on these loans had reached Rs.212.79 crores, as there had been no payments. The waiving of the loans would enable the small borrowers to apply for fresh loans, as regarding the borrowers above Rs.50,000, an interministrial committee was being constituted to look into the question of moratorium and rescheduling of repayments and other reliefs like reduction in interest rates. There are 27,000 migrant families from the valley living in camps. Government would provide an additional sum of Rs.6.6 crores to provide the additional facilities, the Prime Minister announced.[17]

1996s State Assembly Election : Return of Democracy

On New Delhi's offer of "Maximum Autonomy", Farooq participated in the Assembly election held in 1996.[18] The National Conference Party fought these elections on the autonomy platform with the following Manifesto:[19]

"We pledge that if we are elected, our party will be bound to accomplish the following:-

Dignified undiluted and meaningful autonomy which has been inspiring our people will be restored and made unatterable. We will strive to bring it to the shape which was kept before us at the time of accession. We will also demand credible guarantees from the federal centre to keep constitutional relationship with the state and its pristine form so that the tragic events through which we had to pass are not repeated in future.[20]

National Conference promised its electorate that autonomy to the extent of pre-1953 position would be achieved if voted to power. However, in the month long election campaign, Farooq Abdullah was not consistent about this position. Interestingly it was Awami League (Political Front of pro-India venegade militants) which vociferously opposed any form of autonomous regional councils for Jammu and Ladakh also.[21]

However, none of the political parties were clear or concrete about their autonomy proposals and none of the political parties had struck any sense with the mood of people, the bitter fall out of Rajiv-Abdullah Accord, is still green in their memories and National Conference and Farooq Abdullah are identified as betrayers.[22]

After seven years of militancy and insurgency and two unsuccessful efforts to reviving political parties in the state, the completion of a peaceful election for the state was a great victory of

Indian democracy.[23] The people of the state returned the party to power with a two third majority. National Conference of Farooq Abdullah turned victorious with a thumping majority of 57 seats out of total 87 seats. Besides this, Congress, Bhartiya Janata Party, B.S.P. and Janata Dal secured 7, 8, 4 and 5 seats respectively. Awami League, Panther Party, AIIC(T) and CPI (M) got 1 seat each, two seats went to independent.[24] Sept. Oct. elections of the State Assembly were regarded as the most fair in the history of Kashmir but the low participation by the people made them fraught within suspicion.[25]

In Oct. 1996, Farooq Abdullah, on returning to power for the third time after state assembly elections, realized that "any one who wants to form a Government in Kashmir cannot do so without sharing power with New Delhi, for the people did not matter much.[26] From the Congress to United Front and the Atal Bihari Vajpayee led Bhartiya Janata Party, he shifted his loyality with extreme cases. In 1996 after Assembly election, he declared that "the accession of Jammu and Kashmir to Indian Union is "completed" and "irrevocable" to prove his loyality to Indian Union more than his predecessors National Conference joined the United Government at the Centre.

Soon after the installation of popular regime in the State in 1996, the first important step that Farooq Abdullah took was to find a State Autonomy Committee to examine and recommend measures for the restoration of autonomy to the State of Jammu and Kashmir. Consistent with the Instrument of Accession, the constitutional application order, 1950 and the Delhi Agreement of 1952.[27] This was exactly with the mandate given to him by Union Governments.[28]

Autonomy Fever and the BJP (An Anti-Art. 370 Party)

In the Election of 1999, no party could gain majority but Bhartiya Janta Party, however, succeeded in forming a Government at the Centre in third time with the help of motley of parties. Many tall claims were made by the BJP leadership and its allies while releasing the election manifesto of the NDA for the 1999 Lok Sabha elections, it was proclaimed that Atal Bihari Vajpayee was quintessentially a believer and practitioner of accommodative political culture of coalitional politics. It was further maintained the regional aspiration of the allies of BJP would be well looked after and that 24 political parties were enthusiastic to accept the leadership of the BJP.[29]

The BJP had claimed, the presence of regional parties in the central government would ensure that specific regional problems would get resolved in the Council of Ministers. But important regional parties and groups like Akali Dal, Asom Gana Parishad, D.M.K., PMK, and National Conference represented in the Council of Ministers have been airing serious grievances against the excessive centralisation of Indian Federalism under BJP led government.[30] The BJP had claimed that a coalition government under its leadership at the Centre would be the best arrangement for resolving centre-state problems. But Lal Krishan Advani stated that "his party was against treating the minority as mere" vote bank, he affirmed that they would be given 'special status'. Advani also indicated that the BJP's election manifesto would highlight crucial issues such as a uniform civil code, a stable government, abrogation of Article 370 (which prohibits non-Kashmiries from owning land or property and from setting up commercial/industrial establishments in Jammu and Kashmir)."[31] But the National Conference, a partner of the N.D.A. Government has formally approached the Central Government for a discussion on 'autonomy' in Jammu and Kashmir.

After BJP succeeded to power, some fundamental changes got introduced into Kashmir politics. Till now the centre was ruled by the Congress according to which not only Art.370 was indisposable as far as Kashmir was concerned but also used to admit that with the abrogation of this Article even residual connection with the State will break down. But as consequences of this election a core Hinduist party like Bhartiya Janata Party came to power according to which this Art.370 was the sole bone of contention. It was of the opinion that because of this very special status and continuous granting of special amenities the tendency of separation originated in Kashmir, with its abrogation it will become easier to merge Kashmir completely with India. But it failed to gather the required majority necessary to abrogate this article. Among the 24 constituent of this alliance, not all were in favour of abrogation of this Article. So in order to prevent a rift in the coalition Bhartiya Janata Party better chose not to pope the matter any further (BJP has already faced the impact of this rift twice, it does not want to repeat the mistake made once in 1996 and 1999). Because of this attitude of BJP Government the demand of Kashmir autonomy took a considerably new shape.

With the change at the centre the expectation of resolving the Kashmir dispute were increased. The New National Democratic Front under the leadership of Atal Behari Vajpayee and Lal Krishan Advani was expected to take some rigid stand on Kashmir's demand of autonomy as was evident from their party manifesto. But to great relief of this party "it could not garner majority in the Parliament and found an alibi of non-action on Article 370, because of the pressure from other partners.[32]

Nonetheless, one specific advantage that came from new alliance Government was in the form of single centre of authority on the issue of Kashmir, L.K. Advani, the Home Minister of India, has complete control over matters unlike his predecessors. In valley in one of his speeches he not only placed Kashmir problem at the top priority of his Government but also remarked that in case he fails to provide security and rights to the people of the valley he would have no right to hold on office.[33]

BJP led Government announced a free point formula to solve Kashmir problem (A) Strengthening democratic process as it happened in Punjab, after the successful election to the state assembly in Kashmir the Central Government has chances of involving local public in sorting out the problems, involving local administration and police who can prove pivotal in continuing the militancy by evolving non-sympathetic attitude towards them; (B) Isolate the militancy from the people so that they do not get local support and hideouts and could be cleansed; (C) Positive approach of giving free hand to forces to attack the terrorists in anticipation of their movements, and (D) To give the state a rapid economic trust by pouring in more money so that development activities could be increased.[34]

To execute the new plan the state requires adequate funds. The centre has already sanctioned an amount of Rs.147 crores in this respect but more funds will be needed to upgraded. The security system and the intelligence cover of the state. This was also the point of complaint of Chief Minister Farooq Abdullah who was already facing the charges of not filling up promised 2600 posts in the state due to financial contraints.[35]

Autonomy Panel Report

The issue of autonomy continued to be voiced by National Conference. After 1996's Assembly election, it was only in end of the decade, that politics on it began in a big way.

After its forced withdrawal from the political scene in the wake of militancy and mass upsurge in early 90's the National Conference used 'autonomy' as its main ideological plank to reclaim its political constituency in Kashmir. In its first central working held in 1994, after a gap of five years, the party held the union of India responsible for destroying the regional constitutional arrangement of the people of Kashmir. It passed a resolution, which asserted that, "The time has come when this state of affairs should be revived in order to restore autonomy to its pristine and original form"[36] was defined with reference to the constitutional status of the state in the pre-1953 period.

So after installation of popular regime in the state in 1996 the first important step that the Farooq government took was to found a state autonomy committee under the Chairmanship of Mr. Karan Singh to "Examine and recommend measures for the restoration of autonomy to the state of Jammu and Kashmir". This report was placed on table of two houses of Jammu and Kashmir legislature on April 16, 1999. It was subsequently adopted by the state legislative Assembly on June 26, 2000 and by the state Legislative Council on June 27, 2000. But centre has rejected the autonomy resolution on July 4, 2000.

In the next chapter we will examine the autonomy resolution of 2000.

References

1. Jana, Anil Kumar, *Indian Politics at the Crossroads*, Commonwealth Publication, (New Delhi, 1998), p. 94.
2. Singh, M.P., Toward a more federalized parliamentary system in India: Explaining functional change, *Pacific Affairs*, Vol. 74, No.4, University of British Columbia – Canada, 2001-02, p. 554.
3. *Ibid.*, p. 557.
4. Thakur, K.K., *Jammu and Kashmir : Integration and Alienation.* Aalekh Pub (New Delhi, 2001), p. 126.
5. *Ibid.*, p. 128.
6. *Ibid.*, p. 128.
7. Nanda, K.K., *Conquering Kashmir–A Pakistani Obsession*, Lancer Publication, (New Delhi, 1994), p. 308.
8. *Ibid.*, p. 308.
9. *Ibid.*, p. 314.
10. *Ibid.*, p. 314.
11. Government of Jammu and Kashmir, *Report of the State Autonomy Committee*, (Srinagar/Jammu), July 2000, p. 100.
12. Autonomy for Jammu and Kashmir : Little to fear, *Asian News Digest* July 8-14, 2000, p. 448.
13. Kumar, Dev. P., *Kashmir-Return to Democracy*, Cosmo Publication (New Delhi, 1996), p. 2.
14. Ibid., p. 3.

15. *Ibid.*, p. 9.
16. Autonomy for Jammu and Kashmir : Little to fear, *Asian News Digest*, July 8-14, 2000, p. 448.
17. Kumar, Dev. P, *op.cit.*, pp. 20-21.
18. Singh, M.P., Toward a more federalized parliamentary system in India : Explaining functional change, pacific affairs, Vol. 74, No. 4, University of British Colombia-Canada, 2001-02, p. 556.
19. Puri, Balraj-The Farooq doctrine-Kashmir's relation with New Delhi, EPW, June 24, 2000, p. 2218.
20. Government of Jammu and Kashmir, *Report of the State Autonomy Committee* (Sringar/Jammu, July, 2000), p. 101.
21. Government of Jammu and Kashmir, *Report on 1996 Assembly Election in Kashmir,* (Srinagar, 1996), p. 8.
22. *Ibid.*, p. 8.
23. Kumar, Dev. P., Kashmir-Return of Democracy, Cosmo Publication (New Delhi, 1996), p. 2.
24. Thakur, K.K., *Jammu and Kashmir : Integration and Alienation,* Aalekh Publication, (New Delhi, 2001), p. 136.
25. *Ibid.*, p. 136.
26. Puri, Balraj – The Farooq doctrine-Kashmir's relation with New Delhi, *Economic and Political Weekly*, June 24, 2000, p. 2218.
27. Chaudhary, Rekha, Kashmir autonomy at Crossroads, *Economic and Political Weekly*, July 22, 2000 p. 2599.
28. Government of Jammu and Kashmir, *Report of the State Autonomy Committee* (Srinagar, Jammu), July 2000, p. 105.
29. Bhambri, C.P., *Bhartiya Janta Party–Periphery to Centre*, Shipra Publication, (New Delhi, 2001) p. 194.
30. Dr. Thakur, C.P. and Kumar, Devender P., *India under Atal Bihari Vajpayee–The BJP era*, UBS Publication, (New Delhi, 1999), p. 448.
31. *Ibid.*, p. 448.
32. Thakur K.K., *Jammu and Kashmir: Integration and Alienation,* Aalekh Publication (New Delhi, 2001), p. 137.
33. *Ibid.*, p. 137.
34. *Ibid.*, p. 1374.
35. *Ibid.*, p. 138.
36. Lamb, Alastair, Kashmir -A disputed legacy 1846– 1990, Oxford University Press, Oxford, 1991, p. 329.

6

Autonomy Demand of June 2000—Politics in Jammu and Kashmir Since 2000 to 2002

The Jammu and Kashmir Government forwarded the 184 page State Autonomy Committee Report (SACR) to the centre and strongly urged the union President to accept it and implement all the 13 recommendations it contains. The SACR has been drafted strictly in accordance with the lines indicated in the October 26, 1947 Instrument of Accession, the January 26, 1950 constitution order and the July 24, 1954 Nehru-Sheikh Abdullah Delhi Agreement.[1]

Preparation of the Report

The Farooq Government set-up a committee to examine the question of restoration of autonomy to the state of Jammu and Kashmir vide Government Order No. 1164 – GAD of 1996 Dated 29.11.1996 with the following composition.[2]

1.	Dr. Karan Singh	Chairman
2.	Sh. Moti-ud-din Shah	Member
3.	Sh. Abdul Azad Vapil	Member
4.	Sh. Abdul Rahim Rather	Member
5.	Sh. Pyarelal Handoo	Member
6.	Sh. Bodh Raj Bali	Member
7.	Molvi Ijtikhar Husain Ansari	Member
8.	Kushok Jhikshay	Member
9.	Shri Teja Singh	Member

The committee had representation of all three regions of the state and different communities. By a subsequent Govt. Order No. 263-GAD of 1977 dated 21.02.79, it was ordered that Shri Teja Singh should be Member of the above committee. Dr. Karan Singh resigned as Chairman on July 31,1997 vide Government Order No. 1303-GAD of 1997 dated 19.08.1997, Shri Ghulam Moti-ud-din Shah, PWD Minister Jammu and Kashmir government was appointed Chairman w.e.f., the date Dr. Karan Singh resigned. By another government order No. 1413 of 1997 dated 05.09.1997 Nirza Abdul Rashid, Former speaker of Jammu and Kashmir legislative assembly was nominated as a member of the committee.

The term of reference of the committee are as follows.[3]

(i) To examine and recommend measures for the restoration of autonomy to the state of Jammu and Kashmir consistent with the Instrument of Accession, the constitution application order, 1950 and the Delhi Agreement of 1952.

(ii) To examine and recommend safeguards that be regarded necessary for incorporation in the union/state constitution to ensure that the constitutional arrangement that finally evolved in pursuance of the recommendations of the committee is inviolable.

(iii) To also examine and recommend measures to ensure a harmonious relationship in the future between the state and the union. The terms of reference of the SACR were very clear which, inter alia, asked the committee to examine and recommend measures for restoration of autonomy to the state, consisted with the Instrument of Accession, constitution application order of 1950 and Delhi Agreement of 1952.[4]

The SAC held nearly 50 settings in two and half years and ever visited New Delhi to interact with major national political parties on the issue of autonomy. The committee completed its report and presented it in the state legislature on April. The copy of report was sent to the centre also. The state cabinet examined the report in its two meetings on January 19 and March 15, 2000 and endorsed its recommendations. It constituted a five member ministerial committee and requested the central government to set up their ministerial committee to dialogue on the report.[5] On 19th June 2000 a special session of the Jammu and Kashmir Assembly started to discuss the report. Both the houses approved the motion by voice vote – Legislative Assembly on June 26 and Legislative Council on June 27.

Main Recommendations of the Proposal

Main recommendations of the autonomy resolution by Jammu and Kashmir as follows:–[6]

1. Change in the title of part XXI and heading of Article 370

The word temporary has been used in the title of past XXI and heading of Article 370 of the constitution of India. Recommendations.

(i) The word 'temporary' be deleted from the title of part XXI of the constitution of India.

(ii) The word 'temporary' occurring in the heading of Article 370 be substituted by the Word 'special'.

2. Constitutional Relation (Part XI)

In the legislative field it is recommended as under:-

(i) Subjects in the union list not connected with the three subjects of Defence, foreign affairs, communications should be removed from applicability in the state.

(ii) All modifications made in Article 246 in its applications to the state subsequent to the 1950 order should be rejected.

(iii) Article 246, 249, 250, 251 whether applied in original or substituted modified form should be omitted in relation to the state.

(iv) As in 1950 and 1954 lists II (state) and list III (concurrent) of the VIIth schedule not be applicable to the state.

(v) Article 254 be restored to the position it had in its application to our state in 1954.

(vi) Article 262 and 263 should not be extended to the state.

Elections – Article 324-329

Since elections to the state legislature are held under laws made by the state legislature, Article 324 should continue to apply in the manner and the way it was applicable in 1950/1954 orders this is particularly so when the state constitution had provision relating to there Recommendation: - Therefore, change brought about in this part after 1954 be reversed and consequential changes in other Articles in this part be effected.

3. Emergency Provisions (Article 352-360) Part XVIII

The following should be added to clause 6 of Article 352: Recommendations:-

(i) "Provided that this request for concurrence of the Government of the state shall be subject to whatever decision the State Assembly may take within two months of declaration of emergency and failing any such decision, the proclamation of emergency shall be deemed to have been revoked."

(ii) Sub-clause (b) of clause (6) of this article should be deleted.

(iii) Article 355, 356, 357, 358 and 360 should be made non-applicable to the state of Jammu and Kashmir as was the position in 1954.

4. Part III (Art 12 to 35)

Fundamental Rights

Recommendations : This part should be deleted. A separate chapter on the fundamental rights need to be included in the Jammu and Kashmir constitution situation where directive principle do not apply and Fundamental Rights is not a happy one. Directive principle in the state constitution apply in the absence of a provision these can hardly near anything to Fundamental rights, which are enshrined in the Union constitution. Fundamental Rights chapter in the state constitution would add weight and worth to the organized law of land and give the citizens satisfaction of even testing worth of Directive Principles of Legislation and governance accordingly to letter and spirit of law.

5. Part– V– The Union

Article – 52-151

Very few Articles from this part were made applicable in 1954 order but the situation was changed with the passage of constitution (Application to Jammu and Kashmir) order, 1960 and thereafter. Normally there can be no dispute now with the extended jurisdiction of Supreme Court over matter in regard to our state, but it has got to be recorded that his aspect of state union relationship was not settled at the time of Delhi Agreement of 1952 and after the events of 1953 quick decisions were forced upon the flamed Constituent Assembly fooled by a Number of Constitution (Application to Jammu and Kashmir) orders. The position which ultimately has emerged is that the state of Jammu and Kashmir has been accorded the same status as the rest of the states except for the above form of Articles 133 and 134 applied to the state. The Judiciary of India has been unitary in character during the British rule and it remained so under the new constitution of India adopted in 1950. Jammu and Kashmir became part of it. Notwithstanding, the fact that strong views to have judicial autonomy were expressed during Negotiations for Delhi Agreement, 1952. In any case divergent views were recorded. The state had at that time a High Court whose judgements were subject to appeal / review before His Highness, advised in his judicial function by a Board of Judicial Advisors consisting of eminent jurists knowledgeable persons.

That has not be end reopening that chapter may not sound appropriate now except, of course, where adopting of provisions of the Union judiciary for the state have in a way infringed upon the corresponding provisions of the state have constitution in regard to the state High Court Recommendations:-

(i) Articles 72 (i) (C), 72 (3), 133, 1354, 136, 138, 145 (a) (C) and 151 (2) should be made non-applicable to the state as has the position in 1950 order.

6. Part VI–The State

Article 151-237

Article 124(4) of the constitution of India, mandates that a Supreme Court judge shall not be removed from his office except by an order of the President passed after an address by each House of Parliament supported by a majority of the total membership of that house and by a majority of not less than two-thirds of the members of that House present and voting has been presented to the President in the same session for such removal on the ground of proved misbehaviour or incapacity. Article 218 has in the course of time been applied to the J and K State. The position as it obtained prior to C.O. 60 was that under the state constitution the removal of a judge of the High Court by the President for proved misbehaviour or incapacity could be on the basic of an address for removal supported by a majority of the total membership of each House of the Legislature of the state and by the majority of not less than two-thirds of the members present and voting. But after the aforesaid application order of 1960, the power to pass an address for such removal rests with the Parliament in accordance with Article 124(4). Part VII of the state constitution deals with the state High Court. The part starts with section 93 (constitution of High Court) of these, we have sec. 95 (appointment and tenure of office of judges) and Sec. 99 (Resignation and removal of a judge of the High Court). The aforementioned provision about removal till 1959 was sub-Section (2) of Section 99 of the state constitution. The constitution of Jammu and Kashmir (First Amendment) Act, 1959 vide its section 4 deleted this provision and the question of removal of a judge for proved misconduct or incapacity was left to be taken care of as in the rest of the country by resort to procedure in section 124 clause (4) thereof this was so vide constitution (Application to Jammu and Kashmir) Order No. 60 of 1960. All provisions about High Court having been retained in the state constitution including one about administrative expresses, salaries, allowances and pensions continuing to remain a charge upon consolidated fund of the state, deletion of the above provisions regarding removal by means of an address being the duty right and obligation of state legislature and not Parliament. It is because all other provisions like 93 to 108 of our state constitution are in their case part of the union constitution itself. We would, therefore, recommend the following in this regard:

Recommendations

(i) Article 218 be omitted in its application to the state, that would enable the state legislature to re-enact the provisions as they existed in such section (2) and (3) section 99 of the state constitution before the enforcement of Jammu and Kashmir constitution (first Amendment) Act of 1959.

(ii) Article 220, 222 and 226 should also be omitted in their application to Jammu and Kashmir state.

7. Part XII–Finance, Property, Contracts and Suits

Article 264–300 A

We have been seen that in 1952 during and after negotiations for Delhi Agreement Article (relating to the consolidated funds of India and public accounts of India and of the state) Article 282 and 284 (relating to the Union or Public Accounts of India), Article 298, 299 and 300 (relating only to the Union or Government of India) were applicable. Exception was made in respect of Articles 264 and 265, clause (2) of Article 267, Articles 268 to 281. Clause 2 of Act 283, Articles 286 to 291, Articles 293, 295, 296 and 297, C.O. 48 of 14th May 1954 made Articles 264, 265, 272, 274 – 281, 285, 293, 295 to 297 applicable to our state Articles 269 and 286 were applied with amendments in 1958.

Law for imposition of tax burden is clearly laid down. The rule in federal policy generally is that if the union levies a tax in respect of matters assigned to it, it retains the proceeds yielded by such imposition it is true of a unit in defecation. There are however, a number of exceptions as under Articles 268 and 269 in the matter of distribution of income tax as also of whole or part of proceeds of excise duty our state also would collect excise and stamp duties as specified in entries 84 and 91 of list I and appropriate the net proceeds. Same is true as a result of application of Article 269 to our state in respect of levies collected thereunder. Even Article 270 applies to our state. What has been incorporated in the constitution of the

State viz consolidated fund and contingency fund of the state as also custody thereof and Public Account of the State is covered by sections, 115, 116, 118 and 119 of the constitution of our state. In fact the position that emerges from the application of India identical to what has been incorporated in the state constitution in sections 115, 16, 117, 118, 119, 120, 121, 122 and 123 do not apply, and for the rest, by and large, provision of part XII of the constitution of India apply to our state as the rest of the state.

On the passage of constitution (Application to Jammu and Kashmir, second Amendment order 1958 (C.O. 56) jurisdiction of the Auditor General and Controller was extended. This brought entry 76 of list I into the picture in its application to the state. Despite allocations available to the state at present, we are firmly of the opinion that in order that the state should be financially viable it needs more financial resources and assistance. It may be recalled that during 1952 Delhi talks, the discussion on financial arrangement between the union and the state remained inconclusive.

Recommendations

It is, therefore, recommended that the matter be discussed in depth between the state representative and the union government.

8. Part XIV–Service Under the Union and the State Article 302-323

Article 308 excluded application of this part to our state. There is hardly any federation in the world where such provisions as those contained in Article 312 and legislative enactments thereunder are envisaged. These were not applicable to the state even in 1954 but have been made applicable thereafter.

Notwithstanding seemingly an attractive proposition one can say without any fear of contradiction that it has dwarfed local latent and made it difficult for local youth to aspire to complete for key civil posts on competitive basis. The weak – kneed attempt to organise Kashmir Civil Service is neither here not there and increasing inflow of all India Service has next pretty little in field for which the services were apparently conceived. No imperial model of civil services in central cadre can be or could be substitute for what the local youth could be expected to have, i.e., local patriotic feeling and passionate attachment on the service of those among whom they live. Even since the application of these provisions of the Indian constitution to our state the number of direct recruits from the state has been negligible. The problem has attained so unpleasant a shape, even in the national content, that demand of greater number of promote from local services all over the country have assumed alarming proportions.

Recommendation

It is, therefore, recommended that in Article 312, the brackets and words " (including the state of Jammu and Kashmir)" inserted by the constitution (Application to Jammu and Kashmir) Order 1958 be omitted.

9. Part XVI–Special Provisions Relating to Certain Classes Article 330-342

Article 339 regarding control of the Union over the administration of scheduled areas and the welfare of scheduled tribes was not applicable to the state till 1985. It was applied in a modified form of the state vide constitution (Application to Jammu and Kashmir) order of 1985.

Likewise, Article 342 has been applied for the first time to the state in 1985.

Recommendation

(i) It is recommended that the powers in respect to the aforesaid matters be restored to the state.

(ii) Articles 330, 331, 335, 336 which were applied by 1950 order should continue to be applicable; Articles 338, 339, 340, 341 and 342 have been applied after 1950. There application to the state should be omitted and corresponding provisions be made in the state constitution.

10. Part XX–Amendment of the Constitution Article 368

Needless to maintain that unlike other states of the union, the state of Jammu and Kashmir has a constitution of its own. Before the constitution (Application to Jammu and Kashmir) second Amendment order 1975 (C.O. 101) the state legislature had unfettered powers to amend it. But vide this order clause (4) was added to Article 368 of the India constitution in its application to our state which reads as under:-

"94) No law made by the legislature of the state of Jammu and Kashmir seeking to make any charge in the effect of any provisions of the constitution of Jammu and Kashmir relating to:-

(a) Appointments, powers, functions, duties, emoluments, allowances, privileges or immunities of the governor, or

(b) Superintendence, direction and control of elections by the election Commission of India, eligibility for inclusion in the electoral rolls without discrimination adult suffrage and composition of the Legislative Council, being matters specified in sections 138, 139 and 50 of the constitution of Jammu and Kashmir shall have any effect unless such law has, after having been reserved for the consideration of the President, received his assent;"

The addition of this clause in the Indian constitution has restricted of the power of the state legislature to amend its own constitution. The uncalled for clog on the constituent power of the state legislature needs to be removed lock, stock and barrel.

Recommendation

It is therefore recommended that:-

(i) Clause (4) of this Article 368 added vide C.O. 101 be deleted.

(ii) Clause (2) of Article 368 should apply with the provision already introduced by 1954 order and clause (I) thereof which was not in existence in 1954 was introduced in 1971 should remain omitted in its application to the state.

11. Part XXII Scheduled First to Twelve

The Indian constitution has twelve schedules, only some of which apply to our state with or without modifications relatable to some of the Articles of the constitution of India. Each schedule which is applicable to the state of Jammu and Kashmir being fathered by a specific Articles in the constitution of the country will naturally suffer modification, charge/substitution depending upon what that Article contains in regard to its application to the state of Jammu and Kashmir.

12. Seventh Schedule

Seventh schedule derives its character and quality from what Article 246 of the constitution reals like. Its corresponding quality in respect of Jammu and Kashmir state naturally will depend upon the form and the content that Article 246 of the constitution of India will assume in its relation to the state of Jammu and Kashmir. In 1950, Article 146 of the constitution of India had one character and quality/ content in its application to the state of Jammu and Kashmir and that was reflected in the number of entries in the union list in the 7th schedule, in their application to the state of Jammu and Kashmir. Later on, this Article suffered changed and consequently various entries in the union list and the concurrent list also suffered radical charged.

Recommendation

It is recommended that:

(a) Entries in the union list which were applied to the state by 1950 Application order should continue and all other entries made applicable to the state by subsequent orders should be omitted;

(b) Concurrent list was not applicable under 1950 order and it was also agreed in Delhi Agreement that this should not apply to the state. Hence all subsequent orders applying various entries from this list should be rescinded.

In some, it is recommended that consistent with the above, requisite changes as may become necessary consequent upon change in the articles of the constitution of India in their application to the state of Jammu and Kashmir, as result of this report be effected in the schedules concerned.

13. Change Required in the State Constitution

In view of what has been stated in chapter XI, this committee recommends the repeal of:-

(i) The constitution of Jammu and Kashmir, (First Amendment) Act, 1959 relating to superintendence direction and control of elections relating to the state legislature and provision relating to the state High Court; and

(ii) The constitution of Jammu and Kashmir (sixth amendment) Act, 1965 relating to the mode of appointment and nomenclature of the Head of the state and nomenclature of the head of the Executive.

The reports without giving any reason, says that the root cause of the 10 years old separatist movement and estrangement of Kashmiri was the deep – engineered by New Delhi in collaboration with its Kashmiri henchmen to bypass these three solemn agreements; under which the state was to enjoy maximum internal autonomy and to bring Jammu and Kashmir surreptitiously within the preview of central laws and institutions like the Supreme Court of India, the Comptroller and Auditor General, the Election Commission, et al, and thereby on a par with other states of the union, and erode "Kashmiri". Again, it puts forth a solution which alone, accordance to it, can assuage the hurts feelings of the Kashmir's and solve the 53 years old Kashmir problem. Its solution: the centre must withdraw all the central laws and institution extended to the state after August 9, 1953, restore without any delay the pre-1953 constitution position and meet all its financial needs.

The SACR makes no reference to the 1975 India - Sheikh accord under which the latter got the chief ministers chair on a platter much against the wishes of the state Congress which commanded an absolute majority in both the legislative assembly and the legislative council and appointed in 1977 a High powered three members cabinet sub-committee under the deputy chief minister, Mr. D.D. Thakur, to go into the whole gamut of central laws extended to Jammu and Kashmir and recommend withdrawal of those which is deemed harmful to the state's special politics—economic and socio-religious right and interests. This committee had produced two highly contradictory reports. One was from Mr. Thakur, who said, "The needles of the clock cannot be turned back" and that "None of the central laws impinged on the state special status or eroded the Kashmiri identity in any manner". On the contrary, he opined, "The extension of the provisions of the Indian constitution had only benefited the people of the state."[7]

The other report was from Mr. Gul Shah son-in-law of Sheikh Abdullah and Mr. Gulam Nabi Kochak (members of the committee) who recommended withdrawal of all central laws and institutions from the state. The upshot of their whole formulation was that 'these were squarely responsible for erosion of internal autonomy granted to the state under Article 370 of the Indian constitution". This profound cleavage of opinion between Mr. Thakur and other members of the committee culminated in a serious controversy in the state cabinet, leave abide the bitter apposition in Jammu and Ladakh to the very idea of the review of the central laws. The controversy was resolved by none other than Sheikh Abdullah. An ardent believer in the doctrine of greater autonomy, when he accepted Mr. Thakur's recommendations in their entirety and even allowed the extension of certain other central laws to Jammu and Kashmir.[8]

Union Cabinet Rejects Jammu and Kashmir Assembly Resolution

On July 4, 2000 the Union Cabinet rejected the autonomy resolution, saying its acceptance would "Reverse the natural process of harmonising the aspiration of the people of Jammu and Kashmir with the integrity of the Nation". It said that most of the recommendations would "adversely affect the interests of the people of the state" and were "tantamount of removal of some of the essential safeguards enshrined in our constitution". The cabinet also disfavoured presentation of the repost in the Parliament.[9]

In the word of Vajpayee " Farooq had played his part by passing the resolution. The centre has played its part by rejecting it".[10]

The Government is committed to the promotion of Federal harmony by ensuring a partnership of the centre and the state as laid down in the National agenda for governance of the National Democratic Alliance. The National Agenda for Governance of the NDA state in no uncertain terms that "there is a clear case for development of more financial and administrative powers and functions to the state". It further says that "suitable states will be taken to ensure harmonious centre-state relation in the light of the recommendation of the Sarkaria Commission... "[11] In the last two years, the government had taken several steps in this direction. The Government reaffirms its commitment to continuing its endeavour to evolve a broad consensus on the implementation of steps for wide-ranging devolution of powers to the states that leads to efficiency in administration, acceleration in development and fullest realisation of the creative potential of all section of our people the setting up of a commission to review the constitution is also a step in this direction. In the above context the cabinet find the resolution passed by the state Assembly of Jammu and Kashmir endorsing the report of state Assembly committed unacceptable. The cabinet feels that the acceptance of this resolution would set the clock back and reverse the natural process of harmonizing the aspirations of the people of Jammu and Kashmir and Kashmir with the integrity of the Nation. Most of the recommendations contained in the report of State Autonomy Committee seek to reverse the application of constitutional provision to the state of Jammu and Kashmir which may not only adversely effects the interests of the people of Jammu and Kashmir but would also tantamount to removal of some of the essential safeguards enshrined in our constitution. Besides, the issue of restoring the constitutional situation in Jammu and Kashmir to its pre-1953 position has been discussed in detailed by Sheikh Mohd. Abdullah with Indira Gandhi in 1974-75. It is noteworthy that the agreement signed after these negotiations had affirmed that "provisions of the constitution of India already applied to the state of Jammu and Kashmir without adaptation or modification are unalterable ." The cabinet argues the people and the government of the Jammu and Kashmir to join hands in the endeavour to address the real problems facing the state to root out insurgency and cross-border terrorism and to ensure accelerated development. The centre will continue to provide all possible assistance for attaining these objectives. The cabinet, therefore, decides not to accept the resolution passed by the Jammu and Kashmir Assembly on the report of the state Autonomy Committee. The Government is of the firm conviction that national integration and devolution of powers to state must go together printing out that the country had came a long way since 1953. The focus of attention in the state should now be on the development, good government and better facilities to improve the living conditions of the people. Adequate power were available to the Jammu and Kashmir government under the states list to take care of matters such as heath, education, social welfare, roads, communications, agriculture and other allied activities.

What's Controversial in the Report[12]

- Substitute the word 'temporary' in Article 370 with 'special'.
- Centre to look at defence, foreign affairs, communication and ancillary subjects.
- Head of state to be renamed Sadar-e-Riyasat.
- Article 356 not to apply to state.
- External emergency only with concurrence of state.
- Separate chapter on Fundamental Rights to be included in Jammu and Kashmir constitution.

The Most Unacceptable Part in the Report

According to V. Sudarshan, the following suggestions and recommendations will be helpful to solve dispute's between centre and the state of Jammu and Kashmir.[13]

1. All amendments in the J & K constitution made vide the constitution of J&K (First Amendment) Act in so far as they relate to superintendence, direction and control of Election to the state legislature and to the state High Court be repealed and regional origional of J&K constitution be restored.
2. The centre would find it impossible to concede a separate chapter on fundamental rights to J&K.
3. The proposition that the Election Commission have no role whatsoever in J&K may not get off the drawing board.
4. The State Autonomy Committee recommendation with respect to the emergency provision could well run into a brick well.
5. Considering the financial arrangements between the centre and the state and considering that the 1952, Delhi agreement was not the conclusive word on this matter there is scope for discussion. It doesn't, however, appear that the role of the Comptroller and Auditor General with respect to J & K can be easily or radically redefined unless the matter is discussed, it won't be apparent as to why the centre should give up its

claim with respect to provisions of financial emergency vide Article 360.

6. There could be give and take on the policy of deployment of a All India Services.
7. Article 356, which relates to provisions in case of failure of constitutional machinery in the state, is a matter of herce debate even outside the scope of its applicability in J&K.
8. The impasse with respect to nomenclature of Head of State and Head of Executive (Sadar-e-Riyasat) and (Wazir-e-Azam) is a reheaded outtake from point 6 of the Kashmir accord of 1975, which, noting the lake of agreement on this point, remitted the matter to the principals. Does nomenclature really matter? Narasimha Rao had taken a very lenient view on this.

View of Political Parties–Major political formations have strongly apposed the Jammu and Kashmir package that calls for return of the pre-1953 situation.

Bhartiya Janta Party–BJP welcomed the Union Cabinet rejection of the Autonomy resolution passed by the J&K Assembly.[14] BJP is totally against any move that snakes of autonomy. Party says "the mistake committed by Jawaharlal Nehru by granting special status to the state cannot be allowed to be repeated" any talk of autonomy should be based only on the 1975 Indira Gandhi-Sheikh Abdullah accord. It should be people oriented, reinforce the country's secular traditions and safeguard its national interest of the people of the state. BJP feels that if the state gets back its status of 1952, the country's bond with state will weaker.

On June 23, the BJP emphatically rejected the National Conference demand for allowing Jammu and Kashmir to revert back to the pre-1953 status. However, the party said it was willing for discussion on greater devolution of powers to the state. Party general secretary K. Venkaiah Naidu states that while the centre had yet to formulate its stand on the demand raised in the Jammu and Kashmir assembly special session, the BJP had decided that such a thing would never be acceptable to it. "One cannot turn the clock back nor will it help anybody" the leader stressed." He also stated that the party is enable to understand what the national meant by talking of autonomy for the state, if they wantd greater decentralization of powers, the party was all for discussion on the matter, he said "we are ready for devolution of powers up to the Zila Parishad and Panchayati Raj level. The focus of alternation in the state should now be based on development, good governance and better facilities to improve the living condition of the people".

The Autonomy resolution passed by the assembly appears to have left the ruling BJP throughly confused.[15] Shiv Sena supremo Bal Thakrey has urged the centre to dismiss Dr. Abdullah led Jammu and Kashmir government for passing the controversial resolution seeking restoration of greater autonomy in the state and thereby "threatening the territorial integrity of the Nation"[16] But BJP said that it would not be a good idea. Party also said that the NC remains a part of NDA and there is no proposal to ask them to quit the Union Council of Ministers. Dismissal of the Abdullah ministry would not solve the problem. BJP pointed out that a similar demand has already came from Punjab and there is likelihood of such demands coming from the north-eastern states. The BJP and National Democratic Alliance government are willing to consider greater devolution of powers including Jammu and Kashmir but if they want to revert to pre-1953 status then no party will back it, Parliament will definitely reject it, party said.

BJP President Kushabhau Thakrey termed the retrograde a reactory step. "Greater harmony between the centre and the state is the need of the hour", we believe in the co-operative federalism"[17] Mr. Thakrey points out that "autonomy has been discussed for the last fifty years, but is the scope of autonomy that has to be considered. If it means greater powers to the state they were already on the way. We recently shared 19 per cent of central revenue with states but if they want separation then they are not going to get it under any circumstances[18] asserted party General Secretary M. Venkaiah Naidu who sought to wider the issue to include devaluation of the powers to states. " It is well known that the per capita central assistance for Jammu and Kashmir is 14 times that of Bihar, 11 times that of Tamil Nadu, 6 times that of even a state like Assam which faces as a threat"[19]

Congress Party–Congress party is ready to discuss the issue if it is based on the 1975 Indira Sheikh accord, which maintains the country's secular tradition and uphold National interest.[20] BJP and Congress party are against greater autonomy. The common viewpoint of the two national parties is that the clock can not be set back. They feel that a situation where in Jammu and Kashmir gets back, Its greater autonomous states of 1952 will weaken the country's bond with the state. But Atal Bihari Vajpeyee's views and the Bartiya Janata Parti's stand on the Kashmir autonomy issue came in for sharp criticism from the Congress which said that there was a "sharp contradiction" between the two. Party said that National Democratic Alliance Government should clarify its position on the Kashmir Assembly resolution. The BJP has vociferously apposed the autonomy package but both Mr. Vajpayee and Mr Lal Krishan Advani are talking about the discussion on the package".[21]

The party pointed out that the issue of autonomy has had a cascading effect and similar demands were not being made in Punjab and Tamil Nadu, which went against the interests of the nations.

Congress Party said "the government's inaction and inept handling of the issue and opened a Pandora's box as is evident observations of various politicals parties. The demand for more autonomy, made by everyone from G.T. Tohra to Prafulla Kumar Mahanta had serious implications. It would make more difficult talking cross border terrorism and effectively countering insurgency in some part of the country.[22]

The Congress party said that the 1975 accord along should be the basis of any autonomy package, time is not ripe for raising the autonomy questions, as the state is in the grip of large scale terrorism.

Shiv Sena Party–Shiv Sena Supremo Bal Thakeray has demanded Farooq Abdullah's dismissal.[23] he has argued the centre to dismiss Dr. Farooq Abdullah led Jammu and Kashmir Government for passing the controversial resolution seeking restoration of greater autonomy in the state and thereby "threatening the territorial integrity of the nations".[24] He said "By passing a resolution for greater autonomy for the J and K, Abdullah has taken a step to secede from India."[25]

C.P.I (M)–The CPI is ready to discuss the issue if it is based on the 1975 Indira Gandhi – Sheikh Abdullah accord. The CPI(M) on its part made it clear that "it was for greater autonomy for the state within the framework Article 370 of the constitution of India". The party said in the case of Jammu and Kashmir the demand for autonomy had a specific background. The state had a special status. It was a fact that over a years, government at the centre had eroded and whittled away the scope and content of autonomy within the ambit of Article 370. This was recognized in the Indira Gandhi – Sheikh Abdullah accord.

The Party does not subscribe to the scope of autonomy as defined in the resolution adopted by the State Assembly, which is going back to the pre-1953 status. Over the decades, development in the political system and the political administration structure in the country have warranted certain changes that are justified.

"It is not possible to accept the definition of autonomy which assigns the centre only External Affairs, Defence and Communications, However the reality is that ever within the ambit of Article 370, there was a steady erosion of the right of Jammu and Kashmir" the party stated.

Janta Dal (United)–Janta Dal (United) strongly opposed the autonomy demand raised by the J&K Assembly. Saying it had "dangerous implication" and announced its decision to raise the issue at the National Democratic Alliance coordination committee meeting in July 2000. The Janta Dal (United) was in favour of devolving more powers to the states in accordance with the recommendations of the Sarkaria Commission on centre-state relations.

The party was against the autonomy demand. The party said that any solution to the Jammu and Kashmir problem should be found within the constitutional framework and "nothing should be done which may jeopardize the country's unity and integrity".

The Vishwa Hindu Parisad– The Vishwa Hindu Parisad has strongly opposed the National Conference move for greater autonomy the party said, that greater autonomy would end unity, the people of Jammu and Ladakh would feel alienated. By pressing for a pre-1953 status the Farooq Abdullah government was only sending wrong signals to separatists, VHP central secretary Mohan Joshi said. Asked if the VHP would demand the dismissal of J & K government, Mr. Joshi said it was up to the centre to decide that.[26]

Asom Gana Parishad–The autonomy resolution by the Jammu and Kashmir assembly has sparked off an intense debate in the Northeast, particularly in Assam where the ruling Asom Gana Parishad (AGP) had advocated autonomy for the state in its 1996 election Manifesto "demanding Autonomy for the state is certainly nor anti-national or secessionist as some political parties including a section of BJP mention" told Chief Minister Profulla Kumar Mahanta. "But yes, autonomy must be within the preview of the constitution".[27] In 1996 election manifesto, the Asom Gana Parishad said it would strive for Assam's autonomy in all matters. However, defence, foreign affairs, currency and communication were the exceptions, besides state regulation in all administrative and financial affairs without central interference.

It differs from Jammu and Kashmir package on a separate national flag and constitution. It also differs in redefinition the government and the Chief Minister as per the pre-1953 arrangement.

Mr. Mahanta declined to comment on these aspects of the Jammu and Kashmir package owing to "our limitations as a regional party" but he felt that all items in the autonomy charter were within the scope of negotiation, he however, hinted at these demands being tools for bargaining with the centre. "There are two strong reasons why Assam needs autonomy: to tackle insurgency and to control our own natural resources toward development" the Chief Minister said.

"Insurgency in Northeast has gone international, and states of this region need certain powers to take up the issue directly with neighbouring nations where leaders of banned outfits have taken shelter." Mr Prafulla Kumar Mohanta regretted that centre was not willing to let the North Eastern states to deal directly with the neighbouring countries on the insurgency issue. "On the other hand, New Delhi insists insurgency is a regional problem that should be solved regionally".

AIADMK–The AIADMK wanted the imposition of Presidents rule in the state following the passage of the "condemnable resolution",[28] AIADMK leader Jayalalita demanded dissolution of the Jammu and Kashmir Assembly following the passage of the autonomy resolution. She said if the centre did not act against the Farooq Abdullah Government, the demand of autonomy would spread like wild fire and lead the country's fragmentation. The AIDMK leader accused the BJP led government of adopting a "Free for all" approach toward question concerning the country's integrity. Her party was steadiest in its commitment to the country's integrity even though it favoured greater devolution of the powers to the states. Her party believed in the position: "We will not live as slaves, but at no time will we seek separation".

Rashtriya Swayam Sevak Sangh (RSS)– The autonomy resolution passed by the Jammu and Kashmir Assembly was on the top of the RSS agenda. The RSS demanded imposition of Presidents rule in Jammu and Kashmir, and effect correction in the economic policy that has drawn a blank response from the BJP.

The party said that the Vajpayee Government's economic policies need to be changed and the centre must clamp President's rule in Jammu and Kashmir and do away with Article 370.[29]

In an interview to Zee TV the RSS Chief K.S. Sudarshan said "whatever we find unacceptable in the Vajpayee government's economic policy we will place before the people".

Sudarshan Speaks –[30]

- Scrap Article 370, clamp central rule in Jammu and Kashmir.
- Convince Muslims to hand over Ayodhya site for Ram Temple "The Ram Mandir will be build. No one can stop it.
- Do not hand over nation to foreigners.
- Sheikh Abdullah worked for separation from India.
- Economic policy, not beneficial to the country.
- Allowing 100 P.C. FDI e-commerce is dangerous.

Shiromany Akali Dal– Punjab Chief Minister Prakash Singh Badal said his party Shiromany Akali Dal supports the devolution of more powers to the states within the limit of true federal system. The time had come to give more powers to the states, as their financial status was very poor. "We are for one country nobody wants to separate from India." Badal replied to a question on the autonomy resolution in Jammu and Kashmir.

He said the Akali Dal and DMK were the only parties, which voiced the need for true federalism in 1962 as it was the only way for progress and prosperity. But we were branded as separatists. He said "we are for more powers under a true Federal structure. The state government has to serve the people directly. The development of the people is mainly dependent on the Financial resources of the states. The Federal system is only way to success and progress",[32] Badal said the policy is now that the state would hold certain subjects while the powers remained with the centre.

Hurriyat–Hurriyat party has rejected the greater autonomy concept, it is fighting for either aazadi and sees role for Pakistan in any dialogue. The All Party Hurriyat Conference (AAHC) described the hullabaloo over the Jammu and Kashmir Assembly resolution, which the union cabinet rejected as a "non-issue" as far as the permanent resolution of the Kashmir problem was concerned.

"We in the Hurriyat attach more significance to the Vajpayee's government's approach on the Kashmir and not what Dr. Farooq Abdullah does, as the people of Jammu and Kashmir have lost trust in his Government."[33] Former APHC chairman Umar Farooq told the *Hindustan Times*.

He said the Hurriyat was not interested in any arrangement aimed at transfer or devolution of more powers. The dialogue should on the core issue and not the grant of the greater autonomy, which was totally irrelevant in the present context. Mr. Farooq said that the

APHC never attached any significance to the development as greater autonomy for Jammu and Kashmir was never on its agenda.

Responding to the cabinet's rejection of the Assembly resolution. Mr. Farooq observed that the Kashmiris were clamoring for a permanent solution to the problem, which can not be achieved through the autonomy route, "when we speak of a solution to the Kashmir problem, our focus is on the entire state (including under PoK occupation). The grant of autonomy touches only a fraction of the problem," he argued.[34] The Hurriyat leader further remarked that the "APHC would favourably respond to any unconditional offer for talks by the Vajpayee Government provided the proposal reflected a genuine desire on the centre's, part to find a lasting solution to the festering dispute. It's for New Delhi to reduce its ever-roing dependence on the armed forces and create a congenial atmosphere for dialogue.[35] Mr. Farooq exhorted the government to start on a positive note and express its willingness to address the core issue of the Kashmir problem. Such an approach would also help the Hurriyat to convince the people of Kashmir about the utility of engaging with the centre.

AFTER REJECTION OF THE AUTONOMY RESOLUTION

Having summarily rejected the Kashmir autonomy resolution, the Vajpayee government found it much harder to satisfy the aspirations of Kashmir and of other states – with its anodyne promise of "devolution of financial administrative powers". The ruling National Conference believes that greater autonomy is the only solution to the problem of militancy in the state but the BJP and Congress against greater autonomy. Legal and constitutional expert says that greater autonomy to Kashmir would require constitutional amendment that may not be possible immediately.

Also, the Ladakhis are against the autonomy as "Srinagar rule" they are to observe a "Black week".

Jammu and Kashmir Chief Minister Dr. Farooq Abdullah says that "I believes that the Centre-State dialogue on the autonomy issue will take place my understanding it that they have kept the door for dialogue open if you don't talk about autonomy today, you will have to tomorrow." Dr. Abdullah said " If other party say it is a political issue why should it not be sent to a political committee of some kind"[36] "Kashmir's solution has to be political and our resolution is the first step in that direction."

The Sheikhs of Kashmir (The Abdullah Family have a history of belong not cold, they took an anti Delhi start when out of power and moved to her extreme when they got powers. [37] But Dr. Abdullah has gone a step ahead of his father Shri Abdullah he is expecting greater autonomy from party that even wants Article 370 abrogated.[38]

But Home Minister Lal Krishna Advani promised "suitable to ensure harmonious centre-state relation in the light of the recommendations of the Sarkaria Commission".[39] Justice Sarkaria submitted his report in 1988, but his recommendations have yet see the light of day, curiously the Vajpayee government has not though tit fit to expedite the suggestion the BJP itself made it commission, such as on financial autonomy and the appointment of governors "from a panel prepared by the Inter state council in consultation with the concerned state" [40]

The BJP may consider the autonomy resolution secessionist but for several constituents of the NDA–notably the DMK, AIDMK, PMK and the Akalis what the Kashmir assembly is demanding is not different from what they themselves asked for in the past[41]. The three Tamil Parties are still officially committed to the Rajamanner committee recommendations, as endorsed by the Tamil Nadu assembly in 1974. The resolution was moved by M. Karunanidhi, Chief Minister of the state. Its content was the same as the Kashmir resolution: "The Federal government should have only powers relating to defence, foreign affairs, inter-state communication and currency" like the Kashmir assembly the Rajmannar Committee wanted the Supreme Court limited to constitutional cases and Election Commission to conducting national and not-state elections.

But in politics, context is everything. There was no insurgency, no cry for separation. The union cabinet did not rush to reject the Tamil Nadu resolution. Indira Gandhi simply ignored it, as she had the equally radical 1973 Anandpur Sahib resolution sponsored by the Akali Dal. It was only in the early 1980's –with the shettering of the Congress hold on the south–the centre states problem became important. When the four southern chief ministers met in Bangalore in 1983 to demand equitable sharing of fiscal revenues, Indira Gandhi reaction was to appoint the Sarkaria Commission. Since then, the salience of regionalism had dramatically increased. What has changed, also, is that the BJP has supplanted the Congress as the main defender of a centralised polity. The irony is that the BJP is forced to rule in alliance with regional parties, all of whom, to some extent, want a radical overhaul of centre-state relation.

Interview of Farooq Abdullah by Arun Joshi of *The Times of India*, on June 25, 2000.

What is this autonomy and for whom?

The autonomy is a commitment.

But what will the people of Kashmir gain out of this autonomy?

You need food to satisfy hunger of your stomach. There is another kind of ago that you need to satisfy the aspirations of your head and heart. It is the question of our *izzat* and *abroo* (dignity and honour) not something new that we are asking. It was there. It was taken away from us. We simply want that to return to us.

Don't you think that this kind of politics will weaken the State's ties with rest of India especially when there is already violent atmosphere around?

Let me tell you, what we are asking is within Indian constitution. We are Indians. Every day my party workers are getting killed for India. Why we are being suspected when we are asking only what we had and that too within the sovereignty of India. If Government of India is willing to talk to those asking for Azadi or freedom and Pakistan, we are only asking something from our own country. What is wrong in that?

The people in Jammu and Ladakh are opposed to it?

First, we are discussing the State Autonomy Committee Report. It is debate. It is to clear many doubts. Secondly, we are open to discussion with the Centre and with other parties at all levels. We have already constituted a committee of ministers to discuss the matters. Let there be a national debate on the issue.

What about the intra regional tensions, Ladakh is already agitating?

Don't say Ladakh. It is only part of Leh district. There is Kargil also in Ladakh. Ask them. They all want autonomy. The Leh agitation is being sponsored by some elements. I know them. They are sitting in north block (in Delhi). They are directing the anti-autonomy agitation. That is not going to help the matters. It is a matter of debate, let it be solved through debate.

There is also a suggestion to trifurcate Jammu and Kashmir. How do you react to that?

Do that. Leh district union territory status, that is what they are asking for. Let two and half districts in Jammu form a separate state, rest of Dodi, Udhampur, Rajouri, Poonch and Kashmir will become greater Kashmir. Independence is there. But I will not allow the State to be divided, we are committed to its unity and integrity. God knows, what kind of politics is being played.

What about finances? Jammu and Kashmir is a poor state depending on centre for its small and big needs. How can you open a chapter of confrontation with Centre?

There is no confrontation in the first place. Let there be no doubt on this account. Autonomy doesn't mean that we will move out of India. We are very much part of India and as part of the country we are entitled to our share. We are working on our power projects and I hope the day comes when others come to sign MoU (memorandum of understanding) for money from us.

There is an impression that this autonomy issue has been raised at this time to scuttle the talks between Centre and Hurriyat Conference.

Let it be clear to everyone that we are not opposed to any talks with anyone in the democratic set up. Let there be talks but within the Constitution of India. Autonomy has been our plank since long and no motives should be attached.

There were other promises too made to the people. What about those?

Yes. We have worked hard on those. Open the days of Governor's rule. They left debt of Rs.600 crore for us in power sector alone. No one would collect taxes then. We are collecting taxes and power tariff. The tax revenue has gone four times high in the past three and a half years." Schools and hospitals have started functioning. The malaise of copying has been eradicated. Now officer's function. People get their work done. Yes, we have not been able to do as much as we had expected in curbing militancy. That is because of many other reasons. There is infiltration from across. Pakistan has stepped up its campaign against us. Then there are certain things that the Centre has to do.

One of the charges against your government is that it indulges in wasteful expenditure and the central funds are not utilised in the sectors for which those are meant.

Each and every penny is accounted for. Let them come and see. How without proper utilization of funds the damaged bridges and schools have been reconstructed and how new bridges have come up. How new water supply schemes are coming up.

One fails to understand that the maximum criticism against your government comes from BJP, the party with which you have an alliance at the Centre and your government is not getting funds from the Central government where your party is part of it. Isn't it strange?

We are partners in National Democratic Alliance (NDA). BJP is also there. We have no intentions of entering into any confrontation with centre. We are only asking for our rights. Whatever has been done is for the interests of the State.

Some of the BJP leaders are also saying that Article 370 is to be abrogated. It is still on their agenda.

Prime Minister Atal Behari Vajpayee told a huge gathering at Tangdhar that Article 370 is a reality and no one can change that.

Hurriyat leader Mirway Umar Farooq in an interview with Vidya Subrahmaniam, he discusses the prospects for talks and explains why such negotiations would be meaningless if they did not include Pakistan.

Azadi is Once Again Back as a Slogan

People cannot define *azadi.* It is a vague concept *hum chahte hain azadi* is a slogan that has caught the people's imagination. But it is not necessarily for a separate state.

Are you saying that the people of Kashmir really don't want aazadi ?

When people here talk of *azadi*, what they are saying is that they don't want to take this relationship (with India) any further. In reality, there is a reason why we have not been able to resolve the impasse. Historically speaking, we have always spoken about the two Kashmir's as one. For us, PoK's not Pakistan. It is a part of the Jammu and Kashmir state. There is no difference of opinion in the Hurriyat on this. The two Kashmirs have to be together. Whatever is decided has to be decided from the entire former princely state of Jammu and Kashmir.

So where do you go from this position ?

We have proposed that the governments of India and Pakistan set up an intra-Kashmir dialogue between all the regions of Jammu and Kashmir on both sides. Half of my family is in PoK. I have never met some of my relatives. More than-a political issue, it is an emotional issue for us.

Do you see a solution soon?

We would definitely like to see the world community arrive at a solution that has acceptance in both Kashmirs. There have been certain other attempts. British MP Lord Eric Avery has been planning to have an intra-Kashmir dialogue in Kashmir, but this has never happened. Most of us do not have travel documents. Besides, India and Pakistan must give us permission to hold the dialogue.

The government of India and Pakistan should not hesitate to meet. That is the only forum where we can put forward our views. We are entering a phase where the world community is getting together. European Union unity between the two Germanys and now the two Koreas and Israel and Palestine.

Are there any specific proposals?

A number of solutions are in circulation. Buffer state confederation, State within a state, these are all in the air. However, for any proposal to be considered, it has to be discussed across the table. There is a lot of talk about holding talks with us. But we have not been approached officially or unofficially.

What are your Suggestions?

The Indian government must give us space. We must be allowed to go to Azad Kashmir, it is silly to stop us at airports, impound documents etc. In the Internet era, when there are practicalily no communication barriers, does it make sense to impose restrictions, like these? They must also understand that when we talk of Kashmir, we talk of the two Kashmirs. It is a human issue involving 30 million people.

What are your comments on the Kashmir study group proposal?

It is a good ground to start with. It is a proposal worth considering. However, ultimately you have to refer any formula to the people, they must decide who'll administer the state.

Can the first step be greater autonomy of the kind proposed by the Abdullah government ?

We are against this. Once you take away finance, defence and communieation, there is very little autonomy left. In any case, you know very well what happened, how early safeguards about autonomy and Article 370 were eroded.

May be we can start from cessation of hostilities by both the militants and the security forces?

When we talk in terms of cessation of hostilities, we have to be in a position to convince the Mujahideens that this is a meaningful first step. And for that we must be allowed to go to PoK and talk to the people there and convince them that the Indian government is sincere. If New Delhi is willing to take this first step, we'll respond.

Do you see any change at all in the environment?

There was a feeling after Clinton's visit that something will happen. A lot is being said about American interest in Kashmir. Definitely, we were released because of Clinton, though, I do hope I'm wrong and the move came out of a genuine desire to find a solution.

But the, signals we get are negative. The Indian leaders have approached Israel. For what ? Obviously to gather tactics. It is difficult to be convinced about their sincerity in this situation. There has been no let up in atrocities committed by the security forces. In the last two months alone, 18 young boys have been killed. They were no doubt militants once. But they had come back to politics. Unless this situation changes, dialogue cannot work out. That can happen only if the environment is right.

Are you in favour of dividing the state into three or more parts?

We are proud of our Kashmiriyat. The secularism of this state is an example for the whole world. I want a solution that includes all religions, and people, Hindus, Muslims or Buddhists. But once we come to the negotiating table, we may not be able to hold this position. For instance, we are told that Ladakh wants to be administered directly by Delhi. If they don't want to be a part of the new solution, then they have a right not to we have to respect their choice.

So, it is all hopless?

No, I have a solution, but it is for the government to consider it. 1 say instead of the bipartite approach, have a tripartite approach. Let the Hurriyat talk to the people of Pakistan and India. We will do our best to break the mistrust and bring the two countries together.

Surely, after Kargil, India is justified in harbouring mistrust?

Kargil was definitely a misadventure. It was a disaster. It gave the peace process a jolt. But it must start again. WhenVajpayee went to Lahore it was the first to welcome it. Unfortunately, that effort failed. I have a lot of hope in Vajpayee. I feel he is sincere.

Ram Jethmalani's interview with kidya subrahmaniam.

You have said that the autonomy resolution passed by the Jammu and Kashmir assembly negates 'Pakistan's Claim'. What claim is this and how is it negated?

Ever since independence in 1947, Pakistan has been raising the Kashmir issue in the United Nations as well as other for a claiming that the state was forced to accede to India fraudulently. However, through this resolution the elected representatives of the people of J & K have unequivocally succeeded in negating Pakistan's claim. The elected representatives have made it clear that they are proud of the bond that unites the state with India. They have also said that even though accession is final and irrevocable, India's jurisdication should extend strictly to just three subjects: that of defence, communications and external affairs. Even this fact completely makes nonsense of the Pakistani claim. There is no reason for Pakistan to be happy about this resolution. In fact the resolution hasn't even made the Hurriyat happy. The elected representatives have also praised constitution of India for being democratic-which recognises basic human freedom. We are democracy and the National Conference is a constituent of our government. We cannot and must not slam the door on the prospect of dialogue. What makes the assembly resolution unacceptable, is its present form and content. At one place it unfortunately declares that everything that has happened after 1953 is unconstitutional and immoral. Incidentally, this will also include the agreement reached with his father.

Looking at the issue legally, is it possible to turn the clock back to what happened half a century ago?

Legally speaking, if a law is passed today, it can be repealed tomorrow. But when Farooq talks about erasing history after 1953 totally, it does not make sense. Farooq went overboard and ultimately ensured the resolution's rejection. Even now, nothing is lost. Every legitimate demand which is not inconsistant with the integrity and sovereignty of the country should be seriously and respectfully be considered. Farooq too knows that the test is not a technical one, where whatever developed since 1953 can be wiped clean like a slate. If you feel that Mr. Abdullah has gone overboard, what according to you would have constituted a reasonable demand ?

It is too early for me to answer that. We have a whole committee under Justice Sarkaria to decide. I cannot answer this.

So, where does Farooq Abdullah go from here ? Do you see, any end or solution to this debate ?

What I feel is that in time dust will settle down on this unfortunate controversy. In a sense, it's also an unnecessary quarrel over words. The home minister, used the term "devolution' which means more power to the state, which means an increase in its autonomy. Thus, whether they discuss devolution or autonomy it is very similar. It is a play of words. The Horne Minter has made a statement moderate in tone avoiding all polemics and stridency and left the door open for our ally.

If at all the demands are accepted, how drastically will the constitution of India change?

Marginal changes can always be made. The constitution has already been amended 79 times in the last half century, and it can be very well done now.

There is also a fear that an autonomy call in J & K will find expression in other states. For example, we are already hearing similar sentiments from Punjab and Assam.

This is why we have appointed the standing committee under Justice Sarkaria to put an end to such controversies arising anywhere in the country.

If you did have differing views from the BJP on this question, why did yon not put forward your view forcefully in the cabinet meeting?

"'I have never claimed to have differing views froms the BJP. I respect the cabinet's decision, that in its present form resolution was destined to be reflected.

Criticism of the State Autonomy Committee Report

This report has been rejected by the centre. Many politicians, political scientist, researchers criticized it on various ground. In the next section after analyzing we will examine which criticism is factually correct or not.

Report Presented and Passed in Haste

Restoration of autonomy to Jammu and Kashmir, eroded since 1953, figured in National Conference election manifesto since 1977 (when it re-entered into the electoral pray after Indira –Sheikh accord of 1975). However autonomy was the main plank for National Conference manifesto for Assembly election of September 1996 that returned the party with massive mandate in all the three regions of the state, thereby restoring the democracy in Kashmir after seven years. The party agreed to join the electoral fray in 1996 elections only after explicit assurance of the central government of restore corded autonomy soon after taking over the reins of the administration, the Farooq government set up a 9 members state autonomy committee (SAC) on November 29, 1996 vide Government Order No. 1164 GAD of 1996 under the chairmanship of Dr. Karan Singh, former Sadar-e-Riyasat. The Committee had representation of all the three region of the state and different communities. Meanwhile, Mr. Gh-Moti-ud-din Shah was appointed its chairman on August 19, 1997 following resignation of Dr. Karan Singh on personal grounds. The terms of reference of the SAC were very clear which, inter alia, asked the committee to examine and recommend measures for restoration of autonomy to the state, consisted with the instrument of accession, constitution application order of 1950 and Delhi agreement of 1952.

The SAC held nearly 50 sittings in two and half years and even visited New Delhi to interact with Major National Political parties on the issue of autonomy. The committee completed its report and presented, it in the state legislature on April 13, 1999. The copy of the report was sent to the centre also. The state cabinet examined the report in its two meeting on Jan. 19 and March 15, 2000 and endorsed its recommendations. It constituted a five member ministerial committee and requested the central government to set up their ministerial committee for dialogue on the report. A resolution, endorsing these decisions and seeking dialogue on the report with the centre, was introduced in the state legislature on April 8, 2000. The debate on the motion remained inconclusive and on the demand of the members, a special session on the state legislature was convened on June 19, 2000 to enable the members to debate on this vital issue. Both the houses approved the nation by voice vote – legislative assembly on June 26 and Legislative council on June 27. The criticism of rushing through the motion is, therefore, unfounded and smacks of ignorance of basic facts, critics unfortunately presume and reflect in their analysis that the issue was rushed through in great haste, which is factually incorrect.

Autonomy will open a Pandora Box and may lead to disintegration of the Country

The position of Jammu and Kashmir is different from other states of the country. It has a separate constitution and a separate flag. The instrument of accession acceding Jammu and Kashmir to the Union of India clearly restricts the jurisdiction of the Union to only three subject, i.e., defence, foreign affairs and communication, J&K's position in the union of India is unique which is a historic reality and no amount of diatribe can change it. This position was gradually changed through 42 constitutional orders since 1953.[42]

By restoring the original position and giving more powers to Jammu and Kashmir there is no danger to the integrity of the country. Moreover, devolution of more powers to the states is part of the National agenda of Governance and this also needs to be discussed at National level. The states like Tamil Nadu are already demanding devolution of powers. To use the word of prime minister, India is a strong enough to face all these situations, its no good to run away from the reality.

Autonomy will Weaken State's Tie With the Country

Removing mistrust and fulfilling regional aspiration will never weaken the state's tie with rest of the country. In fact, it will strengthen the tie as there would be based on trust and fair play, leaving no room for suspicion and consequent alienation of the people. Jammu and Kashmir was, is and shall always remain a glittering crown of India, Jammu and Kashmir's accession with India is final and irrevocable and its people had once for all, rejected the two nation theory and there is no going back on it. Today the world is heading for federalism and in the present political scenario, India too can't escape from it any more with such demands already coming up and NDA's National agenda of governance explicitly speaks about devolution of powers to states which is nothing but autonomy to states. The centre must respect its promises and safeguard states special status (in its original form, i.e., undiluted Art 370) and its identity India will definitely emerge much stronger with its federal units, each satisfied with its regional aspirations.

Timing Inopportune for Autonomy Resolution

No time is inopportune for realizing commitments. Once the process is initiated it has to culminate at some stage. Its not a political gimmick, as is being made out by some elements for the assembly election are stated for 2002, i.e., two year ahead (life of Jammu and Kashmir Assembly is six years). It is a sincere effort of the SAC to complete the task assigned to it. When the report is finalized it had to come before the legislature for debate. After all, it's a very important issue associated with sentiments of the people who started feeling alienated since 1953 when their most popular leader Sheikh Abdullah was sacked and erosion of autonomy started.

Autonomy Will Flare up Secessionist Activities and Communal Tendencies

The state is already confronted with secessionist activities of some elements fuelled by pro-Pak Hurriyat leaders. These do not stem from settlement of political issue within the Indian constitutive but deprivation of these rights provides a breeding ground for such activities and the situation thus created, easily explained by Pakistan to its advantage. What Jammu and Kashmir is asking for is only the restoration of eroded autonomy under the framework of the constitution. Autonomy is not secession. Those who sought to link it with secession are either ignorant of the difference of these words or willfully mixing it to create confusion and to paint Jammu and Kashmir people in bad light. This is bigger danger. In fact. Resolution of the legislature reiterates the finality of Jammu and Kashmir's secession with India and has unnerved the secessionist leaders in the state as well as their mentors across the border. Otherwise why did it (resolution) evoke wide spread condemnation from Hurriyat leaders, Pakistan government and PoK Assembly? They known well that it has taken away their thunder. Today autonomy has touched hearts of the people. They feel that anything can be discussed in a democratic India and this makes India different from Pakistan. The autonomy resolution does not promote communal tendencies. It guarantees unity of the state under the framework of Indian constitution and negates the move on trifurcation of the states. Some elements are, however, spreading dis-information on the issue by distorting facts and creating misgiving in the minds of the people for political expediencies. The National debate proposed by the Chief Minister Dr. Abdullah to debate the report will clear all these misgivings on restoration of autonomy in Jammu and Kashmir.

Autonomy Resolution is An Anti National Act

What is anti national in asking for eroded political rights within the constitutional framework. More over the resolution asks for positive and effective steps for implementations of the report. It includes debate at the national level and dialogue with the centre. The resolution should not be mixed up with the Bill. Its not a piece of legislation. To appreciate the report, it is essential to known the historic and political events of the post-independence era. What the state is asking for is restoration of its eroded autonomy and not secession. It is paradox that there is not furore on centre's talking with those asking for secession but lots of voices are being raised on the autonomy demand which is under the framework of the constitution. Some are even asking for the arrest of Dr. Abdullah and dismissal of his government for demanding restoration for constitutional provisions, which were available to the state in the past. Some elements are spreading disinformation, which will do more harm to the nation than the national debate on autonomy to Jammu and Kashmir. It is more appropriate for the critics to read historic documents, letters exchanged between the central and the state leaders and debate that took place between 1947 and 1952 on the constitutional relationship of Jammu and Kashmir with India. The Chief Justice of India, Dr. A.S. Anand's book *The Development of the constitution of Jammu and Kashmir* is recommended for everyone to appreciate the genesis of the demand for restoration of autonomy.

Had the demand for autonomy been anti-national in any manner, then the united government at the centre would never have incorporated it in their common minimum programme (CMP) and "devolution of powers" would not have been incorporated in the national agenda of governance for NDA.

Supreme Court and Election Commission Jurisdiction Restricted and there will be Separate Supreme Court for Jammu and Kashmir

The report does not bar Supreme Courts original jurisdiction over Jammu and Kashmir under Article 131. What the report asks for is omitting the application of Art. 218 extended to Jammu and Kashmir by the first amendment Act 1959. This will restore power of the state legislature under sub-section (2) and (3) of section 99 of the state's constitution as it existed prior to 1959 in respect of removal of Judges of the state High Court on the ground of proved misconduct or incapacity. There is no recommendation to set up state's own Supreme Court or bar Supreme Court's original jurisdiction the impression is erroneous and mischievous. While all provisions about High Court are in the states constitution, including its administration and expenses, salaries, pensions etc remain a charge on state's consolidated funds deletion of powers of the legislature about removal of judges was unfair and unjustified. As regards the jurisdiction of Election Commission of India, it is not known to many that Jammu and Kashmir has its own People's Representation Act of 1957. Election to the State Assembly are held under the state act and not under the centre act. Prior to amendment in Jammu and Kashmir constitution, state election organisation used to conduct elections. The report seeks to restore it to original position. But elections to the Parliament are held under the centre act and will continue to be conducted by the Election Commission of India.

Resolution of a Play to Cover up Non–Governance

It is absolute incorrect to say that autonomy report and motion on it in the legislature was a play to cover up the alleged non-governance of Dr. Abdullah government in last three years. First of all, there is nothing like non-governance and the question of covering it does not arise at all. One cannot be blind to the discernible change in the over all scenario—both on law and order and development fronts. On the security scenario, while there is no denying the fact that militancy continues with active abetment of Pakistan, it is also a fact that over all situation has gone a sea change in last three and a half years of Dr. Abdullah's government, notwithstanding killing and continuous militant violence. The security bunkers, which four years ago doted the Srinagar city and urban areas, are nowhere to be seen today. There number has almost to be reduced to near negligible now. The fear of fun is waning and is much less than what it was four years ago. The political activities has gained a greater momentum despite militant targeting national conference workers. There is no "liberated" Zone anywhere in the valley and political leaders including BJP who had no base, are visiting every nook and corner of the valley without any problem. This itself speak volumes about the change. The political leaders who criticize Farooq Government day in and day out in the length and breadth of the valley, could not have dreamt of visiting the areas of four years ago. The pressure of militant is mounting and killing, mostly through grenades or explosion, is no yardstick to measure ground situation. The fully galvanized local police have taken over the lead role in combating militancy and achieved many successes, giving sacrifice while hitting hard militants.

It is because of improved situation that administration at every level is now fully functional and attending to the accumulated multifarious problem of the people, mostly arising out of the prolonged spell of militancy. The de-railed education system was put back on the rails and menace of copying, an offshoot of militancy, was sternly curbed.

Tourism, backbone of Jammu and Kashmir economy, was reviewed. The pace of development accelerated despite all odds of particularly financial constraints.

Restoration of work culture, enforcement of accountability, drive against corruption, waning fear a guns, relaxed atmosphere, instilling confidence in the people and creating an atmosphere of trust, are the hallmark of political dispensation of Dr. Farooq Government. The earlier situation presented a grim picture of anarchy prior to his taking over all the reins of the government. This should be enough to make critics introspect and appreciate the realities, which of course will not die merely because it is not to their liking. As for the governance is concerned the following achievement despite financial constraints could well indicate the endeavours being made to put the state back on the path of development.

1. 124 militancy – damaged bridges constructed, work in progress of on another 75 minor and major bridges.
2. As many as 2600 bridges/culverts constructed under rural development scheme.
3. 1500 kilometre road upgraded. More than hundred villages connected by new roads.
4. 700 link road completed under border area development programme, 1800 school buildings constructed under different schemes. In addition over 500 Panchayat Ghars, 632 Anganwari Centres, 523 passengers sheds, 7200 works under various rural development schemes completed.
5. More than 31000 houses constructed under Indira Awas Yojana.
6. Over 400 lack mandays works generated in rural areas under rural development department.
7. About one lakh unemployed youth provided employment.
8. 7.5 MW power added by completing four micro power projects. 105 MW upper Sindh Hydel Project, Kanagar and 42 Chennai Hydel project being commissioned shortly.
9. First ever mega hydroelectric power project at Baglihar taken up by the state government to tap the available hydro potential. It will generate 450 MW power at the cost of Rs. 4000 crore. The state Government is also taking up another mega 600 MW Sawalkote Project.
10. The state government entered into agreement with the NHPC for Rs 16000 crore.
11. The state government entered into agreement with the NHPC to unable it (NHPC) to take up seven others Rs. 16000 crore Hydel Projects with over 2800 MW on BOOT (Build, own, operate, transfer) basis.
12. Over 1600 kilometre HT transmission lines and 650 kilometre LT transmission lines completed. Addition capacity of 650 MVA added to the power distribution system.

13. More than 100 drinking water schemes completed, work in progress on another 500 schemes.
14. Over 11 million-galloon per day water supply augmented in Srinagar and Jammu cities. 1600 hamlets provided drinking water.
15. 1800 hectares of additional land brought under irrigation system, 26000 irrigation wells dug under million wells scheme.
16. Above 24000 cases sponsored for loans under self employment schemes.
17. Most ambitious scheme of Rehbare– Taleem launched in the state over 6000 five member village committees involving over 30,000 non-official members constituted to supervise the functioning of the primary schools and recommend appointment of local eligible youth for post of teachers.
18. 600 new primary schools opened. 250 schools upgraded. 500 militancy damaged school buildings reconstructed work in progress on another 153 buildings. Drinking water and toilet facilities provided to entire primary and middle schools.
19. 20 sub-district hospitals, 50 primary health centres, 90 sub-centre established work on several major health projects in progress.
20. The food production of the state increased 13.28 million tons in 1996-97 to 16.88 million tons in 1998-99.
21. Tourism revived, special packages given for revival to tourism, first national winter games organised in Gulmarg in January 1998 and more 20 conferences and conventions held. Gandola lift project commissioned.
22. New industrial policy introduced to revive industrial culture cash assistance to the migrants got increased to Rs. 600 per member subject to the maximum of Rs. 2400 per month per family sufficient one room tenements constructed and no migrant living in tent. Ambitious multi-crore package for return of migrants formulated and sent to the centre for funding.
23. Dal development project formulated and conservation measures taken up.
24. Efforts in mapping up internal resources exhibited government's grit to collects fees and taxes which the Governor's administration could not do in seven years rule. The revenue receipts increased from Rs. 493 crores in 1995-96 to Rs. 1040 crores in 1999-2000.

25. A 3 member women commission constituted to take cognisance of excesses against women and solving their problems.

Abdullah Won Last State Assembly Election with Autonomy as an Issue What About Other Election Promises

True many pledges were made in the manifesto and action almost every pledge has been taken.

- *Restoration of greater autonomy and regional autonomy.* Restoration of autonomy adopted by the legislature and sent to the centre for further debate and implementation. Regional autonomy report also prepared and placed on the table on the state legislature, a committee constituted to find out lacuma, if any. An expert committee to minutely look into this issue and recommend measures for the devolution for the devolution of power to different regions of the state.

* *Activating District Development Boards.* The district development boards reconstituted with a cabinet minister as its chairman made fully representative and effective in formulating and monitoring district plans under decentralized system of planning.[45]

* *Revival of administration and weeding out corruption.* Administration revived, made responsive and accountable, functional at every level, stringent measures taken against corruption, scores of cases registered against corrupt officials of every level.

* *Appointment of ombudsman.* Action yet to be taken.

* *Human Rights Commission.* The state is first in the country to have its own statutory Human Right Commission. Over 700 complaints are before the commission.

* *Rebuilding militancy damaged infrastructure.* The magnitude of progress is enormous requiring crores of rupees, so far 124 bridges reconstructed, work in progress on 75 bridges, 500 militancy damaged primary and middle schools buildings reconstructed, work progressing on another 153 such buildings.

* *Tackling unemployment.* Nearly one lakhs educated youth absorbed in government departments and semi government organisations. Self employment schemes reinvigor ted, about 24,000 cases sponsored for loans under various self employment schemes. Openings in private sectors ensured, industrialization speeded up, several centrally sponsored projects with employment opportunities got sanctioned, agreement made with NHPC for

absorption of locals, including skilled and unskilled hands besides technocrats in seven new mega hydro electric projects.

* *Solving problem of migrants.* A high powered apex body constituted for solving day to day problem of migrants, special package implemented to improve their condition in camps, cash relief increased, ambitious package for their return and rehabilitation in the valley formulated and sent to the centre for funding, no migrant now living tents, adequate ORTs constructed.
* *According top priority to power generation.* The Rs. 4000 crore Baghliar HEP installed capacity of 450 MWs taken up in the state sector, Rs. 6500 crore sawalkote project with the capacity of 600 MWs also being taken up, MOU signed, agreement entered into with NHPC for taking up seven mega HEPs with installed capacity of over 2800 MWs and investment of Rs. 16000 crore on Boot Basis, to be completed in five to seven years.
* *Saving Dal Lake.* An ambitious save Dal Lake project formulated and launched with central funding, a separate lake and water ways development authority set up for its effective implementation, mechanized deweeding taken up in a big way, encroachments checked, rehabilitation of Dal dwellers mooted.
* *Improving state revenue.* Godbole committee constituted and report submitted for economic reforms and financial reforms.
* *Panchayat elections.* Elections twice announced, once postponed due to non-availability of adequate security forces required in the militancy hit valley and oodoc district, second time due to mid-term Lok Sabha poll, again delayed due to census operations which are in progress, 38 per cent seats reserved for women.
* *Inclusion of Dogri in the 8th schemed of the constitution.* Included in the 8th scheduled of the Indian constitution.
* *Improving security scenario.* Local police reactivated and strengthened with modern weaponry and greater man power, police taking role in combating militancy and achieving successes, intelligence network improved, co-operation of people solicited general atmosphere relaxed, unnecessary security pickets removed, life returned to normal, political activity revived and tourism started picking up.

Will Restoration Strengthen Democracy

The basic question is: will the restoration to the pre-1953 constitutional position strengthen democracy or provide what the

SACR calls " a democratic framework" and redress the grievances of the alienated Kashmiris? Or, will re-empower the people to shape and control their political and economic future themselves?

It is obvious that a return to the pre-1953 constitutional position will grievously harm the legitimate political and democratic rights of the Kashmiri and non-Kashmiries and enslave them once again. The roots of the Kashmiri alienation and solution of the Kashmir problem lie not in the central clouts, introduced after August 9, 1953 (with the concurrence of or at the request of the state government) but in the gross misrule, bureaucratic bungling and denial of a legitimate expression of the popular will. The centre must repudiate outrightly any such suggestion that seeks to re-establish dictatorship, render the people ineffective for all practical purposes and widen a gulf between Jammu and Kashmir and New Delhi. It should also ensure that state government provides a clear, efficient, fair and responsive administration – which is accountable to the people. This and the re-organisation of the state's polity on a regional basis and the elimination of Pakistan sponsored militancy are the fundamental demands of the people.

Political Scenario in Jammu and Kashmir after Rejection of the Autonomy Demand

The question arises again, " If Farooq Abdullah really advocating an independent Jammu and Kashmir or is he attempting to maneuver India into the position of being guarantor to a feudal freedom run by Abdullah family?" How many of the recommendation of the state autonomy commission are serious and how many are just potential bargaining points.

The action of NDA cabinet has put both the Vajpayee's government and Farooq in a blind. Farooq is in political trouble in Jammu and Kashmir. His authority is being eroded by allegations of corruption, increased custodial killing and other human right violences. Major constituencies in Jammu and Ladakh are protesting violently against actions of the government appropriating nearly all resources to serve the interest of only Kashmiri Muslims at the expense of others. Many politicians are calling for Farooq to severe his ties with the NDA as he is regarded as the NDA's man' in Jammu and Kashmir while many have judged the passing of the state autonomy commission report to be only a means of starting debate on the status of Jammu and Kashmir and have condemned its outright rejection by the central government of India, the implications of those actions are further reaching. The centre has limited its maneuvering room by slighting the CM who has been regarded as its own representative, Farooq has been left as the loser in a gambit designed to really support by fulfilling a 1996 election promise. For many Kashmirs' what faith they may have had left in both state and central governments, has been further eroded.

The larger question, however, is if Jammu and Kashmir can press for independence, what about other groups? What about Nagaland, Assam or Bodoland? For that matter, how about Punjab and the Sikhs? The list of organizations demanding independence for their regions is lengthy indeed and includes. United liberation front of Asom Bengal Liberation Army (which demands the secession of West Bengal—Bodoland Liberation Force (which demands an independent Bodoland created from Assam): Dalistan organization (which demands independence for predominately Dalit Scheduled Tribes areas): Gujrat Swaraj Sangh (which demands an Independent Gujrat): Council of Khalistan (which demands an independent Sikh Khalistan): Maratha Rashtra Parishad (which demands the restoration of Shivaji's 18th century empire): Revolutionary Party of Manipur (which demands an independent Manipur):Hezb-e-Muglistan, Pak Islamic Mughlistan and Jihad-e-Mughlestan (which want to restore the Muglistan Khilafat which would involve the Union of Pakistan and India as well as Bangladesh, Nepal, Afghanistan); Oriya Kahasabha (which demands an independent Orissa); India National Front for smaller states (demanding the creation of Bodoland from Assam, Gorkhaland from West Bengal, Purwanchal from eastern Uttar Pradesh, Panchal from western U.P., Bundelkhand from Southern U.P., Telengana from Andhra Pradesh, Vidarbha from Maharashtra, Saurashtra from Gujrat, Malowa from Madhya Pradesh and Kodagu from Karnataka), All this in addition to the already committed formation of Uttaranchal (Northern U.P.), Jharkhand (Southern Bihar) and Chhattisgarh (Eastern Madhya Pradesh).[46]

The list goes on, some of these groups are smaller annoyances and others are large, very vocal and potentially dangerous. The point is that if any form of independence is considered for Jammu and Kashmir, it will only stock the fires of other radical groups who perceive some benefit for themselves and feel they have an equally valid claim.

Following is a brief summary of some other recommended action of the Autonomy Resolution by Jammu and Kashmir Assembly:[47]

That the Kashmir valley be divided into three provinces: Kanraz provinces (Baramullah and Kupwara), Nandbad province (Srinagar and Badgam), Maraf province (Anantnag and Pulwara);

That Ladakh, be divided into two provinces; Leh (Buddhist regions north of Indus) and Kanuul (includes Buddhist Janskam and regions south of Indus).

The Jammu be divided into three provinces; Chenab valley (Doda and Mehore Tehsil), Jammu Provinces Jammu, Uddhampur and Katha) Pir Panjal province (Rajouri and Poonch).

If one look at the map and overlays the territory with the predominant demographiy it is not hard to see that these recommendations divide the state into communal areas. The Kashmir Valley being almost totally Muslim. Ladakh with many Buddhists, and Hindus and Sikhs in Jammu and segregated into other areas except in Pir Panjal where the Hindus are combined with majority Muslims, this would pave the way for a potential plebiscite to send all of Jammu and Kashmir with the possible exception of the Leh and Jammu provinces to Pakistan.

Demand for the Trifurcation of the State Into Jammu and Ladakh and Kashmir

Recently, the Akhil Bhartiya Karyakari Mandal (All India Leader's Committee) of the Rashtriya Swayamsewak Sangh passed a resolution demanding that the region of Jammu be made a separate state and Ladakh a Union Territory.[48]

This kind of divisions is meant to scuttle the demand for regional autonomy within the state[48]. The demand for a division of the state is not new, the United Nations mediator, Sir Owen Dixon, had recommended a partition of the state in 1950's had also sought that Ladakh and Jammu be detached from the valley if full integration of the state was to be achieved quickly. But, in its new avatar, several factors have coalesced to produce a potentially explosive situation. Most important is the widespread feeling within Jammu and Leh of deprivation as well as political and economic discrimination by politicians from Kashmir. While this feeling of deprivation may have some grounds, it is being exploited by sectarian political groups who are demanding separate statehood for Jammu and Union Territory status for Leh they argue that now only separation from Kashmir will ensure better governance, more economic opportunities and a greater share of political powers.

The dangers of the debate on the division of the state are many, but the proposition becomes even more clear when one looks at the specific instances of the regional discrimination listed in the fact sheet of 12 allegations of discrimination, several are so vaguely phrased as to be meaning less. It claims that there is "35 per cent education in Kashmir and 65 percent in Jammu". There is no explanation of what education is being referred to, and the numbers do not even remotely resemble official literacy or school expenditure figures. Others discrimination is claimed that only 30 per cent of all state expenditure, including central assistance, it continues, is used in the Jammu Zone, the remaining 90 per cent being utilized in Kashmir. It is also alleges that only four of 35 commissioners and secretaries to the government are from Jammu, and that all central and state corporations have their headquarters in Srinagar. The RSS data also suggests that just 20 megawatts of the 350 MW of power generated goes to Jammu, and the figures of 350 MW refer only to production in Kashmir.[49]

This kind of discriminations are spreading in Jammu and Ladakh and they are opposing the demand of greater autonomy because these regions suffer from an acute feeling of regional deprivation. Among the most common complaints voiced here are those related to disproportionate share of political powers, development grants, bureaucratic positions and employment opportunities among the three regions of Kashmir. It is generally felt that Kashmir gets a bigger piece of cake, leaving the other two regions perpetually deprived. Since no mechanism of internal devolution of powers is suggested in the report, it is felt that the autonomy for the state may actually come to mean autonomy for Kashmir only. The state, in any case, is known for its centralized structure of power.

It cannot be denied that there is as much need for a devolution of powers from New Delhi to Srinagar as there is for a transfer of authority from Kashmir to Ladakh and Jammu and beyond to the grassroot level. Only then can empowerment and autonomy have any real meaning. Regional harmony can not be insured through partition but through a decentralization and devolution of financial and economic power that will treat the Panchayat as the primary unit of governance.

The issue of autonomy in the state is complex in nature. It not only involves the question of the fair principles of the centre-state relation but also the question of internal devolution of power and inter-regional relations. The two issues of the state autonomy and the regional autonomy are, in fact, logically interconnected, it is not possible to achieve the one without aiming at the other, the politics of autonomy of the regional or of the state level, somehow has failed to carry this logic forward. Those who demand regional autonomy oppose the demand of autonomy for the state and those who demand state autonomy hesitate to talk about the regional autonomy.

The state of Jammu and Kashmir needs a multi layered package of autonomy that extends beyond the state to the regional and sub-regional levels. The sub-regional discontent in the state is as acute as regional discontent. The backward and peripheral parts, both in the Jammu and Ladakh regions, often complain of political and economic neglect. Regional autonomy, therefore, has to flow further to the sub-regional and the Panchayat levels, only then can autonomy have any real meaning.

References

1 Hari Om, "Jammu and Kashmir Autonomy Report: Disastrous consequences of pre-1953 position", *Koshur Samachar Magazine*, Vol. XXL1V, No. 3, June 2000, p. 8.

2 Government of Jammu and Kashmir, *Report of the State Autonomy Committee* (Srinagar/ Jammu, July) p. 6.

3 *Ibid.*, p. 7.

4 "Kashmir's puppet Regime Demand Autonomy", *Information Times,* 26 June, 2000.

5 "The Autonomy Report", *India Today,* June, 2000.

6 Government of Jammu and Kashmir, *Report of the State Autonomy Committee*, (Srinagar/Jammu, July 2000) p. 103.

7 Hariom, "Jammu and Kashmir autonomy report; Disastrous consequence of pre-1953 position", *Kashmir Samachar Magazine*, Vol. XXLIX, No. 3. June 2000, p. 8.

8 *Ibid.*, p. 9.

10 *Outlook*, 17 July 2000, p. 27.

11 "Kashmir's puppet regime Demand Autonomy". *Information Times,* 26 June, 2000.

12 Sharma, S.D., *Kashmir Autonomy – An exercise in centre-state relation*, Subhi Publication, (New Delhi, 2002), p. 141.

13 *Ibid.*, P. 142.

14 *Mainstream* 27 July 2000, p. 26.

15 Sharma, S.D., *op.cit.*, p. 136.

16 Francis Bernier, "Twist with destiny, *India Today*, 10 July, 2002, p. 26.

17 *Ibid.*, p. 28.

18 Sharma, S.D., *op.cit.*, p. 137.

19 Francois Brinier – "Twist with destiny", *India Today*, 10 July, 2000, p.' 28.

20 Sharma, S.D., *op.cit.*, p. 119.

21 *Ibid.*, p. 156.

22 *Ibid.*, p. 170.

23 Francois, Brinier, "Twist with destiny", *India Today*, 10 July, 2000, p. 27.

24 Sharma, S.D., *Kashmir Autonomy – An exercise in center state relation*, Subhi Publication, (New Delhi, 2000), p. 137.

25 *Ibid.*, p. 137.

26 *Ibid.*, p. 121.

27 *Ibid.*, p. 169.

28 *Ibid.*, p. 166.

29 *Ibid.*, p. 171.

30 *Ibid.*, p. 171.

31. *Ibid.*, p. 158.

32. *Ibid.*, p. 167.

33. *Ibid.*, p. 168.

34,35. Francois Bernier " Twist with destiny", *India Today*, 10 July, 2000, p. 27. Dr. Sharma, S.D., *op.cit.*, p. 178.

36. Francois, Bernier., *op.cit.*, p. 29.

37. *Kashmir Samachar Magazine*, Oct. 2000, p. 13.

38. Francois Bernier, *op.cit.*, p. 23.

39. Sharma, S.D., *Kashmir Autonomy – An exercise in center state relation*, Subhi Publication, (New Delhi, 2000), p. 174.

40. *Ibid.*, p. 174.

41. *Ibid.*, p. 174.

42. Jammu and Kashmir, "Turning the tide", *The Times of India*, 9.10.2000, p. 11.

43,44. Kashmir's puppet Regime Autonomy demand, *Information Times,* 26 June, 2002, Jammu and Kashmir – "Turning the tide", *The Times of India,* 9.10.2000, p. 11.

45 Chaudhary, Rekha , "Autonomy Demand: Kashmir at cross borders", *EPW* 20.7.2002, P. 2603

46 Sawhney, Karan, A, *Kashmir–how far can Vajpayee and Musharraf go?* Peace Publication, (New Delhi, 2000), p. 55.

47 *Ibid.,* p. 86.

48 Swami, Praveen, "The RSS game", *Frontline,* 2.10.2002, p. 29.

49 Swami, Praveen, *op.cit.,* p. 29.

7

Fiscal Problem of the State of Jammu and Kashmir—A Clear Cut Policy Needed

The story of J & K state's relations with the national identity at constitutional, political and emotional levels, in its totality and with its dramatic ups and downs, presents a tantalizingly complex but fascinating picture. The multiplicity of factors that influenced the singularly uniform course of Indian federalization in the state baffles the sharpest of minds. But no study of the subject can be quite complete without adequate consideration of the economic factor. Economic factors are vital part of popular aspiration all over the world.

So much work have been done on J&K's relation with the Indian union in political perspective but a vital component of political relation is its economic relation. Political relation or autonomy will be more meaningful if it is accompanied by economic autonomy, which means power to raise resources, power to decide priorities and an objective and equitable formula for allocation of funds by the centre to the states. The allocation should not be based on arbitrary and subjective considerations but should be based on objective factors like population, area, backwardness and contribution to the state exchequer in proportion to its income. But J & K, which occupies an extremely strategic position on the Indian frontiers, is the only state in the Indian union that is the most pampered state and totally depend on central grant and assistance.

Indeed, in liberalized India, autonomy especially fiscal autonomy is an idea whose time has come, states today are competing for foreign projects, multi lateral aid, infrastructure investment and sprucing up their records book to present a better face and fiscal autonomy could greatly help.

None of the states of Indian union would be fiscally viable on their own resourses because their revenues, and money are not enough to cover even day to day expenditure, staff salaries and poor revenues efforts are the biggest problems facing India's state. Most of which are poorly managed and, therefore, over dependent on central funds. As the state of J&K faced financial problems due to destruction and devastation caused by militancy, industrial sickness and loss of tourism industry. The central government made generous allocation of grants loans etc.

Hundred thousand crores of rupees in the form of central assistance has been given to fulfill the aspirations of the peoples of Jammu and Kashmir. But it is not known to anyone where the hundred thousand crores of rupees have gone?

But before giving any other grant-in-aid and central assistance to J&K central government should examine where the hundred of thousand crores of rupees invested in Kashmir have gone? This paper is the first attempt to examine the wide spreading grave dissatisfaction in the state of Jammu and Kashmir within a economic framework. It aims to test the following hypothesis: Central Assistance and central grants benefited only Jammu and Kashmir state than any other state of India.

Kashmir is a Multi-ethnic, Multi-religious state with 64 per cent Muslims, 33 per cent Hindus and 3 per cent Buddhists, Sikhs, Christian and others. There are three distinct geographical regions. Ladakh (with 58 per cent of the area and 3 per cent of the population), Jammu (26 per cent area and 45 per cent population) and Kashmir (16 per cent area and 52 per cent population). Kashmir is a land scarce and labour abundant state, with less than 30 per cent of its total area suitable for cultivation. The majority of the land comprises mountains and hillsides. In the 19th century, a rural elite dominated Kashmir, with rich landlords exploiting the landless peasantry that comprised the bulk of population.

The state has been categorized as one of the union's special category state due to its level of economic backwardness, difficult climatic conditions, hilly terrain etc. In 1969 when the Gadgil formula for distribution of central assistance for state plan was evolved, there were only three special category states viz., Jammu and Kashmir, Assam and Nagaland.

At the time of independence the state of Jammu and Kashmir has been categorized as one the special category states, due to its economic backwardness. By instance, over 85 of the population was engaged in agriculture, only 11 per cent was literate and installed power capacity was a mere 6 - Megawatts. The government of India attempted to overcome these handicaps heavily subsidizing the state with grants in early years and it was increased in the decade of 1990s.

Between 1950 and 1970s nearly 90 per cent of the state's five year plan were funded by the centre, while other backward states such as Bihar only received 70 per cent aid one major side effect of this policy was that it failed to give the state an impetus to mobilize its own resources for economic growth. As a result, Kashmir has not tapped its potential tax revenue and developed into the lowest taxed in India.

However, in the early 1970's, the center reversed its aid policy to 30 per cent grant and 70 per cent loans. As a result 50 per cent of the state's expenditure began to comprise of debt and interest repayments. In 1978-79 out of the total budget plan outlay of the Rs. 108 crores, 56.8 crores were directed toward department re-servicing.

Today Kashmir is enjoying maximum fiscal autonomy and the telling fact is that the Kashmir is the most pampered state in India. The beginning of militancy in 1990, the state has managed to get the lion's share of central resources-over Rs. 35,571.3 crores in grant and assistance. Kashmir that is demanding more and more fiscal autonomy from the centre is creating more and more problems for the union government.

It is clear that grass is greener in the state of Jammu and Kashmir. Jammu and Kashmir is the least poor-state in the country with a rate of poverty of about 3.4%, compared to 26 percent for the country as a whole. Central assistance both plan and non plan to the state of Jammu and Kashmir have gone up sharply from 1244 crores in 1990-91 to Rs. 4603 crores in 1999-2000. This included central assistance to the state plan and devolution of finance commission and the non-plan revenue deficit grants. If all this is to put together then per capital central assistance to the state of Jammu and Kashmir is approximately Rs. 6000/- per year. Between 1990-2000 the centre paid Jammu and Kashmir Rs. 2432.59 crores as grant-in-aid look at the — magnitude of the largesse: fiscal year amount (Rs. in crores), 1991 (1,244Cr.), 1992 (1,393Cr.), 1993 (1,569Cr.), 1994 (1,820Cr.), 1995 (2,627Cr.), 1996 (2,672Cr.), 1997 (3,208Cr.), 1998 (3,624Cr.), 1999 (3,833Cr.), 2000 (4,604Cr.), 2001 (3,437Cr.), 2002 (4,578Cr.), CAGR= 1991-2002 14%.

Jammu and Kashmir gets 10 per cent of all central assistance and J&K has received more than any other state since 1995! For out of proposition to its fair share, which by population should be about 1 per cent: that is, J&K gets roughly ten times what it deserves.

To put it another way, the per capita central assistance is Rs. 8,092 per man, women and child in Jammu and Kashmir. Kindly compare this to the per capita GDP in India roughly $460 or Rs.22,000. Therefore, each man and woman and child in J&K gets eight to ten times more money from the centre than citizens from other states. This is true rip-off. And all this money is given by the centre to the state directly, to use as it pleases per capita assistance 1992-1993 per capita assistance 2000-01 CAGR

Other states	5761,137	8.8 per cent
J&K	3,197,092	12.3 per cent

For all that talk of autonomy or azadi, the fact is that J&K cannot sustain without the centre's support. In 2001-02, the state spent Rs.7, 516.6 crores of which 4,577 crores or 60 paisa of every rupee spent come from the centre. The state's non development expenditure was Rs. 2,829 Cr. including a salary bill of Rs.1,193 Cr. while its own revenues were barely Rs.1,095 Cr. The state could not have paid even the wages of its employees without the centre's help.

In fact the center also pays for the financial assistance to Kashmiri migrants, the ex-gratia paid to people killed in terrorist acts and public works related to security plans, while other states get central assistance in the ratio of 70 per cent debt to 30 per cent grant, J&K (as a special category state) got 90 per cent of its assistance as grant and only 10 per cent repayment criteria has been removed and the centre has been —funding the entire plan expenditure of Jammu and Kashmir or Rs. 11,400 crores in five year.

Though the state of Jammu and Kashmir has enjoyed privileged position as far as central assistance is concerned yet it is still backward and demand for more grant, however, is still on. They already have more fiscal autonomy than any state of Indian union. So the next time some 'secular' 'progressive' asks for why there is a object poverty in India, the answer is 'because we spend all our money on keeping Jammu and Kashmir well fed and well protected, of course, the 'secular', progressive will then ask the question, 'why don't we give up J & K to Pakistan? The answer is if we do so, very soon we'll be repeating the very same conversation about West Bengal, U.P., Tamil Nadu and Kerala because the Islamic terrorist are looking for Jammu and

Kashmir alone. They want nothing less than to complete conquest of India.

Significantly, grass is greener in the valley. If the Kashmiri feel alienated, it has more with the quality of local administration. Before demanding more and more grant from the centre, state government should try to distribute this assistance and grant and resourse to regional levels and sub-regional levels.

Mere demanding more and more grants from the centre, state government should try to resolve the basis problems like poverty, unemployment, illitracy. Does the state government really have the policy to meet the "aspiration" of the people? They want employment security from intimidation, life with dignity and honour, local rule, alinination to corruption, free and fair election and the recognition of their regional aspirations.

8

Regional Autonomy—Pre-Requisite of Unity: Jammu, Kashmir and Ladakh Relation Need Revision

The post modern thought recognizes two basic human urges; urge for identity and urge for unity. Both would be crushed in a forcible uniformed communities.The process of modernization, democratizations, information explosion and technological revolution, it has been universally acknowledged, sharpens urge for identity. Unity and identity are quite different things. Unity is international in references, international perspective and rooted in political feeling. Whereas identity is local and regional, rooted in imagination and work of culture. National unity is a statement about politics; it is affirmed or challenged by political activities and the measure of its achievements ranges from political stability or instability, the absence or presence of commitment to the survival of the national political experiment.

The new concept of identity have captured the stage of social science. The identity aspiration and sense of identity have offered a new dimension to the assertiveness of ethnic group, a sense of identity means a sense of being at with oneself... It means, at the same time, a sense of affinity with a community's sense of being at one with its future as well as history or mythology.[1] But there is no singular construct of identity. Identity has multiple Nature making people live many identities at a time. This is probably because of the crosscutting nature of social cleavages and oceanic evolution and formation of identity. Yet what is more pronounced is regional identity. Even the individuals objective marker of identity acquires regional specificity. It is the performative variation in identity that distinguishes one region from other. We may presume that the regional identity and entity has significant bearing on approach taking towards the demands, or the regional configuration. These regional identities—it's formation, expression assertion, has been a very complicated phenomenon. Most surprisingly, regionalism or autonomy movement are based mainly on the concept of identity.[2]

1 would like to respond to two questions in this chapter. Firstly, what is the definition of a 'REGION' and 'REGIONALISM' and how regional identity distinguished one region from other? Secondly, does regional identity regionalism erode national confidence and threaten national stability or regionalism as a challenge of establishment of Nation-state. This chapter also seeks some answers of these questions. Why are men and women willing to die for their identity? Why do they identify so strongly with their region? Is regional character or nationalism universal? Or is a 'region' a purely modern phenomenon and a product of strictly modern social conditions? And what, in any case, do we mean by the concept of the 'Region', 'Regional identity', 'regionalism', 'nation building'and Nation-state.

Many writers on the concept of identity, ethnicity, Regional identity and regionalism, Nation building and Nation-State have done great jobs. Paul Brass[4], Rajni Kothari[5], Narman, D. Palmer[6], K. Sheshadri[7], R.N. Mishra[8], Morries Jones[9] and Balraj Puri[10] have explained problems of regionalism as one dimension of the net result of the impact of modernization. These theorists link the emergence of regionalism as a result of modernization. According to Balraj Puri, regional and sub-regional consciousness' is likely to grow with the process of Modernization and democracy. He thinks that the "technological revolution', instead of wiping out smaller identities, has led to rootless ness, alienation and atomization of the individuals". The vacuum is filled by his urge for identity which he seeks in smaller culture, language, group history and region with which he identifies himself[10] Paul Wallace argued that historical and cultural environment of a region shaped the distinctive relationship between region and Nation in India. He concludes that Indian civilization and regional culture are the two realities of Indian federalism. This observation echoes the thoughts of many others. Suri Ratnapara Ian Copland and John Richard in their work on federalism regards federalism, 'as a response to Ethnic-regionalism', they explain federalism provide a means of accommodating regional ethnic diversity and in federal system regionalism can promote inter-ethnic harmony. These ethnic-regional diversity does not create challenge to a federal system.[11] Cynthia Enloe, argued that regional identity and elienation spring from cultural heterogeneity, which produces intense consciousness of ethnicity, a peculiar feeling among persons that causes them to consider themselves a group distinguishable from other.[12] Navnita Chadha Behera says that root causes of the regional alienation and suffering among different regions lie in the organization of the Nation-

State.[13] One stream of political scientists including Dr. Behera argued that Nation State itself is facing pressure from the regional and sub-regional level and some other theorists think that subject of region, regional identity and regionalism involve many kinds of problems—social, cultural, political and historical. These aspects manifested in the demand for secession, demand for separate statehood, demand for regional autonomy, demand for state autonomy and center-state dispute.

The aim of this study is to support the hypothesis that individuals generally act in their own self-interests, these self-interests and sentiments promote ethno-regional sentiments and identity. But it does not mean that these ethno-regional sentiments and regional identity create challenge to national feelings or national-identity. I wish to prove it further with the aid of tools provided by evolutionary theory. To understand the problem in its proper perspective regionalism, it become necessary to define the various concept like region, identity, regional identity, national identity and nation-state'.

The term "Region" becomes an analytically relevant category for comprehending the process of state formation and federal nation-building. Defining the region as a concept is an essential prerequisite for the analysis of the phenomenon of regional. Identity or regionalism. This is very difficult task because their is no particular defination of the term region. A region may be defined in many different ways as the objectives of enquiry or the questions under study. The choice of the definition of region is, therefore, constrained by the purpose for which delineation of set of regions is required, and by the overall structure and degree of the integration of the regional system considered as a whole[14]. The term 'region' is undoubtedly one of the catchword of our day among both popular and scientific writers[15]. To the practical man of affairs a region is simply an area with certain characteristics, in virtue of which it is suitable unit for some particular purpose of business or administration. Geographer have been accustomed to the 'formal region'[16] because their discipline was born in consideration of physical features and climate. The identity of an area as a 'Region' in the field of geographer is an old concept of space-explanation, the formal region is defined as an area with similar features, topography, compactness, population, duration of working season, existing level of development and the resource endowment to ensure mobility of working machinery for effective implementation and supervision of project in execution. Geographical definition of a region assumes uniformity of composition, a territorial presence and boundaries.

A region is an areal concept, a nucleus of social aggregation on a well demarcated and identifiable expanse of territory which is to be understood in a time space context.[17] People living in a particular region over a period of time are opt to develop an identity affiliation with it. Continued stay in that area creates a common new identity which provides a self image. This image identification is a resultant of an interplay of several dependant variables, such as religion, language, ethnicity, a common past rooted in history, and a common desire to live together in future.

However, region has got different meanings for different scholars. A geographer tries to emphasis on geographical area, an anthropologist on cultural area, while for a sociologist it is composed of a constellation of communities characterized by "homogeneity of economic and social structure". Nonetheless, for a political scientist, it is a political sub-system with components of its own and interactions among these components laying a boundary within the national system.

A region becomes significant in a nation only when it becomes a unit dominated by a widely prevalent sentiment of "togetherness", a sense of particularistic and separate identity.

When the particularistic attitude of the region claims recognition of its cultural identity, it is better understood as "regionalization" or regional movement. Thus Prof. Haqqi writes, "whatever the context or parameter, 'region' may be said to denote an area, at least sufficiently large in size, which is differentiated and / or distinguishable from others by a variety of factors (or at least a combination of some of them) such as language, culture, religion or caste/creed, socio-economic life, political background, historical background, geographical continuity, and certainly, group consciousness and of being neglected, deprived and/or discriminated by the majority and/or those in authority".[18]

Hence, regionalism is a multidimensional phenomenon a feeling or sentiments backed by objectives factors like language, culture, economic development, etc. It is manifestation of emotional, psychological and sub-rational socio-cultural forces confined to a particular region within a large political set-up.

Some writers feel that regionalism denotes a relation pattern based on conflict between the core federal centre and peripheral units, and shall continue to dominate so long as political boundaries continue to impinge erratically on ethnic, linguistic and political alignments. The interplay of these variables give rise to a kind of aggressive activism resting on native -migrant dichotomy, religious fundamentalism, linguistic chauvinism, cultural pluralism, geographical attachment, caste dominance, economic deprivation, political discrimination and a real exclusivision[19]. Since the end of Second World War, there has been a growing academic and political cancer with the problem of regionalism. Today there is hardly any country including the developed ones which has escaped this problem. Even the states widely considered to have passed the threshold of National integration, like Great Britain. The USA, France, Belgium, Italy and Canada, have been suddenly confronted with basic issues relating to the fundamental unity and integrity of their constituent national components.

On the other side, the erstwhile socialist world including the Soviet Union, Poland and Yugoslavia, which claimed to have resolved the complex "national question" by eliminating national oppression, ensuring equality among various nationalities and other ethnic groups, and creating conditions for their free development, have suddenly been threatened by a resurgence of regional identities to the extent that the very existence of their political systems has been put into doubt.[20] The situation is still worse in the old societies and the new states of Asia and Africa which, as Rupert Emerson has pointed out, "are not yet nations in being but only nations in hope.[21]

The older States of Latin America, which have had more than a century to establish some form of accommodation with the forces of socio-economic change, in fact, tried to consolidate their real independence after the collapse of colonial system and the change in the global realignment of political forces. Many of these countries like Uruguay, Bolivia, Brazil, Peru and Ecuador suffer from the lack of feeling of national identity on the part of the inhabitants of the whole territory.[22]

What follows from the above arguments is that the emergence of regional consciousness or concern with regional identity, appears to be a nearly universal phenomena, across Europe and North America, indeed around the globe. Put differently, the regional problems of each country have their own specific character; and in each period of historical development they may assume a different significance and content.

In order to understand the problem in a right perspective, a brief look at the problem of regionalism in various countries where this phenomenon is more alarming, is desirable. Such an analysis becomes more important at the present point of time when regionally-based ethnic, tribal, cultural or religious subgroups, have begun to make demands which at time border on separation.

Let us first take the care of United States of America. The vastness of its size and multiplicity of cultural groups have engendered regional cleavages on many occasions. The civil war between the northern and southern states which was fought for a long period of time was one of the most remarkable inter-regional cleavages in the history of the USA.[23]

In France, in spite of the polarization of politics between left and right which has helped to moderate the process of the emergence of regional consciousness, in many less developed regions like Lorraine, Occitania, Corsica, and Catholic regions like Brittany, regionalism is re-emerging and getting a footholds.[24]

In Italy also the conflict between northern regions like Lombardy and Piedmont which took the lead in industrialization and the relatively less developed southern areas, especially the Frulia, though not so strong yet, had definitely some impact on the Italian politics.[25]

In West Germany though politics is dominated by issues that cut across all regions, Bavaria still retains the strong regional identity and is conscious of economic and political dominance by the Rhine-Westphalia region. The Union of the two Germanys after 45 years of separate and mutually hostile existence is likely to add another dimension to regionalism in United Germany.

In Canada, the problem of regionalism is very serious in Quebec where economy is controlled by the Anglophones but numerically the region is dominated by Francophones. The Quebecois have charged the Qntario government controlled by the Anglophones for the bias in the industrial development and consider the cause of their economic problems as a consequence of cultural division of the country and Anglophone dominance.[26]

The question of regional identity in the Soviet Union involves non-Russian groups which constitute more than half the Soviet population residing in different geographical regions. These include small tribal groups in remote areas, non-western peoples with ancient litrary and artistic traditions such as the Uzbeks, large Slavic groups such as the Ukrainians, small but highly educated and advanced populations -as in the Baltic states which are closer to Central Europe or Scandinavia than to Moscow. The Soviet Union claimed to have resolved the vexed problem by granting cultural autonomy to these regions but the unilateral declaration of independence by Armania and Ukraine threaten the unity of the Soviet Stateds.[27]

Regionalism is one of the most common features of the politics of most of the Asian, African and Latin American countries where lack of integration is evident among the several religious cultural, ethnic or tribal groups which are generally regionally-based and are relatively autonomous, self-contained and traditionally hostile towards one another. Frequently, these groups are stratified within the state along social, economic and political lines, further complicating the problem of nation-building because the different identities both cross cut and converge. Above all, the problem of regionalism also assumes special importance in the context of the third world countries because of the low level of socio-economic development, the incompleteness of the processes of class formation, the mixed character of the economy, characteristic of most of the developing countries, the continuing dominance of foreign monopolies and the retention of many of the archaic forms and traditional institutions of pre-capitalist society. Hence a brief study of the problem in the developing contries like India becomes more important.

In Indian federation fight is actually between regional identities and National Integrity and the point is how to have both. Regional identities are a reality of Indian federal polity. And at the same time it would be unirealistic to expect total integration in a country as diverse as India. On the political level, rise of regionalism as a force cannot be ignored.[28] The wide variety of cultures and languages have given rise not only to different identities but also to a multiplicity of identities that an Indian generally possesses. What gives a particular significance to these identities is the fact that most of them are specio-cultural meaning thereby most of cultural identities are associated with specific regions. The specio-cultural identities became a vehicle for political phenomenon called regionalism and sub-regionalism both of which are sub-group phenomena, the main difference being of the level at which they manifest.

Many western scholars have raised doubts about the very survival of India as a nation-state because of the multi-ethnic character of Indian polity. The development of regional forces in India is a natural consequence of the given tremendous heterogeneity in Indian Society which is "a continent of many communities united through shared experiences but powerfully motivated by parochial and regional considerations". But because of having multi diversity Indian political system is passing through a 'multiple crisis stage' and simultaneously is facing all the crisis such as "crisis of identity, legitimacy, penetration, participation and distribution. These crisises can be noticed in many states of the country like Jammu & Kashimir, Tamilnadu, Andhra Pradesh, Assam, Nagaland.[29]

The concept of regionalism in Indian politics "has generally been regarded as something that is anti-system, anti-federal and against the basic interests of a well-integrated and well developed polity.[30]

In the Indian context and following Iqbal Narain's typology we can classify regionalism into three types.[31] First type, which he calls supra state regionalism that refers to that manifestation of regionalism which cuts across state boundaries or in which states or parts are grouped together in term of regional identity. The conflict between north and south India and Jharkhand movement can be cited as example of supra-state regionalism. Second type of regionalism is called inter-state regionalism in which "the regional identity of one state is in competition with the regional identity of another state mostly for economic development, sharing of benefits and allied purposes". The various movements and agitation involving the issues such as river water disputes, boundary disputes, etc., are some of the examples.

The third and final type of regionalism is characterized as intra-state regionalism which is the reflection of "a psychic deprivation on the part of a portion of the state which feels alienated from the whole". This intra-state regionalism has been defined as subregionalism.

Regionalism as the Challenge to Nation State or Nation Building

Regionalism is a multi-dimentional phenomenon at once psychological, geo-cultural and politico-economic in its nature and manifestation with negative and positive overtones. On the negative side it represents real or perceived deprivation on the part of people of an area. It is negative aspect which makes regionalism quite militant, agitational and violent and on the positive side regionalism means the urge of the people living in a particular territory for self identity and self-fulfillment.

It will not be out of place here to distinguish regionalism from nationalism. Regionalism may thus, be understood as the extension of nationalism at the regional level or national can be defined as the extension of regionalism at the nationalism level. However, regionalism is distinguished from the nationalism in that it recognises a higher unity and superior national interests transcending the attachment to the local region. Regionalism also cannot be equated with the term 'Sectionalism' because it is not merely based on regional economic and class interests but other ethnic factors like culture, religion or language are equally essential for the emergence and growth of regional consciousness.

What follows from the above argument is that regionalism and nationalism both are interdependent, and it is not possible to achieve one without aiming at the other.

National unity can genuinely flower out of a healthy reconciliation between regionalism and nationalism. However, it is evident that like national chauvinism, unhealthy regional or sub-regional patriotism is equally cancerous and disruptive both of creative regionalism and also of syncretic nationalism.[32]

It is highly necessary that we discard, once for all, the notion of regionalism as being somewhat unpatriotic or posing a threat to national integrity.

The needless dichotomy between nation/country and sub-national groups has quite often led to sterile and meaningless debates and discussion, even at the decision-making levels. The unavoidable historical process is forgotten: that in a country of manifest diversities and varieties like India, unity does not mean uniformity, nor integration means centralization.

As a matter of fact, the current role of nationalism in India can be rightfully visualized as one capable of generating a process of both aggregation of sub-national groups, whether based on regional, linguistic cultural, communal, caste or other identities and their coalescence into a national political integration.

In this connection, it should also be appreciated that the process of democratic diffusion and panchayati raj has brought to the forefront the question of regional and sub-regional identities and their reconciliation in the federal framework.

Conceived in any form, regionalism and sub-regionalism are unavoidable in a country as vast and expansive as India. The existence of regional and sub-regional consciousness is not only a prelude to and a pre-requisite of genuine national sentiments, but logically it is generated precisely by the euphoria created by the establishment of a Nation-state. Nothing is more basic to the very concept of federalism than regionalism and sub-regionalism."[33]

Man is a territorial animal, he is born with loyality to the soil from which he had sprung, and in course of social living imbibes loyalty to the region of which that soil is an emotionally integral part. This regional identification is not necessarily antagonistic to the loyalty to the nation of which he calls himself a citizen. These loyalties are to be viewed as being basically complementary, not competitive, very currently did the State Reorganization Commission (1953-55) remind '"National loyalties do not demand that other loyalties should be eliminated". Both region and Nation represents symbols to which people in different situations identify with and use them to achieve a particular purpose.

Thus, there is no obvious dichotomy between national and state identity so long as one does not raise secessionist slogans. As long as one believes in national unity and integrity, regionalism will not create any horizontal split, because nation building is generally understood as the process of integration of sub-national and regional group, enthusing in them all unified identity so that they might think of themselves as a Nation State.

Today there are many writer who willing to do amendment in the concept of Nation State because Nation State demand total loyalties from its citizens. But in diverse society it is not possible, citizens also want to be loyal to their regional identity. Every region carries a split personality. People make no secrete of being Kashmiri, Punjabi, Bihari, Rajasthani, Gujarati, Marathi, Tamil or Malayalee when asked to specify their place of domicile. But this is no reason to feel dependent. To be an Indian is not necessary to be a non-Rajasthani or to a non-Bengali. But it can be understood in a different way. If a Bengali visits Delhi and people ask him who is he, he would be perfectly within his right to say that he is a Bengali. But if the same question is addressed to him in London or Washington, his answer would be that he is an Indian. That is the spirit in which one's state identity should be understood. Lokenath Misra explained the alleged state nation dichotomy in a convincing manner, when he said, "my first ambition is the glory of Mother India. 1 know it in my heart of hearts that I am an Indian first and an Indian last. But when you say you are a Bihari. 1 say 1 am an Oriya when you say you are a Bengali, 1 say I am an Oriya, otherwise 1 am an India.[34] This attitude of identity often used to being anti-Nation State. Rajni Kothari has refused to rise of identity and ethnicity as a Negative phenomenon to Nation State.[35] Dr. N.C. Behera argued that modern Nation state allows recognition of a single, presumably unified Nation but this is inherently-problematic because the single nation tents to be identified with the dominant majority. With the state being the sole repository of all things different ethnic communities tend to feel alienated and marginalized and they feel that their identity in a single state is not safe.[36]

Paul Wallace says that when National Identity and Nation State claims supremacy and demands total loyalty, local and regional communities lose their silence.[37] The superior claim of the Nation State is unfit in a diverse cultural society like India.

Much more important in this respect is the fact that if the nation-state in fact reflects nothing more than the supremacy of a dominant socio-cultural group and becomes a tool of oppression and repression in its hand, so can a region. Its probability is much stronger in a region which is heterogeneous. But even in an ethnically or otherwise homogeneous region, the probability of using the State as an instrument of repression will not be less pronounced if the collision of particular interests threatens the peaceful but ineffective tenor of political order. Regionalism, whether as an autonomous political entity or as a part of a larger political system, can be as aggressive, as oppressive and as destructive as nationalism.

We can say that the challenge and opportunity lies in maintaining the will and the tolerance, the sacrifice and the mutual support, that sustain a nation. We should not forget the fact that regionalization and federalization are two mutually reinforcing process of Federal Nation Building. Undermining any of them may only weaken the "Union of India".

Every urge for regional identity and Regional autonomy is not a demand for destroying national unity and it should not be taken as a call for disintegration of the National Sovereignty, but it is re-integration and now the mind of people is changing. The earlier attitude of looking upon every demand for demanding greater authority to states as secessionism is fast disappearing. In the backdrop of this changed attitude towards state autonomy, regional urges and aspiration do not pose any real or imaginary threats to integration. Regionalism opens new channels of communication and create a new perception of collective selfhood among people. The aim of this chapter to support the hypothesis that regional autonomy and state autonomy are interconnected. Regional identity and autonomy should not be used to being anti-nationalism. Before giving any solution, it is necessary to know full history of the demands of regional autonomy. This chapter will try to present the regional consciousness of the people of Jammu, Kashmir and Ladakh region and how this regional consciousness and identity influence the political, economic and cultural life of the state. The focal point of this chapter to trace the root causes of regional imbalance suffering is economic, cultural, political. What are the political demand resulting from social, cultural ethnic demands of different regions. This chapter carefully examine differentiation between three regions on the ground of ethnicity, language, religion, culture, caste ideology and how far these factors give birth to regional political movement for the realization of socio-culture and politico-economic objectives. Before any thing it is necessary to have full details of all three regions about their political, cultural, economic and social development.

Below mentioned details/tables presents the political, social and economic development which is based on comparative study.

Regional Grievances and Autonomy

The issue of the autonomy is complex is nature. It not only involve the question of evoling the fair principle of centre state relations but also the question of internal devolution of power and inter regional relations.

State governments always demand more and more power from the centre but they hesitate to talk about regional autonomy. In their own case they argued in favour of the virtue of federation but they often dubbed regional movement as parochial and fissiparous. They used double and contradictory standard in applying the principle of decentralisation of power within their own boundaries.

One of the serious flaw of the Indian Constitution is that it does not provide for regional autonomy whereas its Article 3 explicitly provides for the creation of new States in simplest possible manner- by a bare majority of those present and voting in Parliament. But if a regional identity is to be recognised in any form, it involves constitutional amendment as was done in case of Series of additions to clauses of Article 371. There has been very little debate on the constitutional provision for regional autonomy. At the time of Constitution making, a noted scholar D.R. Gadgil had mooted the idea of Sub-states and drawn a list of subjects which should be retained by the states. The brief paper he wrote on the subject remained completely obscure and nobody even mentioned it. In 1977, the socialist leader Madhu Limay had moved a resolution in Parliament for Similar provision in the Constitution. It was just talked over and never heard again.[38]

Thus the regional aspirations were left with two choices either to be assimilated and homogenised with dominant community or seek separate statehood. Both may not be possible or desirable. In many cases forced uniformity not only kills creativity and healthy potentialities of regional identities but is also surest way to disunity.

The other alternative of separate statehood, if certain conditions are not fulfilled; like total homogeneity in separated parts, can spell disaster for these parts. The unnatural division of Punjab and Bengal in 1947, under momentary communal frenzy, is an instance which resulted in greatest massacre in the history of the subcontinent. Jammu and Kashmir State is another instance that cannot be divided through a neat operation without generating communal troubles and creating other grave implications which can have repercussions in the rest of the country.

This leads to the inevitable third alternative of extending the federal principle to the internal set up of the State viz, providing autonomy to its constituent regions. Though public opinion has been mobilised and assertive in favour of decentralisation below district level and three tier Panchayati Raj has come into operation in almost all the States, there is a conspicuous missing link of the fourth tier of the region, in between the district and the state. The empowerment of district, block and panchayat will not be fully effective without a similar politically empowered regional tier. A bureaucratic

Table 1.
Population (1981) Area and Representation

Region	*Population*	*Area*	*Representation From*	*Assembly Seats*	*Inhabitants per seat*	*Lok Subha seats*	*Inhabitants per seat*
Kashmir	31,34,904	15,948 lq.cm.	Kashmir	42	74,000	3	10 lakh
Jammu	27,18,133	26,293 lq.cm.	Jammu	31	90,000	2	About 14 lakh
Ladakh	1,34,372	96,701 lq. cm.	Ladakh	2	67,000	1	1.34 lakh

authority like a Divisional or Regional Commissioner cannot properly perform the task of coordinating the fictions of the districts and give their combination strength enough to assert their rights. Transfer of power from centre to states, regions, districts, blocks and panchayats is, therefore, a federal continuum.[39]

We should accept that without getting regional autonomy, We cannot get state autonomy. Jammu and Kashmir might be the first state in India where the idea of regional autonomy was mooted. It has been debated some time acrimoniously and on other times cordially, since almost soon after the establisment of popular government in the state in 1947. Many people in Jammu and Ladakh in their representations to the committee and public expression, have argued the case for regional autonomy on the basis of a catalogue of regional grievances, neglect and discrimination, over the last 50 years. But even if the state government treats all regions equitably, such impressions can persist.

Regional Autonomy is needed to inspire confidence of the people, to make the system more democratic, to ensure speedier and balanced development and to make the administration accountable to the people and thus more efficient and above all, to evolve a composite and harmonious personality of the State. None of these objectives can be achieved in the present unitary constitution of the State and by centralisation of power and administration.

It is for this reason that champions and supporters of regional autonomy, as will be clear from the foregoing account of the prolonged debate on subject, have all along been totally secular and enlightened people within and outside the state who were equally sympathetic to the aspirations of Kashmir, Jammu and Ladakh and whose commitment to unity of the state was most important categories.[40]

Historical Background[41]

Many commissions were set-up on the issue of regional grievances and tensions. These were; the Gajender Gadkar Commission (1967), the Qadri Commission (1972), the Sikri Commission (1979), and Wazir Commission (1981)[41]. The commission of inquiry headed by Shri P.D. Gajender Gadkar was appointed in november 1967. Its terms of references were[42] :

(i) to make an assessment of development programmes apportioned to the various regions of the State and to recommend measures necessary to give assurance that the resources available are being shared equitably and also to ensure a feeling of equal participation in the integrated development of the State;

(ii) to examine the recruitment policies of the Government and to recommend measures for giving an equitable share in Government employment to the various regions and communities, having special regard to the claim of Scheduled Castes and other economically and socially backward communities, classes and groups among the citizens of the State consistently with the maintenance of efficiency of administration;

(iii) to examine the policies of the State Government regarding admissions to institutions of higher education and the schemes of assistance by way of scholarships and loans, with a view to ensuring an equitable distribution of the available facilities to the various regions and communities, and having special regard to the claims of scheduled castes and other backward communities; and

(iv) to consider generally the causes that lead to irritations and tensions and to recommend remedial measures.

Other Recommendation

1. To have regional development boards and religion and district-based service cadres: it is meaningless without decentralisation of political power. Otherwise this will only strengthen the bureaucracy.
2. The Commission had suggested formation of Zilla Parishads and Village Panchayats in this context. It had asked for reservation for economically and socially backward classes in the services and in technical institutions.
3. The recommendations of the Commission for opening, technical colleges in the Jammu region and a degree college each at Leh and Kargil are to be welcomed. To stress the need of development of Ladakh in general and Leh in particular is only timely. The recommendations for a uniform quantum of ration and review of foodgrain prices are only logical. At present foodgrains are cheaper in Srinagar than in Jammu and Leh. Also the quantum of ration at Srinagar is higher.
4. There are some other recommendations which reduce the economic and other disparities between various regions. The reference of the Commission to the Big Landed Estates Abolition Act and Tenancy Act was uncalled for Jammu and Kashmir State was the first to abolish zamindari without any compensation. To review this is to put the clock back by two decades. It may be a cause for irritation to the big landlords, mostly from Jammu. For a new social order, one has to ignore the sensitivities of the capitalist class.

5. This commission had also suggested free and fair elections so that a genuine leadership for the various regions could emerge, such as to protect the regional interests. At present, the representatives of Jammu and Ladakh in the Government are the "yes" men of the leaders of the valley, and the leaders of the valley are at the mercy of the Central Government.The Commission has agreed that "the doubts on the manner in which the elections have been conducted" "is a cause of irritation and tension and a note of this feeling is to be taken." It further adds, "we should, therefore, like to add that as the Jammu and Kashmir State occupies a strategic area, it is necessary to nurture the faith of the common man in democracy and democratic institutions in the State." Thus a case has been made for a thorough review of the elections in the State. Any ostrich-like attitude will only complicate the issue.

The PSP had further submitted that the elections to the local bodies are long overdue, which amounts to suppression of the legitimate democratic rights of the citizens. In this case, the Commission has specifically recommended, "the State Government should immediately take all steps to arrange for the holding of elections to the local bodies as early as possible. These elections should be held regularly in future."

Result of the Gajender Gadkar Commission's report

A material change has taken place after the submission of the Gajender Gadkar Commission's report, the feeling of step-motherly treatment by the people of Jammu and Ladakh was hitherto ignored without any foundation; it has been now established by the Commission that there are reasons for the grievances. Now the common man in Jammu and Ladakh is more aware of his neglect asd discrimination.

Sikri Commission (1979), the Wazir Commission (1980) and the Singhal Committee (1998) were also appointed to look into the grievances of regional imbalance to provide a valuable guidance. All acknowledged that the complaints of the people were not groundless. The recommendations of the commissions remained unfulfilled. No appropriate action was taken to ensure social, political and economic justice to the people of three regions. These commissions suggested a few sweeping changes in the states politico-administrative and economic setup in order to meet some of the requirements of the people of Jammu and Ladakh. These, inter-alias, included the setting up of three regional development boards, one each for Jammu, Kashmir and Ladakh; creation of three more districts of Reasi, Kishatwar and Samba (Bahu) in the Jammu Region; equal representation to Jammu in the state cabinet, and reservation of all the seats in the professional colleges located in the Jammu region for Jammu boys and girls and recommendation of a similar mode of admission for the Kashmiri students in the valley based on professional institutions.

However, what was most striking was the observation of the Gajendergadkar Commission. It reads; "The main cause of irritation and tension is the feeling of political neglect and discrimination from which certain regions (Jammu and Ladakh) suffer. Even if all the matters are equitably settled, we feel that their would still be a measure of discontent unless the political aspirations of the different regions (of the state) are satisfied.

Valley leaders did not take any notice of these observation nor did they implement the reports which various commissions had submitted.

The Sikri Commission which followed the agitation started from Ponch, against mal-practices in recruitment and spread over to whole Jammu region, was led by an All party Jammu commitee. Its demand for statutory, political and democratic setup at regional, district block and panchayat level has already been refered to. The Sikri Commission, which submitted its report in 1980, examined all measures for equitable share in government employment to various regions and district administrative units within the region, it came to he conclusion that "the commission had found no imbalance, apart from imbalance in individual items". As fas as individual items are concerned, it said that Jammu faced imbalance in three areas, while Kashmir faced imbalance in nine areas on the basis of indicators it selected. The commission made recommendation on a large number of individual demands like construction or improvement of a piece of road, setting up a housing colony in particular towns, construction of an industrial sheel, review of abiana rates at some places and so on. But none of the commission addressed itself to basic causes of tensions and considered systemic changes. The Regional Autonomy Committee (RAC) was also appointed to examine regional alienation and grievances within the region under the chairmanship of Balraj Puri. This report work was based on 'Regional and sub-regional autonomy within the state constitution'. The National conference after assuming power appointed the Regional autonomy commission. The Regional Autonomy Committee Report suggested two approaches on regional autonomy. First, setting up of District Council, second, breaking up of the existing regions; Jammu and Kashmir into three parts. It also gives some suggestions to remove regional grievances, and differences. It raised many questions like, what are the subjects that should be delegated to the regions? What should be the basis of allocation of funds between and within the region and what should be the institutions to deal with the subjects delegated to the regions? What steps should be taken for the promotion of language, literature and culture of various linguistic and ethinic groups and what posetive measure apart from constitutional provisions including political, cultural and social should be adopted to promote emotional harmony and unity of the state and to remove all causes of tensions between ethnic and religious community and what special measures are needed to identify and protect interests of various groups and community. These recommendations were also not implemented. But the fact that the RAC was constituted in response to the compelling political circumstances prevailing in the regions of the Jammu and Ladakh. The report negates the very notion of the regions of Jammu and Ladakh. The central argument of the report, ironically, revolves around the logic of counteracting the existing understanding of the regions. We are reminded time and again about the inaccuracy of the term 'region' to define the political status of Jammu and Ladakh or for that matter even Kashmir. The committee comes to the conclusion that there is an urgency in demarcating regions in the state for the purpose of political and economic decentralization of power, it was argued by the ethnic groups that administrative classification of the provinces should be recognized as the genuine and real classfication of the regions. Seen from this perspective, the RAC report exists in a political vacuum. By problematising the claims of Jammu and Ladakh to their regional status it annihilates the political setting in which the committee was appointed and jettisions the whole political logic of 'regional autonomy'. And in order to do that it has taken upon itself the task of redefining the 'regions' and on the basis of the definition 'mapping' the regions of the state. It is interesting to note the sense of urgency that the committee feels in accomplishing this task. The word urgency has been, in fact used more than once in the RAC report for justifing its 'conclusion' that their should be fresh demarcation of the regions into three regions, the report suggests eight regions, namely Kamraj (Baramulla and Kupwara district); Nundbad (Budgam and Srinagar districts); Maraaz (Anantnag and Pulwama districts); Chenab valley (Doda district and Tehsil Maohore); Jammu (Jammu Kathua and Udhampur districts excluding Mahore Tahsil); Pir Panchal (Punch and Rajouri districts); Ladakh (Leh and Kargil districts). The Committee by suggesting the above classifications has introduced into the area of reorganisation of the states[43].

The Committee, by suggesting the above classification, has intruded into the area of regional reorganisation of the State. This is going far from its brief. The Committee was given specific terms of reference. These terms of reference were:[44].

1. To examine, consistent with the integrity of the State and to promote better involvement and participation of people in different regions for balance, political, economic, educational, social and cultural development, evolving of instrumentalities like local organs of power, at all levels.
2. To examine the powers that such organs need to be vested with to achieve the objectives set above.
3. To examine whether any change in the State Committee structure, obtaining at present, is required.

These terms of reference are quite self-explanatory and do not include the task of either defining/ re-defining the regions or suggesting internal reorganisation of the State.

The Regional Autonomy Committee Report is very feeble in its argument. It tends to undermine the plurality and complexity that marks the identity of Jammu region. It fails to understand that rich diversities that define this region, rather than fragmenting the society, do provide it a plural base. It points to the assertion of emerging identities, divergent political aspirations and developmental lag within this region.. and uses these as the basis or argument in favour of its division into three regions. In suggesting this re-classification, the sub-regional aspirations are played against the regional ones assuming somewhat communal overtones. Otherwise what can be the justification of excluding tehsil Mahore from Udhampur and including it in Doda district.

It is pertinent to note that plurality being the hallmark of Jammu region, there is no necessary antagonism between regional and sub-regional identities and aspirations. These sub-regional identities, rather than leding to the logic of carving of this region into three distinct regions, lead to the logic of regional autonomy of Jammu as a whole. What is needed is a pluralistic and a federal set-up extended upto the grass-roots level. It is only such a set-up that can reconcile diverse type of identities within the State. Long ago in his address to the Constituent Assembly, Sheikh Abdullah had pledged to give "maximum autonomy for the local organs of the state power which are the ultimate source of authority in the State while discharging obligations as a unit of the federation".

Sushma Chaudhary feels that the fear of domination by Kashmir over the other two regions of Jammu and Ladakh persisted mainly due to the absence of any institutionalized mechanism of devolution of power at the regional level. The autonomy of Kashmir actually come to mean autonomy for Kashmir only. It may not flow to the regional or sub-regional levels. She says solution of Kashmir problem neither lies in trifurcation of state nor state autonomy. She suggests that state needs a multilayered package of autonomy that extends beyond the state to the regional and sub-regional level.[45]

All recommendations of the commissions (including RAC) remained unfulfilled. No appropriate action was taken to ensure social, political and economic justice to the people of the three regions. Both region (Jammu, Ladakh) with all their diversities facing different type of regional imbalance with effects on their political life and these regions are seeking for two solution, regional autonomy or trifurcation of the state. First option has failed to carry this logic, Because state government is not interested in this. Now, both regions are seeting for second solution.

Is the trifurcation of the state a way not? No, certainly not, we must be guided by the experience of the North-East where the creation of smaller states have not solved the problem, on the other hand, the North-East is facing an increasing clamour for more status. In the state of Jammu and Kashmir, Jammu and Ladakh regions are facing many political economic and cultural imbalances, Which influence the regional autonomy.

Armed with absolute and unbridled political powers under Art 370, the valley leaders ruled the state roughshod, completely ignoring the general political rights and interest of the people of Jammu and Kashmir and created an environment in which no Jammuite or Ladakhi could reside and serve in Kashmir or become the Chief Minister of the state. This was not merely a lapse on their part. The immediate consequences of the policies the valley leaders evolved and pursued ruthlessly were allotment of 43 seats (now 46) to Kashmir in the 75 member (no 87) State Legislative Assembly as against 30 seats (now 37) to Jammu and a paltry two (now four) to Ladakh ignoring the fact that Jammu and Ladakh were and continue to be superior both in terms of land, area and population, wholesale transfer of Jammuites and Ladakhis from Kashmir to Jammu and Ladakh, appointment of thousands of Kashmiri in Jammu and Ladakh against vacancies caused by retirement, death or dismissal of the incumbents and additional requirements, closure of the agriculture and Ayurvedic colleges in Jammu, transfer of the dental college and artficial limb centre which were earlier sanctions for Jammu to Kashmir, diversion of funds allotted for Jammu and Ladakh to Kashmir, creation of a Muslim majority Doda district out of the Hindu Majority Udhampur district in 1948, division of the Buddhist Majority Ladakh district in 1978 in order to set-up a Muslim majority Kargil district and so on.

It was under these circumstances that the people of Jammu and Ladakh engineered one agitation after the other with a view to achieving what they called their 'legitimate due in the state's political and economic process'. Strong and popular were some of the struggle like the 1952-53 Praja Parishad Movement, the 1966-67 students agitation, the 1978-79 Poonch revolt..

The state is divisible into three different regions Muslim majority regions of Kashmir which is the most homogeneous region. Jammu and Ladakh are Hindu and Buddhist majority regions respectively. The geographical composition of the state has an obvious bearing on its politics which manifests in complex and varied form. The people belonging to different regions do not react uniformly to political developments and pulls from the state, which effects adversely their relations with one another.

Jammu is a land generally of low hills, with a few territory producing maize and wheat in most of its areas and rice in some, and inhabited by people belonging to all the major religions in substantial number, known generally as the Dogras, with wheat at their staple diet, Kashmir is a valley, enclosed by high mountains, endowed by nature with a very fertile soil, most suitable for the cultivation of rice, peopled nearly 100 percent by men of one faith, that is Islam, who are known as Kashmiris, and consume rice as the best part of their diet. Ladakh is a country of high and dry mountains, with little vegetation and, therefore, precarious conditions of living, inhabited by followers of Budhism and Islam, and girm, a kind of barley, forming chief article of their diet. All these regions are facing different type of political, economic and cultural problems, so they need different type, of treatment Now they don't want to live in a single state, they are demanding trifurcation of the state. The demand for a division of the state is not new, the United Nations mediator, Sir Owen Dixon, has recommended a partition of the state in 1950, and elements within the Praja Parishad agitation of the early 1950s has also sought that Ladakh and Jammu be detached from the valley if full integration of the state was not achieved quickly.

On, June 22, 2003 at Haridwar, the Kendriya Margdarshak Mandal of Vishva Hindu Parishad called for a division of the state, including the creation of a separate Union Territory for Kashmiri Pandits carved out from within the valley. Similarly, on June 30, at Kurukshetra, the Akhil Bhartiya Karyakari Mandal of Rashtriya Swayamsevk Sangh sought separate statehood for Jammu and union territory states for Ladakh. In addition, the Jammu Mukti Morcha and the Ladakh Buddhist Association were leading the local campaign for this demand.

The negative approach of the National Conference toward the issue of internal autonomy has led many in Ladakh and Jammu to think in terms of opting out of the state. The demand for the division of the state has become quite vocal in Jammu and Ladakh. The Leh Autonomous Hill Development Council (LAHDC) has recently rejected the 'Autonomy Resolution' of the National Conference government and has passed a resolution demanding the union territory status for Ladakh. In Jammu also, the demand for a separate statehood has found greater popular approval and organisational support. RSS and BJP have come out openly in support of this demand. The 'Panun Kashmir', the political organisation of displaced Hindus of Kashmir has also staked its claim for a separate 'homeland' in Kashmir, with a union territory status. The idea of the division of the state is independent of and precedes the autonomy debate. Yet, it has been fuelled, to some extent by the recent discourse of the pre-1953 constitutional status of the state. The failure of the National Conference to evolve a consensus in Jammu and Ladakh around this discourse has led to many apprehensions in these regions. These apprehensions have reinforced the demand for division of the state. What is alarming, though, is the activation of reactionary forces around this demand. Not merely the RSS but the Jamat-i-Islami also, appears , to be quite favourably inclined to the idea of division. The ex-chairman of the All Party Hurriyat Conference and the ideologue of the Jamat-i-Islami, Syed Ali Shah Gilani, has suggested the possibility of 'trifurcation' of the state if it can help resolve the Kashmir imbroglio. A similar suggestion has been made by the Kashmir Study Group headed by America-based Kashmiri billionaire, Farooq Kathwari. It has recently come out with a Report entitled *Kashmir — A way Forward* which taking the clue from the Dixon Plan propounds the idea of reorganisation of the state and its division on the basis of re-ligious lines. It suggests a separate Muslim state of Kashmir incorporating the Muslim dominated areas of Jammu regions like Doda and Poonch-Rajouri. The Hindu-dominated districts of Jammu and Buddhist-dominated district of Leh are proposed autonomous zunits.

The solution of Kashmir problem will have to be found for meeting the aspirations of the people Jammu and Ladakh for local self governance. They do not want to look up to the government in Srinagar for meeting all their needs. An effective devolution of governance to the glass roots level is the best means of meeting their aspirations. A more federalized and bottom up approach is needed to solve the problem of this state.

References

1. Sajal Basu, *Regional movements: Politics of Language, Ethnicity and. Identity*, Pub by Indian Institute of Advance Study, Simla, 1992, p. 48.
2. Eli Mandel, "Image of praise man" in Richard Allen (ed.), *A Region of the mind*, Regima, 1973, p. 206.
3. Fyre's view cited in Gerald Frieser. *Regionalism and National Integration.* The Canadian and Indian experience in M.P. Singh, p. 38.
4. Brass, Paul, R., *Ethnicity and Nationalism.* Theory and Comparison. Sage Pub. ND. 1991.
5. Kothari, Rajni, *Caste in Indian Politics*. Orient Longman Pub. New Delhi 1970.
6. Norman, D. Palmer, *The Indian Political System*, Houghton Mifflin Company, New York, 1971.
7. Sheshadri, K, *Indian Politics. Then and now*, Pragati Prakashan, Delhi, 1976.
8. Misra, R.N, *Regionalism and State Politics in India*, Ashish Pub. New Delhi.
9. Morries Jones, *The Government and Politics in India*, Houghton Miffling Company, New York, 1997.
10. Puri, Balraj, "Sub-National Identities and National integration" *Economic and Political weekly*, June, 1976, pp. 945-48.
11. Ian Copland and John Richard, *Federalism Comparative Perspective from India and Australia*, Manohar Pub., N.D. 1999.
12. Cyhthia H. Entoe; *Ethnic Conflict and Political Development*. Little Brown Pub., Boston, 1973.
13. Behera N.C., *State, identity and violence, Jammu and Kashmir*, Manohar Pub. Delhi, 1999, p. 277.
14. Verma, Ramesh, Kr., *Regionalism and Sub-regionalism in state-politics Social, Economic and Political bases*. Deep Publication, New Delhi 1994, p. 23.
15. *Ibid.*, p. 23.
16. Shah, Gulam Mohd. Prakash, *Toward Understanding of Kashmir Problem*, Gyan Publishing House, New Delhi 2002, p. 17.
17. Singh, Bhavan, *Regionalism and Politics of Separation*, Printwell. Jaipur, 1993, p. 1.
18. Prof. Haqqi's view cited in Sharada Path '*Regionalism and Political Development in India*' in Bhawani Singh's *Regionalism Political Separation in India,* Printwell, Jaipur, 1993, p. 59.
19. Singh, Bhawani, *Regionalism and Political-Separation in India*, Printwell, Jaipur, 1993, p. 1.

20. Verma R. Kr, *Regionalism and Sub-regionalism in State Politics-Social Economic and Political Bases*, Deep Pub., Delhi, 1994, p. 1.
21. Ropert Emersion, *From Empire to Nation*, Cambridge Harvard Uni. 1960, p. 94.
22. Verma R. Kr., *op.cit.*, p. 2.
23. *Ibid.*, p. 2.
24. *Ibid.*, p. 3.
25. *Ibid.*, p. 3.
26. *Ibid.*, p. 3.
27. *Ibid.*, p. 4.
28. M.P. Singh, Chandra Mohan (eds); *Regionalism and National Identity Canadian and Indian Perspective*, Pragati Pub. Delhi, 1994, p. 38.
29. Verma, R.K., *Regionalism and Sub-regionalism in state politics, social economic and political bases,* Deep Pub., 1994, p. 8.
30. G.R. Reddy, B.K. Sharma, *Regionalism in India*, Concept Publishing Company, ND 1979, p. 3.
31. Eqbal Narain; "*Regional Politics in India*" in P.C. Mathur *Government and Politics in South Asia*, Printwell Pub., Jaipur 1985, pp. 84-85.
32. Bombwall, K.R., *National Power and state Autonomy*, Meenakshi Pub., Meerut, 1978, p. 1I7.
33. *Ibid.*, p. I 17.
34. Lokenath Mishra's views cited in Bhawani Singh; *Regionalism and political separation in India,* Printwell Pub., Jaipur, 1993, p. 184
35. Rajni Kothari, *State against democracy*, Delhi 1998, p. 6.
36. N.C. Behera, *State identity and violance. Jammu and Kashmir*, Manohar Pub, ND. 1999, p. 217.
37. Paul Wallace (eds), Region and Nation in India, Oxford, ND. p. 276.
38. Puri, Balraj, *Jammu and Kashmir—Regional Autonomy,* (A report) p. 3.
39. *Ibid.* p.3
40. *Ibid.* p.4
41. *Ibid.* p. 4
42. *Ibid.* p. 5
43. *An Inquiry into the state of Jammu and Kashmir,* (Gajendragadkar Commission report-1968)
44. Puri, Balraj, *op.cit.*
45. Regional Autonomy Committee Report, p. 23.
46. Sushma Chaudhary, RAC (Regional Autonomy Committee Report) A critiques, *Mainstream*, August, 12, 2000, p. 10.

9

Kashmir Problem Re-examined; Towards A More Federalized Solution in Jammu and Kashmir

(Summary and Conclusion)

One of the most important developments of the twentieth century has been the liquidation of colonialism and emergence of a large number of states in Asia, Africa and Latin America. This development led to a great deal of enthusiasm and optimism about the future development of these countries in term of national consolidation, modernization, state formation and industrialization. But there have been more failures than successes. It was mainly due to the fact that nationalism came in these countries as a negative phenomenon. Unlike the Western states, where nationalism accompanied or followed industrial and democratic revolutions and where common culture and language were the key elements in the growth of National states, the new states of Asia, Africa and Latin America found the mixed seeds of their nationalism planted in essentially diverse traditional social soils. Self determination has become the major plank of the various diverse communities in these states. India makes no exception to it. The growth of state system in India very much like the developing states, is not on the pattern of the west. The feeling of Nationalism arose here mainly, as a reaction a negative feeling against the foreign rule and not as a positive phenomenon, i.e., a process of internal assimilation and integration. It has therefore failed to infuse a sense of oneness and unity in the Indian Society, which is pluralistic in character. Pluralism lies principally in the diversities of our caste, creeds, religions, languages and ethnic origins and thus offer a tough resistance to the process of internal integration and synthesis, secessionism is the extreme form of such resistance process is further facilitated if the ethnically distinct community is concentrated at the peripheral areas such as Punjab, Kashmir and North Eastern states of India.

Federalism is intended to be a solution for multifarious problems like ethnic, social, cultural and lingual diversities that resist national unity. On the basis of such problems a federating unit may bargain constitutional autonomy to maintain its individual identity.

In a federal structure there should be two constituent units to maintain their relationship in a administering development and peace through the Institutional mechanism, there shall be division of powers between the central government and the provincial governments. Likewise, there shall be sharing of resources between the central and state governments, but now there is a third institution which has come into being as constitution of self-governance with distinct and categorical political, financial and administrative powers to administer development and social justice. Now the concept of federalism brings a new meaning which explains the relationship among the three institutions, namely, federal, regional and local. Hence 73rd constitutional amendment brought a new phenomenon in Indian federalism.

The Indian federal system has entered a stage where serious conflicts shall emerge between centre and the states. Autonomy for the state is an important agenda of Indian politics in the 21st, and it has to be tackled with great sensitivity on the part of central government. Federalism is always a balancing system between the powers of the centre and the status of the state government and a new dimension has been added to this issue because of globalisation of our economic politics, the demand for autonomy can not be rejected without proper negotiations with a spirit of give and take by the centre and the state government.

The Indian federal system provides various provisions to solve its long-standing and intricate problems, pertaining to the minorities, the backward classes, scheduled castes and tribes in a democratic manner.

The maximum flexibility of Indian federal system can be seen in the special status enjoyed by the state of Jammu and Kashmir. Thus the state alone involves a variation of the federal principles of the Indian constitution. Under British India also state of Jammu and Kashmir used to enjoy a 'special status' which is still continued. This phenomenon of the special status and greater autonomy being enjoyed by the state of Jammu and Kashmir has its roots in the history of its accession with India.

This concluding chapter is divided in four sections. The first section deals with the political developments on the time of Kashmir Accession to India, to July 2002 (When the demand for division of Kashmir was raised). The second section deals with the shortcomings of politics in the centre and the state on Kashmir. In the third section some suggestions on Kashmir autonomy have been given. The fourth section proposes the future Kashmir policy and describes the scope for further research.

Kashmir continues to be a problem, almost as intractable as it has been right from the time the question of its relationship with India arose in 1947. Ever since Jammu and Kashmir acceded to India the state has been provided special status and special help from the Indian Government. Accession of Kashmir with a Muslim majority of Muslim population into India was an incident which defined the two-nation theory, brought forward on communal basis. Pyare Lal, Gandhi's Secretary, in his book *The Last Phase* writes "The question of Accession of Kashmir into the Indian federation become decisive element in proving Indian federation secular" Kashmir's accession into India was the greatest victory of Indian Secularism. The immediate reason for Kashmir to join India was the was the attack on border by the Pak. Before this attack Indian Govt. and National Conference both were of the opinion that the decision of accession with India or Pakistan should be done only by the people of Kashmir, for this, as an internal arrangement and Interim representative government was needed. Govt. of India and NC were wanted to leave it on the decision of Maharaja. NC did not want to take an immediate decision to accede with either India or Pakistan, it just wanted both of these. In 1945 in a session of National Conference, Sheikh Abdullah announced "The future of the Riyasat of Jammu and Kashmir is linked with the future and construction of Independent India".

Sheikh Abdullah wanted to test in the then condition that in the new situation with one of the two countries, namely, India and Pakistan will allow greater freedom to Kashmir or acceding to it and from which one of the two it will be possible to option better benefits for Kashmir and there was nothing wrong to it. The Tribal attack was definitively a blackmail. Because of this attack Kashmir was left with no option except taking resources of Indian army. The Indian federation even before providing militarian assistance, placed a condition that it should accede to India. Here the policy of deal between India and Kashmir determined their relationship. And the same policy is still deciding the relationship between federation of states in the Indian federal system.

The Dominant leaders of the National Conference are of the opision that it would be more beneficial for Kashmir both economically and politically if it become a part of the Indian federation. From the economic angle, Kashmir is more dependent on India for goods than Pakistan. Also political perspective was that India is a more developed country than Pakistan and this will help Kashmir in developing according to its talent and nature.

This thought of Sheikh Abdullah was the thought of a Kashmiri, he was unable to think from a integral Indian angle. So Jammu and Kashmir might have proved to be a special paradigm of the relationship between the centre and the state in a federalism system. The special condition under which Kashmir acceded to India on 27th Oct 1947 makes its relationship with Indian federation considerably different from relationship of the other states with the federation. This special paradigm could have saved for a wider federalization in the Indian subcontinent.

This state followed the same process for its accession to India was followed by the other princely states, making its accession legal, rightful and constitutional beyond dispute. This state leadership desired the issue of accession to remain open at least to unable them to obtain a greater amount of internal autonomy. This special and different kind of status and internal autonomy can be seen in Art 370 of the Indian constitution. In response to their demand for autonomy, they were ensured a constitutionality guaranteed within the federal structure of India. In accordance with this special status, the logic of the state relations with India was defined by a limited applicability of the constitution of India and a restrictive jurisdiction of the Union Parliament within the scope of Instrument of Accession. The state was to be governed by its own constitution.

The Delhi agreement of 1952 also provided special autonomy and status to the state of Jammu and Kashmir. In this agreement it was decided that the state has complete freedom for internal affairs, and Kashmir continued to have the right to elect its own need of the states and Kashmir also continued to be outside the preview of provisions authorising central intervention embodied particularly in Act 356, enabling the President to take over the administration of other states. This was also decided that the Supreme Court have the limitation only for the interstate matters, fundamental rights, foreign affairs and communication.

At the time of Delhi agreement, it was decided that Jammu and Ladakh will also be given regional autonomy. But in both the regions, feeling against Abdullah went on increasing. President of Janasangh Shyama Prasad Mukherji at that time contributed to the movement of complete dissolution of Jammu Praja Parishad. The slogan was 'one symbol, one constitution, one head of the state', on acceptance of greater autonomy to Jammu and Kashmir back tracked from his opposition to Act 370, but his Kashmir Yatra and arresting played a major role in spreading the communal tension in Jammu.

The Praja Parishad agitation of early fifties to abrogate the special status for the state and its opposition to Delhi Agreement of 1952 was one of the major stimulants that caused several suspicions in the minds of Kashmiris. Kashmiris were in no mood to compromise the autonomy they had bargained to protect their separate identity. The PP agitation that channeled the discontent of Jammu based Dogra elite caused misgivings in the minds of Kashmiris, who had so far fought against Dogra Rule and it was mainly due to these developments that Sheikh started speaking of Independent Kashmir.

Sheikh Abdullah because of this atmosphere felt so much disturbed that 7th August 1953 he said "The poison of communalism that is spread in Jammu and Kashmir in relation to India has forced us to rethink over our relationship with India". Because of this statement Delhi apprehension regarding Sheikh Abdullah increased manifold. In this atmosphere of apprehension, on the order of Sadar-i-Riyasat Karan Singh, Sheikh Abdullah was arrested under "public safety act".

Balraj Puri, commenting on the arrest of Sheikh Abdullah, has said "Whatever might have been the condition and how much ever responsibility be shouldered upon Sheikh Abdullah, Praja Parishad, Janasangh, imperialist powers, it is beyond doubt that Abdullah's arresting was the biggest blow from Indian federation to Kashmir after its accession to India".[1] Burtend Russel said "In the case of Kashmir all the ethics of Indian government put on the self".[2]

Today even after 50 years, it does not seem that Indian Government is sympathetically ready to attend the wounds inflected upon Kashmir inspite of its being a Muslim dominant state it decided to accede to India rather than Pakistan. Sheikh Abdullah's arrest in 1953 was the new turn in Kashmir politics, such a turn that influenced the whole course of Indian politics. Just after four years of independence this incident signaled a weakening democracy instead of a strengthening one.

The story after the arrest of Sheikh Abdullah is the story of unauthorized intrusion, treachery and continual perseculion of central government. This is story of declaring Kashmir an inevitable part of India making it India's 'Sairgah' and declaring the national feeling of Kashmiri people's Pakistan inspired till Sheikh Abdullah was in power, Kashmiri used to feel that they are not going to stop beyond Delhi, but after Sheikh Abdullah the series of puppet Prime Ministers acceded to power in Kashmir because of the autonomy of Kashmir next on being scraped. The voices of dissent were suppressed and centre started playing freely on his wheel.

After Sheikh Abdullah, B.G. Mohd became Prime Minister of the state in a conditions under which he became Prime Minister had no chances of development or betterment of relationship between India and Kashmir. B.G. Mohd had acceded to power with the blessing of Delhi. Sheikh Abdullah had no such blessings, but he had a representative base in the state. In the next ten years Bakshi extended all types of support to the central government and in lieu continued his individual reign in Kashmir with the help of treachery, corruption, suppression and electoral bargaining. The worst part of it is that he made central leaders believe that in Kashmir also they can do the same things that they can do in other states. Drunk with power, the central leaders failed to understand that in the specific condition of Kashmir the seeds of seccession will degenerate into insurgance.

The constitution of Jammu and Kashmir framed in 1956 did not have that kind of autonomy which was imagined on 30 October 1947. After the arrest of Sheikh Abdullah in 1953 the President issued 28 constitutional orders to award his former orders between 1957 and 1977. Through these orders more and more articles of the Indian constitution were forced upon Jammu and Kashmir.Of course, keeping Art 370 in view, all these orders were implemented with the consent of the state.

In the Parliament also upto 1973, 262 central laws were implemented in state with the consent of the state governments of the periods concerned. On 21st Dec. 1964, two other articles of the Indian constitution 356 and 357 were implemented to the state (through which the President is given powers of making laws and presenting budgets of the state in case of constitutional machinery of the state collapse). This move was much opposed in the state till 1966, Indian government decided that it could keep Jammu and Kashmir under its rule only by resolving to dispolicy measures and not by democratic measures.

After assuming office in 1975, Sheikh Abdullah had appointed a committee to study the prospects of reviewing the parliamentary laws extended to the state in the post-1953 period. Nothing much came out of it because the committee failed to evolve a consensus, the issue, however, continued to be voiced by the National Conference in the subsequent period, thought it was only in 9th decade, that political thinking on it began in a big way.

The insurgence of the decade of 90's gave a clear indication that it was impossible to keep Kashmiri people with India by coercing them. So in this decade for the first time those facts came to light that were earlier repressed on the name of patriotism and blind Nationalism. On the name of keeping terrorists at bay central government came out with such laws that played havoc with the life and dignity of the Kashmiri people. These laws not only transgressed the autonomy of Kashmir but also frequently violated human rights.

The major reason behind this insurgency in the valley is the lackadaisical approach of state and central government. The policy of Indian leadership since beginning has been to keep Kashmir under its control no matter whether this can be done by fair and democratic means or not. From the time of exit of Sheikh Abdullah in 1953 to the forcing of Farooq Abdullah to resign in 1990, the political history of the state is abundant with the instance when state leaders were replaced, allured, installed and even demoralised to fit the designs of the centre. These shortsighted policies of the centre were also accompanied by the use of unfair means in elections to the state Assembly, and the union Parliament. The ouster of the Sheikh from power in 1953, forced resignation of Bakshi in 1963, compelling of Mir Qusim to resign in 1975, installation of G.M. Shah as new Chief Minister of the state in 1984 and his replacement again by Farooq who had been removed earlier in 1986, and imposition of Governor's rule in 1990 are few among many instances of political manoeuvres of the union governments.

After its forced withdrawal from the political scene in the wake of militancy and mass upsurge in early 90s, the National Conference used 'autonomy' as its main ideological plank to reclaim its political constituency in Kashmir. In its first central working committee meeting held in 1994, after a gap of five years, the party held the union of India responsible for destroying the original constitutional arrangement of the state and for alienating the people of Kashmir. It passed a resolution, which asserted that, 'the time has come when this state of affairs should be reviewed in order to restore autonomy to its pristine and original form'. Autonomy in its 'pristine form' was defined with reference to the constitutional status of the state in the pre-1953 period.

The party contested the 1996 assembly elections with the slogan of 'autonomy' and proclaimed its massive victory in this election as a mandate for restoration of the pre-1953 constitutional position of the state soon after forming the government, it constituted the State Autonomy Committee (SAC) to "examine and recommend measures for the restoration of autonomy to the state of Jammu and Kashmir consistent with the Instrument of Accession, the constitutional Application order, 1950, and the Delhi Agreement of 1952". The report of the SAC made public in April 1999 was recently discussed in a special session of the state legislative assembly. The session concluded with the 'autonomy resolution' demanding that the union and the state government take positive and effective steps for implementing the report. The resolution triggered a controversy with many apprehensions expressed against its pre-1953 status. While forces like RSS and the BJP Law minister desined for secessionism in the report, others dreaded its consequences for the National integration with similar demand pouring in from other states. The union cabinet in response to these apprehensions, summarily rejected the report. The debate on autonomy, however, is still on.

Weaknesses in Indian's Kashmir Policy

In this section we will examine the shortcoming of politics in the centre and the state on Kashmir.

The Central government give the impression that they know the answer best, but, they know so little. Neither the Congress leaders nor the BJP and other parties have so far shown that know how to deal with the situation, they have only been groping in dark since 1947, merely changing governor and power brokers does not constitute a policy or strategy. We did not have a policy in 1947, we don't have one today. Our politicians have made many mistakes while dealing with Kashmir. Pt. Nehru was undoubtedly a great man, but like all great men he had his weaknesses. His closeness to Sheikh Abdullah created terror in the mind of Maharaja Hari Singh, who did not want to be humiliated by Sheikh. If Kashmir has became a problem, it is because we chose to live in a make believe world, we made a mess of accession, we allowed personal factor to determine national issue, we did not know how to dealt with a Muslim majority state. We thought that we had purchase the loyalty of Kashmiri Muslims by giving them concession. Even after two nation theory had brought about partition, we accepted the "Separateness" of Jammu and Kashmir by instituting Article 370, this was a great error. We went too far. We have made concessions to Goa, Nagaland, Mizoram and some other states too, but only Kashmir valley has remained insatiable. Its plea for autonomy has turned into a demand for separation.

In the last five decades we Hindu, Muslim, Sikh, Christian and other have failed to arrive at a clear understanding of what is expected of a citizen of this country of immense diversity. If you want to be an American, you have to first to all be an American, then only everything also follows, but here in Bharat a man is an Indian last of all.

Only in Kashmir, the question of autonomy has became a matter of life and death, whereas in all other states, there is a recognition that autonomy is the product of an evolving centre-state relationship of a process of give and take. But we failed to tell the Kashmiri that they already have more autonomy than any other states of India, we started haggling with their leaders on the "quantum" of autonomy to be given to the Kashmiris! The Sarkaria Commission report showed how the autonomy question could be solved, but we hardly given this report any importance.

Indian policy regarding Kashmir is that at any cost it should annex to India. 'How and Why' is becoming insignificant. because of this, Indian rulers have greater respossibility to fulfill the aspirations of the Kashmir people. But this sense of responsibility seems to be completely absent in them. The feeling of dejection of the Kashmiri people needs to be understood by the central government and Indian people. The state which could have proved a paradigm of Hindu Muslim unity and harmonious state centre relationship has instead become a state of curfew, search raids and clashes. Centuries ago Kalhana wrote in Rajtarangini "Kashmir can not be won by force but only by altruism, habitant here fearful only of the second world and not of military". This think needs to be understood most by Indian rules who are not respecting Kashmir subnationality.

Kashmir needs to adopt such an attitude towards India which will help it integrate with India not only economically but politically and emotionally because a good politics binds even the broken nations and a wrong politics fractures even a united one.

Weaknesses in Kashmir's Policy

Kashmir was part of Indian civilisation from time immemorial. No one is going to extinguish Kashmir's identity of Kerala, the fear of losing Kashmir's identity is a false alarm.

Sanskritisation of India over the past 1000 years has failed to destroy the unique elements in cultural life of our states. Then what is it that Article 370 tries to protect. It has certainly failed to promote democracy or self-government, not to speak of a good and efficient administration. In fact, the leaders of Kashmir misused autonomy from New Delhi to run the most obnoxious government in the country. Nothing better could have been expected.The Kashmiri politicians did not suffer from the natural inhibitions common to rest of the people. They were not restrained by any consideration this explains the rampat corruption in every walk of eye. But this is not to say that Article 370 should be abolished. Indeed, we should proceed with the process of integration through a gradual process of adjustment. There are several odd elements in the Jammu and Kashmir situation. How is that the valley seems to dominate all discussion? How it is that we hear of little of voice of Ladakh and Jammu? All the six Chief Ministers were from the Kashmir division; most of the President of political parties were again from the Kashmir division. That is so because the Sheikh Abdullah had given the valley a pre-dominant place in the affairs of the state. Kashmir has enjoyed a large number of autonomy. In any case more than in any other state. Kashmiri leaders have been at the helm of affairs so how can the centre be blamed for the lapse of their own leadors. The people of Jammu and Ladakh, however, have legitimate economic and political grievances. The question is, why did Dr. Abdullah through autonomy dice while other regions of the state expressed their opposition? The Ladakhis are against the autonomy as "Srinagar rule", there are Ladakhis, Buddhists, Punjabi, Muslims, Sikhs and Hindus in Jammu who are anti-autonomy. Where is the autonomy majority opinion that Farooq claims. Sayed Ali Shah Gelani (The Ex-chairman of the APHC) said "people of the state do not attack any importance to the autonomy issue... over 70,000 Kashmiri have not given their blood for security the right of self-determination. Autonomy has never been the goal of Kashmiris.[3]

Farooq Government should realise that the issue of state autonomy and the regional autonomy are interconnected. It is not possible to achieve the one without aiming at the other. Jammu and Ladakh should have adequate regional autonomy. In other words, there is as much need for a devolution of powers from New Delhi to Srinagar as there is for a transfer of authority from Kashmir to Jammu and Ladakh, and beyond to grassroots level only then can empowerment and autonomy have any real meaning.

Dr. Abdullah is also a factor contributing to anger in the state. His regime and all regimes previous to his have institutionalised corruption, secondly, the administration is so centralised in the state government that there are no local Panchayats nor do the regions enjoys any rights. Developments is only for show, and the problems of unemployment become graver every day. While educated youth abound, having received education from outside the state, there are no revenues of employment for them anywhere die he (Farooq Abdullah) discussed this entire scenario with the union government, does he really have a policy to meet the "aspiration" of the people? They want employment, security from intimidation, life with lenity and honour, local rule, elimination of corruption, free and fair election, and the recognition of their regional aspiration.

Farooq Abdullah should be realised that the people of the state of Jammu and Kashmir do not want autonomy, they want peace, education, dignity and honour.

Suggestions :

It is necessary to take steps which are easy and effective, the reckless competition for power has been at the root of the most of the troubles. This competition must be stopped.

To work out a solution which will restore peace between centre and the state, the following salient features must be kept in view.

- Autonomy debate is not yet over.
- Several regional parties also have autonomy dreams.
- Many of them are BJP's partner at the centre.
- Sarkaria Commission report on power devolution is still in the cold storage.
- BJP has ignored its own recommendations to the Commission as Jammu and Kashmir state is enjoying special status and special treatment from the centre unlike any other states of Indian Federalism.

This section outlines a road map for the future.

1. Kashmir is unique and must be dealt with specially

The first solution of the problem lies in the recognition by the union government of "Kashmir different history, needs and circumstances" and grant of a different status to the people of Jammu and Kashmir.

Jammu and Kashmir's uniqueness is obvious for a variety of historical reason recognised even by Indian Supreme Court. In 1984 in Khazan Chand versus the state of Jammu and Kashmir, the Court unambiguously held that the state holds "a special status in the constitutional status of the country".[4] The 1983 Srinagar Declaration adopted by the opposition conclave that included Jyoti Basu, Inder Kumar Gujral, Chander Shekhar and Prakash Singh Badal stated that "The special constitutional status of Jammu and Kashmir should be preserved and Protected in Letter and Spirit".[5]

More important, however, is not Kashmir's singular importance to the very idea of India, which has often been forgotten, is now re-entering the consciousness India in 1947 lent tremendous strength to the construction of India as a vibrant, secular and pluralistic state. The battle, therefore, to win back hearts and minds of the Kashmiri people must be seen as being critical not just for recovery of the ideals that inspired Indian nationhood, but central to the war against obscurantism and fundamentalism especially of the Islamic variety. In other words, there must be a realization that Kashmir must no longer be dealt with the kind of political ineptitude and bureaucratic inertia that has often characterized New Delhi's policies toward many other states over the last decades.

Instead, New Delhi, taking cognizance of the serious situation prevanling, in the state, must give it the attention it deserves, a special task force, which is constituted by the highest political authority of the country and enjoys its confidence and is dedicated full time to Jammu and Kashmir must be appointed in the near future. The task force should be made responsible for initiating and furthering a political dialogue and monitoring and assisting in governance and development activities.

2. Autonomy is not a dirty words

The second solution of the Kashmir problem is seen as giving greater autonomy. The autonomy envisaged under Art 370 was the one factor that had helped bring Kashmiris closer to India. Unfortunately this article was tempered with and misused till Kashmiri youth decided to wield weapons. North-Eastern states also enjoy some special constitutional special status and relaxation and instead of demanding abrogation of provisions other states should also be brought at par with them. For this review of our constitution and turning present set up into presidential one should also not be out of sight. This would help curb the demands for more autonomy from other corner of the country too.

The autonomy ensured under Article 370 should be reaffirmed. This can be done by evolving a 'moderate autonomy formula' under which less important extensions to the state could be withdrawn such as nomenclatures of Chief Minister, Governors, Rashtrapati and Pradhanmantri, entering relating to Welfare of Labour, trade unions, social security, social insurance and cinematograph; laws relating to custom, excise and P & T etc. But the Parliament to impose Governor's rule and President's rule on failure of law and order. And the Election Commission, Comptroller and Auditor General of India should not be compromised at any cost. After all it was Sheikh himself who had justified and endorsed the necessity of extension of these laws to the state. Art 356, if used rationally is the hinge of our constitutional system that keeps the fissiparous tendencies at the other end. This is the extreme to which the country can afford.

There is growing realization today, despite the ruling Bhartiya Janata Party's earlier commitment to fully integrate Jammu and Kashmir within India, that granting autonomy to the province will not weaker its relationship with India. Today, autonomy is seen as being about empowering people, making people feel that they belong, and about increasing the accountability of public institution and services. It is seen as being synonymous with decentralization and devolution of power, phrases that have been on the charter of virtually every political party in India. In Jammu and Kashmir, autonomy, it is realized, carries tremendous resonance with the people because it is felt that puppet leaders from the state colluded, over time, with the central leadership and gradually eroded the autonomy promised by the constitution. And that there is no contradiction between wanting Kashmir to be part of the national mainstream, and the state's desire for autonomous self governance. if this balance is struck, Jammu and Kashmir could become a model of 'co-operative federalism', a special model that could be gradually applied to other states in the union.

Separatism grows, the argument runs, when people feel disconnected from the structures of power and the process of policy formulation; in contrast, devolution ensures popular participation in the running of the polity.

Restoration of autonomy in Kashmir, it must be understood, does not require elaborate reports or reference to past agreements and accords. They obfuscate rather than clarify the issue of meaningful self-governance. Autonomy, as has been suggested by a high-level study group, can be achieved in the state through a simple six-point plan. First, restore the nomenclature. The term Sadar-i-Riyast and Wazier-e-Azam, which were used until 1965, for the Governors and the Chief Minister of the state, still have an important symbolic value for people of the state, literally translated they stand for Head of the state and Prime Minister. This nomenclature should be restored. In substance, this change will neither enlarge nor demish the powers of the Governor or the Chief Minister. This will also not lead to a shift in their order of precedence.

Second, give the state a role in the selection of the Governor. According to Article 155 of the Indian constitution the "Governor of the state shall be appointed by the President by Warrant under his hand and seal." Until 1965, the Sadar-i-Riyasat in Kashmir was elected by the state legislature, but it was clear that he should be a person acceptable to the centre and appointed by the President. The Governor is widely viewed in Jammu and Kashmir as an instrument through which the centre and more often the political party in power has furthered its interests in the state. The office of the Governor, in whom the constitution rests the executive power of the state, should be above narrow partisan polities. The Governor could be elected by the state legislature and be appointed by the President and by virtue of Article 156(1), hold office at the pleasure of the President or alternatively, the state Government could submit a panel of names and the President would appoint as Governor the person he finds most suitable from the panel, who would hold office at the President's pleasure. Third, prevent the misuse of Art 356, this article deals with "provisions in case of the failure of the constitutional machinary in the states". The misuse of Article 356 is a matter that has caused widespread concern in all the states. The Inter-state Council is considering the matter and some agreed modification and safeguards might emerge. While some might argue that it would be prudent and impractical to exempt Jammu and Kashmir from the purview of the article altogether (although the state was brought under its purview only in 1964), it is still possible to modify it significantly, to prevent its misuse without compromising on measures that might be needed to deal with real emergencies. In case of a constitutional breakdown, provisions should be made for holding election within a maximum of three months, and for the appointment of an eminent persons group from within the state to review the situation in case elections cannot be held with three months because of violence or other disturbance. The verdict of the group should be final. Fourth, give state services more authority and increase the quota in the All India Services, Part XIV of the constitution which deals with the services, did not apply initially to Jammu and Kashmir. But the provisions of Art 312 relating to All India Services were ended in 1958. Under the Scheme, entry into the IAS and the IPS is both by direct examination and selection of promotes from the civil service by the Union Public Service Commission. In most states thc state quota has been around 33 per cent. But in the case of Jammu and Kashmir this has been 50 per cent. The bulk of direct recruits to the Indian Administrative Service (IAS), Indian Police Service (IPS) and the Indian Forest Service (IFS) are from just about twenty five colleges/universities in India. There is reason to expect that, as elsewhere, with improvements in the quality of education in Kashmir, the number of direct recruit from the state will increase in the years ahead. Even otherwise, the Jammu and Kashmir selection quota (from within the state services) could be increased for a period of twenty years to 75 per cent given the disruption that the educational system in the state has faced over the last decade. The Kashmir Administrative Service and the Kashmir Police Service have faced and suffered severe neglect and margilaization over the last decade, part of the problem has to do with training, but it is critical that KAS and KPS officers are given promotions and positions of authority, which have a career track similar to IAS and IPS officers.

Fifth, appoint a Regional Election Commissioner for the state.

The impartiality of the Election Commission has come to be gradually respected, despite certain electoral aberrations in the past, particularly in Kashmir. However, it would be prudent if a Regional Election Commissioner is appointed for the state, as provided for in Article 32(4) of the Indian Constitution, to assist the Election Commission in the conduct of elections in the state. This appointment should be made on the recommendations of the state government before each election.

Sixth, provide guarantees for the future. Many people genuinely feel that even if a package for autonomy is worked out, a future central government may, in collusion with the state's political leaders, renege on an agreement that is made today. This is based on the past experience of the state's relationship with the centre. It is essential therefore; the special constitutional guarantees are introduced to ensure that the state's autonomy is not eroded. It may be necessary, for instance, to introduce a provision in the constitution which would provide for a referendum in the state before any major amendment that would affect the state's ties with the union becomes a law.

3. Devolution of power within state

Let us not forget that many Indian states are demanding greater autonomy.... there is no doubt that India needs to be more federal than it is today, there is also no doubt and India is one country and must not become a federation of a large number of countries, within Jammu and Kashmir state, Jammu and Ladakh should have adequate regional autonomy. In other words, there is as much need for a devolution of powers from New Delhi to Srinagar as there is for a transfer of Authority from Kashmir to Jammu and Ladakh, and beyond to grassroots level only then can empowerment and autonomy have any real meaning.

Intra-regional tensions have played upon the minds of Kashmiris. The people of Jammu and Ladakh have traditionally adopted a negative attitude over the special status of the state. The two regions have objected the special status of the state. Instead of this they have been demanding its abrogation. However, living in present states of affairs these two regions have been demanding devolution of more powers under state constitution to them. The state is heterogeneous in character but has been placed under a unitary cost. This has hindered the flow of powers to the all regions of the state because of hegemony of Kashmiri leaders, the other two regions have felt discriminated and as a result they have raised strong protest against special status. Beyond the valley of Kashmir, the demand of 'greater autonomy' has evoked emotions of different kind after the demand of autonomy resolution by state autonomy committee in June 2000. The regions of Jammu and Ladakh, there has been strong apposition to the pre-1953 stance of the report of the state autonomy committee (SAC). The strong wave of resentment against the report has been a result of the Kashmir centric approach of the report that not only ignores the plural realities of the state but also undermines the regional aspirations. The report not only locates the discourse of autonomy in the special history of the Kashmir but also projects the demand for the 'state autonomy' as an exclusive demand of the valley.

The most important reason for resistance to the report of the SAC, within the regions of Jammu and Ladakh, relates to its failure to incorporate the logic of internal devolution of powers. This is a serious flaw of the report because these regions suffer from an acute feeling of regional deprivation. Among the most common complaints noticed here, are those related to disproportionate share of political powers, development grants, bureaucratic position and employment opportunities among the three regions of the state. Kashmir, it is felt, generally gets a bigger piece of cake leaking the other two regions perpetually deprived. Since no mechanism of internal devolution of power is suggested in the report. It is felt that the autonomy for the state may actually come to mean autonomy for Kashmir only. It may not flow to the regional and sub-regional levels. The state in any case, is known for its centralised structure of power and despite persistent regional discontent, the successive state governments have resisted all demands for devolution of powers. The indifference on the part of the state government to the demand for devolution of power becomes clear from the fact that there has been no panchayat election in this state in last 22 years. The state has still to bring its Panchayat Rajs Act of 1989 at par with the 73rd Amendment Act of the constitution of India.

During the 1996's Assembly elections, almost all political parties operating in the regions of Jammu and Ladakh had been compelled to take cognisances of the demand for regional autonomy. The National

Conference had also reaffirmed its commitment to grant autonomy to regions. After assuming power, it had appointed the regional autonomy committee (RAC) to deliberate upon the question of internal devolution of powers.[6]

However, the report of RAC, that was made public simultaneously with the report of the SAC, has not succeded in removing the grievances of people of Jammu and Ladakh regions. Rather than going into the question of autonomy at the regional levels, it has recommended an altogether new classification of regions.

In accordance with this classification of regions, Jammu gets divided into two regions. The suggested division more or less, is communal in nature. In Ladakh, for intance, the division takes place between the Buddhists of Leh and the Muslims of Kargil. In Jammu, similarily, the Hindu dominated districts are separated from the Muslim dominated area of Doda and Poonch, Rajouri. In fact, a part of Muslim dominated area (Mahore Tehsil) is carved out of the rest of the Hindu dominated districts to fit in the Muslim dominated area of Doda.

This kind of division, according to many critics of the report, is meant to secuttle the demand for regional autonomy within the state. By challenging the regional status of Jammu and Ladakh the committee seeks to negate the very basis of regional autonomy. The negative approach of the National Conference toward the issue of internal autonomy has led many in Ladakh and Jammu to think in terms of opting out of the state. The demand for the division of the state has become quite vocal in Jammu and Ladakh. But the danger of the debate on the division of the state are many.

The issue of autonomy in the state is complex in nature. It not only involves the question of evolving the fair principles of centre-state relations but also the questions of internal devolution of powers and inter regional relations. The issue of the state autonomy and the regional autonomy are in fact, logically interconnected. It is not possible to achieve the one without aiming at the other. The politics of autonomy, of the regional or of the state level, somehow has failed to carry this logic forward. Those who demand autonomy for the state and those who demand state's autonomy hesitate to talk about the regional autonomy. The state needs a multi-layered package of autonomy that extends beyond the state to the regional and sub-regional levels. The sub-regional discontent in the state is as accute as the regional discontent. The backward and peripheral parts, both in Jammu and Ladakh regions, often complain of political and economic neglect. Regional autonomy, therefore, has to flow further to the sub-regional and the panchayat levels. Unless these is a surety of power flowing to the grass roots, there is every danger that the divisive tendencies that have been unleased in last few years will reign supreme in this state. In other words, regional harmony, it should be clear from experience, cannot be ensured through partitions, but through a decentralisation and devolution of financial and economic power that will treat the Panchayat as well as primary units of governance. Jammu and Kashmir is not Assam or Uttar Pradesh where the carving of smaller states will provide for better governance, it is in fact a recipe for disaster.

The unitary character of the constitution of the state need to be amended to adapt regional pulls. Until all these regions, especially Jammu and Kashmir join hands and set to work together the regional tensions would continue to mar their relations.

4. Trifurcation of the state into Jammu, Ladakh and Kashmir

There are powerful forces demanding trifurcation of the main regions of the state, Jammu, Kashmir and Ladakh, into separate administrative units.

Posing as an imaginative solution, this demand, if conceded, could lead to violent social disruption in the state and create a communal polarization that would not just irretrievably destroy the cultural and social fabric of the state, but have perilous consequences for communal relations in the rest of India. In addition, trifurcation would forever end the possibilities of reviewing the plural tradition of communal harmony in the state that had once been a symbol of the very idea of India. New Delhi must realize that while it is critical to help to create greater balance, there must be no division of the state.

On June, 22, 2002, at Haridwar, the Kendriya Margdarshak Mandal of the Vishwa Hindu Parishad called for a division of state, including the creation of a separate union territory for a division of state, including the creation of a separate union territory for Kashmir Pandit carved out from within the Valley. Similarly on June 30, 2002, at

Kurukshetra, the Akhil Bhartiya Karyakari Mandal of the Rashtriya Swayamsevak Sangh sought separate statehood for Jammu and Union Territory status for Ladakh. In addition, the Jammu Mukti Morcha and the Ladakh Buddhist Association are leading the local campaign for this demand.[7]

This kind of demand of the state is not new. But in its new avatar, several factors have coalesced to produce a potentially a explosive situation.

Most important is the widespread feeling within Jammu and Leh of deprivation as well as political and economical discrimination may have some grounds, it is being exploited by sectarian political groups who are demanding separate statehood for Jammu and Union territory status for Leh. They argue that only separation from Kashmir will ensure better governance, more economic opportunities and a greater share of political power, but Jammu and Leh will also be able to distance themselves from the militancy. In its most extreme form idealogues of this demand suggest that it is in the national interest to limit the "area of operation" of the security forces to the Kashmir Valley and that division will ensure that only the one-sixth of the whole state will then remain troubled.

This logic is dangerous for atleast four reasons. First, trifurcation will destroy the composite identity of the state, which has existed as one unit since 1846, and send a dangerous message to the whole nation. If Hindus, Muslims and Buddhists cannot live together in one state, can they do so in a larger entity? Second, it will most probably lead to a transfer of Muslims from various parts of the Jammu, not only from parts of the city but also from Doda, Rajouri and Poonch, assuming that the whole province is made into a separate state.

Third, it will lead to such deep communal polarization that bloody communal riots will inevitably follows. It is no coincidence that the only group in Kashmir that has supported the idea of the division of the state in Jamat-e-Islami.

Finally, any plan to carve out a separate enclave for Kashmiri Pandits will not just create dangerous precedent, but ghettoize one of India's most cosmopolitan and dynamic communities.

5. Admission of Mistakes is the first step towards restoring trust between New Delhi and Kashmir

Over the years, the centre has made a number of appalling mistakes in Kashmir. Several elections have been rigged, genuinely elected governments, have been dismissed, puppet leaders have been installed and in the last decade the ordinary Kashmiri has faced tremendous harassment from security forces. Some of these mistakes were available, other inevitable, given the complex situation on the ground. It must be realized that admission of these mistakes will not be construed as an expression of guilt, but will signal recognition that fresh initiatives towards Kashmir will be based on an awareness of past mistakes and a genuine desire not to see them repeated.

Strengthening Secularism : Freedom of religion and religious tolerance are the essential parts of the composite Indian Culture which is neither Hindu nor Muslim more publicity should be given to the concept of secularism as the pillar of Indian polity, and all the mischievous acts of mixing religion with politics should be put down firmly. It was the secular force of the Indian nationalism that had attracted the Kashmiri leadership to accede to India in 1947, and more the Indian projects herself as a secular state, more the chances of the people in the valley, being on our side secularist and egalitarian activists in other parts of the country should frequently visit the valley and the people there organization and such other groups who are fighting for the democratic rights of the suppressed people in other parts of the country should exhibit solidarity with the people of the state. The need of the hour is to create a sympathetic attitude towards the Kashmiri so that the people there could feel that there are their brethren who have respect for them and who are co-sharer of their agony. Stern action should be taken against the elements fanning communalism and religious bigotry.

6. Recovery of Kashmiriyat is vital to sustained peace

While there does seem to be genuine, all pervasive desire within Jammu and Kashmir to recover the social capital lost in the last decade and to restore Kashmir's traditional society based on ideas of peaceful co-existence, pluralism and the common syncretism identity of Kashmiriyat, New Delhi must make the recovery of this central to its efforts to build peace in the state.

7. Evolving Unambiguous Policy

Centre has accredited itself of being guilty of following a vague, incoherent and ambiguous approach towards Kashmir. This has pushed the people of the state into a state of apathy and reduced the faith of the people in the centre, people do not know in the valley what the centre intends to do. For this, an unambiguous and clear cut approach of the centre towards the problem is required. A consensus policy, at least in the ruling party, should be followed which would receive better response from the people in the valley. Special need should be given to the popular Kashmiri sentiment and polities should be formed accordingly.

8. Restoring Democracy

It is the duty of the centre to ensure free and fair elections in the state no matter in which direction the mandate of the people goes. Unless the people of the state, Kashmiris in particular, are assured of free and fair elections and the sprit of democracy restored, any effort of solving the present crisis would be futile. In the present study, one of the causes behind secessionism has turned out to be denial of democracy to the people. Therefore, it is of almost importance to restore democracy by ensuring fair election. The recent assembly elections in Sept-Oct 1996 were to a great extent fair but this practice will have to be maintained strictly in future. Besides, the routine law and order and the development administration should be revamped. The Muslim employees in the Valley should not be looked upon with suspicion. The glaring discrepancies in the number of Kashmir Muslims in the state government needs to be rectified one such anomalies are patched up, it will be easy to create an environment for a settlement of the problem. It will also provide the people with a sense of security and a self-administration, a long cherished demand.

9. Demographic Change

Valley is at present predominantly Muslim. The communal mix up by encouraging people from Jammu to settle in Valley can help some loyal citizens in the Valley. This kind of policy might appear as counter productive but it has productive but it has produced desired results in country like China. This will help not only counter secessionist elements but also develop a popular base in the Valley lending full support to Indian authorities.

Besides these immediate measures which are important to create an environment favourable to solve the Kashmir problem, on part of

India, a distinct and coherent approach permissible under the constitutional provisions needs to followed.

10. Economic Upliftment

There are one other aspect of question of autonomy will the state have fiscal autonomy? In that case it will need financial relations with the federal centre? Indeed, in liberalised India, autonomy, especially fiscal autonomy, is an idea whose time has come states today are competing for foreign projects. Multilateral aid, infrastructure investments and sprucing up their records book to project a better face to the interested. And fiscal autonomy could greatly help.

Says N.J. Kurian, Member, Financial resources, planning Commission "None of the state of Indian Union would be fiscally vaable on their own because their revenues, including the devolution formula. Money are not enough to cover even day to day expenditure".[8] He is right staff salaries and poor revenue efforts are the biggest problems facing India's state. Most of which are poorly managed and, therefore, over dependent on central funds.

As the state of Jammu and Kashmir faced financial problem due to destruction and devastation caused by militancy, industrial sickness and loss of tourism industry, the central government made generous allocation of grants, loans, etc.[9]

Although the state of Jammu and Kashmir has enjoyed a privileged position so far as central assistance is concerned yet it is still economically backward especially the region of Kashmir.

One of the most important things that could be done to build a better Jammu and Kashmir would be rebuild Kashmir's economy and provide employment and career building opportunities to the Kashmiri Youth. India must also commit itself to give adequate autonomy to Kashmir ensuring that the profits of autonomy reach the grassroots level. The Indian Government must take necessary initiatives to ensure that central government will improve the living conditions of the people of Jammu and Kashmir.

This section describes the scope for further research. Though this book deals with Kashmir demand in detail much scope for further research remains because it touches upon the politics of Kashmir from 1846 upto demand of 2002 for trifurcation of the three regions of the state into separate. After that, within the last two years many changes have came in the politics of Kashmir. The September 2002 election to the state Assembly has completely changed the scenario of Kashmir politics.

So the relationship between the state government and the centre needs to be renewed. Because till now the state government has kept airing the demand of Kashmir autonomy in spite of being a constituent of BJP led NDA government in New Delhi. But now the whole chain of incidents has changed. Now the Congress, a party completely hostile to BJP, has come to power in association with Peoples Dominant Party (PDP) what sort of autonomy demand it will put forward, the centre.

After this election that change in political equations in the state is imperative. Because National Congress which was ruling the state for the last 24 years had to go away from power. That this defeat was National Conference's or Farooq Abdullah's can be easily understood Farooq Abdullah has lost the golden opportunity which he had got in 1996. The Kashmiri youths are feeling alienated from the political process for the last six years is much because of Farooq Abdullah.

Why Omar Abdullah, Farooq Abdullah's son was defeated from Gandharbal and his brother Mustaga kamal was defeated in Gulmarg". This can be a topic for further research.

National Conference has basically to face, first of all, it is in interest of Abdullah family, and secondly, there are many leaders in it who are working at the grassroots. They worked in the areas and got reelected. Voters have given a clear verdict that the party will have to search for some new leaders. The basic reason of NC's defeat is that instead of voice of Kashmir in Delhi, it has become the voice of New Delhi in Kashmir. Farooq's image got first shock when he did an agreement with Rajiv Gandhi. After this agreement insurgency in Kashmir picked up speed. The second shock was joining hand with the BJP at the centre. The appointment relationship between BJP and NC was also disliked by the Kashmiri people, as on the one hand NC talks of autonomy, BJP talks of abrogation of Art 370 on the other hand. So the Kashmiri people rejected this relationship.

In the end, the Indian leaders needs to rethink their age old Kashmir policy (If their has been one). If New Delhi sincerely wishes to break the political deadlock in Kashmir, it has no other alternative except to accept and implement what is being turmed as a "Autonomy plus, Independence minus" formula or to grant autonomy to the point where it is almost indistinguishable from independence. By rejecting the autonomy demand of 2000 the centre have not given a proof of any strong will, but have only displayed their weakness to face autonomy demand squintly which is a basic attribute of any federation. The central government needs to understand that Kashmir is not a communal or Muslim problem but is a democratic problem. If the centre gives greater autonomy to Kashmir and other states, the federations only get strengthened. But Kashmir also must keep in mind the dignity of Indian democracy and integrity of the Indian federal union.

References

1. Rajakishore, *Future of Kashmir,* Vani Publication, (New Delhi, 1994) p. 131.
2. *Ibid.,* p. 131.
3. Shastri, Promila "Mind your own Wallet" *Outlook,* July 17, 2000, p. 32.
4 Mattoo, Amitabh, "Next steps in Kashmir" in Sawney. Karan. R, *Kashmir – How far can Vajpayee and Mussaray go*? Peace Publication (2000, New Delhi). p. 35,
5 *Ibid.* p. 35.
6 Chaudhary, Rekha, "From Internal autonomy to division of state" *Economic and Political Weekly,* July 22, 2003.
7 Matto, Amitabh "Dangers of dividing Jammu and Kashmir" *Hindu,* 16 July, 2002.
8 Shastri, *Puromita* "Mind your own Wallet", *Outlook*, July 17, 2000, p. 32.
9 *India Quarterly–A Journal of International affair*, Vol. LVII, No. 2, 2001, p. 193.

Appendix–1

Amritsar Treaty, 1846

Treaty between the British Government on the one part and Maharajah Gulab Singh of Jammu on the other, concluded on the part of the BRITISH GOVERNMENT by FREDERICK CURRIE, ESQUIRE, and BREVET-MAJOR HENRY MONTGOMERY LAWRENCE, acting under the orders of the RIGHT HONOURABLE SIR HENRY HARDINGE, G.C.B., one of HER BRITANNIC MAJESTY'S MOST HONOURABLE PRIVY COUNCIL, GOVERNOR-GENERAL, appointed by the HONOURABLE COMPANY to direct and control all their affairs in the EAST INDIES, and by MAHARAJAH GULAB SINGH in person,—1846.

Article 1

The British Government transfers and makes over for ever, in independent possession, to Maharajah Gulab Singh and their heirs male of his body, all the hilly or mountainous country, with its dependencies, situated to the eastward of the river Indus and westward of the river Ravee. Including Chumba and excluding Lahul, being part of the territories ceded to the British Government by the Lahore State, according to the provisions of Article IV of the Treaty of Lahore, dated 9th March. 1846.

Article 2

The eastern boundary of tract transferred by the foregoing Article to Maharajah Gulab Singh shall be laid down by the Commissioners appointed by the British Government and Maharajah Gulab Singh respectively for that purpose, and shall be defined in a separate Engagement after survey.

Article 3

In consideration of the transfer made to him and his male heirs by the provisions of the foregoing Articles, Maharajah Gulab Singh will pay to the British Government the sum of seventy-five lakhs of Rupees (Nanukshahee), fifty lakhs to be paid on ratification of this Treaty, and twenty-five lakhs on or before the first October of the current year, A.D. 1846.

Article 4

The limits of the territories of Maharajah Gulab Singh shall not be at any time changed without the concurrence of the British Government.

Article 5

Maharajah Gulab Singh will refer to the arbitration of the British Government any dispute or questions that may arise between himself and the Government of Lahore or any other neighbouring States, and will abide by the decision of the British Government.

Article 6

Maharajah Gulab Singh engages for himself and heirs to join, with the whole of his Military Force, the British troops. when employed within the hills, or in the territories adjoining his possession.

Article 7

Maharajah Gulab Singh engages never to take or retain in his service, any British subject, nor the subject of any European or American State, without the consent of the British Government.

Article 8

Maharajah Gulab Singh engages to respect, in regard to the territory transferred to him, provisions of Articles V, VI and VII of the separate Engagement between the British Government and the Lahore Durbar, dated March 11th, 1846.

Article 9

The British Government will give its aid to Maharajah Gulab Singh in protecting his territories from external enemies.

Article 10

Maharajah Gulab Singh acknowledges the supremacy of the British Government, and will Hi token of such supremacy present annually to the British Government one horse, twelve perfect shawl goats of approved breed (Six male and six female), and three pairs of Cashmere shawls.

This Treaty, consisting of ten articles, has been this day settled by Frederick Currie. Esquire, and Brevet-Major Henry M. Lawrence, acting under the directions of the Right Honourable Sir Henry Hardinge, G.C.B., Governor-General, on the part of the British Government, and by Maharajah Gulab Singh in person; and the said Treaty has been this day ratifted by the seal of the Right Honourable Sir Henry Hardinge, G.C.B., Governor-General.

Done of Amritsar, the sixteenth day of March, in the year of our Lord one thousand eight hundred and forty-six, corresponding with the seventeenth day of Rupee-ool-awul 1262 Hijree.

H. HARDINGE F. CURRIE

H.M. LAWRENCE

By order of the Right Honourable the Governor-General of India.

F. Currie

Secretary to the Government of India,

with the Governor-General.

Appendix-2

State Subject Notification

Notification dated the 20th April, 1927

No.I-L/84.- The following definition of the term "State Subject" has been sanctioned by His Highness the Maharaja Bahadur (vide Private Secretary's letter No. 2354, dated the 31st January, 1927 to the Revenue Member of Council) and is hereby promulgated for general information.

The term State Subject means and includes-

Class I— All persons born and residing within the State before the commencement of the reign of His Highness the late Maharaja Ghulab Singh Sahib Bahadur, and also persons who settled therein before the commencement of Samvat year 1942, and have since been permanently residing therein.

Class II— All persons other than those belonging to Class I who settled within the State before the close of Samvat year 1968, and have since permanently resided and acquired immovable properly therein.

Class III—All persons other than those belonging to Classes I and II permanently residing within the State, who have acquired under a rayatnama any immovable property therein or who may hereafter acquire such property under an ijazatnama and may execute a rayatnama after ten year continuous residence therein.

Class IV— Companies which have been registered as such within the State and which, being companies in which the Government are financially interested or as to the economic benefit to the State of to the financial stability of which the Government are satisfied, have by a special order of His Highness been declared to be State Subjects].

Note 1—In matters of grants of the State scholarship, State lands for agricultural and house building purpose and recruitment to State service, State Subjects of Class I should receive preference over other classes and those of Class II over Class III, subject, however, to the Order dated 31st January, 1927, of His Highness the Maharaja Bahadur regarding employment of hereditary State subjects in Government service.

Note II–The descendants of the persons who have secured the status of any class of the State Subjects will be entitled to become the State Subject of the same class. For example, if A is declared a State Subject of Class II his sons and grandsons will *ipso facto* acquire the status of the same Class II and not of Class I.

Note III–The wife or a widow of a State Subject of any class shall acquire the status of her husband as State Subject of the same Class as her husband, so long as she resides in the State and does not leave the State for permanent residence outside the State.

Note IV–For the purposes of the interpretation of the term 'State Subject' either with reference to any law for the time being in force or otherwise, the definition given in this Notification as amended up to date shall be read as if such amended definition existed in this Notification as originally issued.

Notification

(Issued by order of His Highness the Maharaja Bahadur dated Srinagar, the 27th June. 1932/14th Mar, 1989. Published in Goverment Gazetted dated 24th Mar, 1989)

No. 13-L/1989—Whereas it is necessary to determine the status of Jammu and Kashmir State Subjects in foreign territories and to inform the Governments of Foreign States as to the position of their nationals in this State; it is hereby commanded and notified for public information, as follows:—

1. That all emigrants from the Jammu and Kashmir State to Foreign territories shall be considered State Subjects and also the descendants of these emigrants born abroad for two generations:
   Provided that, these nationals of the Jammu and Kashmir State shall not be entitled to claim the internal rights granted to subjects of this State by the laws, unless they fulfil the conditions laid down by those laws and rules for the specific purposes mentioned therein.
2. The foreign nationals residing in the State of Jammu and Kashmir shall not acquire the nationality of the Jammu and Kashmir State until after the age of 18 on purchasing immovable property under permission of an ijazatnama and on obtaining a rayatnama

after ten years continuous residence in the Jammu and Kashmir State as laid down in Notification No. I-L of 1984, dated 20th April, 1927.

3. Certificates of nationality of the Jammu and Kashmir State may, on application, be granted by the Minister-in-Charge of the Political Department in accordance with the provisions of section 1 of this Notification.

Appendix-3

Instrument of Accession of Jammu and Kashmir State

Whereas, the Indian Independence Act, 1947 provides that as from the fifteenth day of August, 1947, there shall be set up an independent Dominion known as India, and that the Government of India Act. 1935, shall with such omissions, additions, adaptations and modifications as the Governor-General may by order specify, be applicable to the Dominion of India;

And whereas the Government of India Act, 1935, as so adapted by the Governor-General provides that an Indian State may accede to the Dominion of India by an Instrument of Accession executed by the Ruler thereof;

Now, therefore, I Shriman Indar Mahandarr Rajrajeshwar Maharajadhiraj Shri Hari Singhji, Jammu and Kashmir Naresh Tatha Tibbet adi Deshadhipati, Ruler of Jammu and Kashmir State in the exercise of my sovereignty in and over my said State do hereby execute this my Instrument of Accession and —

1. I hereby declare that I accede to the Dominion of India with the intent that the Governor-General of India, the Dominion Legislature, the Federal Court and any other Dominion authority established for the purposes of the Dominion shall, by virtue of this my Instrument of Accession, but subject always to the terms thereof, and for the purposes of the Dominion, exercise in relation to the State of Jammu and Kashmir (hereinafter referred to as "this State") such functions as may be vested in them by or under the Government of India Act. 1935 as In force in the Dominion of India on the 15th day of August 1947 (which Act as so in force is hereinafter referred to as "the Act").

2. I hereby assume the obligation of ensuring that due effect is given to the provisions of the Act within this State so far as they are applicable therein by the virtue of this my Instrument of Accession.

3. I accept the matters specified in the Schedule hereto as the matters with respect to which the Dominion Legislature may make laws for this State.

4. I hereby declare that 1 accede to the Dominion of India on the assurance that if an Agreement is made between the Governor-General and the Ruler of this State whereby any functions in relation to the administration in tins State of any law of the Dominion Legislature shall be exercised by the Ruler of this State, then any such Agreement shall be deemed to form part of this Instrument and shall be construed and have effect accordingly.

5. The terms of this my instrument of Accession shall not be varied by any amendment, of the Act or of the Indian Independence Act. 1947, unless such amendment is accepted by an Instrument supplementary to this Instrument.

6. Nothing in this Instrument shall empower the Dominion Legislature to make any law for this State authorising the compulsory acquisition of land for any purpose, but I hereby undertake that should the Dominion for the purpose of a Dominion Law which applies in this State deem it necessary to acquire any land, I will at their request acquire the land at their expense or if the land belongs to me transfer it to them on such terms as may be agreed, or in default of agreement, determined by an arbitrator to be appointed by the Chief Justice of India.

7. Nothing in this Instrument shall be deemed to commit me in any way to acceptance of any future constitution of India or to fetter my discretion to enter into agreements with the Government of India under any such future constitution.

8. Nothing in this Instrument affects the continuance of my sovereignty in and over tills State, or save as provided by or under this Instrument, the exercise of any powers, authority and rights now enjoyed by me as Ruler of this State or the validity of any law at present in force in this State.

9. I hereby declare that I execute this Instrument on behalf of this State and that any reference in tills Instrument to me or to the Ruler of the State is to be construed as including a reference to my heirs and successors.

Given under my hand this 26th day of October Nineteen Hundred and Forty-seven.

(Sd.) HARI SINGH

Maharajadhiraj of Jammu and Kashmir State.

I do hereby accept this Instrument of Accession.

Dated this twenty-seventh day of October Nineteen Hundred and Forty-Seven.

(Sd.) MOUNTBATTEN OF BURMA

(Governor-General of India)

Apppendix-4

The Delhi Agreement, 1952

After the Constituent Assembly of the State had taken important decisions referred to immediately above, it was deemed necessary to receive the Concurrence of the Indian Government. Accordingly, the representatives of Kashmir Government conferred with the representatives of the Indian Government and arrived at an arrangement. This arrangement was later on known as the "Delhi Agreement 1952". The main features of this agreement were :

(i) In view of the uniform and consistent stand taken up by the Jammu and Kashmir Constituent Assembly that sovereignty in all matters other than those specified in the Instrument of Accession continues to reside in the State, the Government of India agreed that, while that residuary powers of legislature vested in the Centre in respect of all States other than Jammu and Kashmir, in the case of the latter they vested in the State itself:

(ii) It was agreed between the two Governments that in accordance with Article 5 of the Indian constitution, persons who have their domicile in Jammu and Kashmir shall be regarded as citizens of India, but the State legislature was given power to make tows for conferring special rights and privileges on the 'State subjects' in view of the 'State Subject Notification of 1927 and 1932: the State legislature was also empowered to make laws for the 'State Subjects' who had gone to Pakistan on account of the communal disturbances of 1947, in the event of their return to Kashmir:

(iii) as the President of India commands the same respect in the State as he does in the other Units of India. Articles 52 to 62 of the Constitution relating to him should be applicable to the State. It was further agreed that the power to grant reprieves, pardons and remissions of sentence etc.. would also vest in the President of India:

(iv) The Union Government agreed that the State should have its own flag in addition to the Union flag but it was agreed by the State Government that the State flag would not be a rival of the Union flag: it was also recognised that the Union flag should have the same status and position in Jammu and Kashmir as in the rest of India, but for historical reasons connected with the freedom struggle in the State, the need for continuance of the State flag was recognised:

(v) There was complete agreement with regard to the position of the Sadar-i-Riyasat: though the Sadar-i-Riyasat was to be elected by the State Legislature, he had to be recognised by the President of India before his installation as such; in other Indian States the head of the State was appointed by the President and was as such his, nominee but the person to be appointed as the Head, had to be a person acceptable to the Government of that State; no person who is not acceptable to the State Government can be thrust on the State as the Head. The difference in the case of Kashmir lies only in the fact that Sadar-i-Riyasat will in the first place be elected by the State legislature Itself instead of being a nominee of the Government and the President of India.

With reward to the powers and functions of the Sadar-i-Riyasat the following argument was mutually agreed upon:

"(a) the Head of the State shall be a person recognised by the President of the Union on the recommendations of the Legislature of the State;

(b) he shall hold office during the pleasure of the President:

(c) he may, by writing under his hand addressed to the President, resign his office;

(d) subject to the foregoing provisions, the Head of the State shall hold office for a term of five years from the date he enters upon his office;

(e) provided that he shall, notwithstanding the expiration of his term, continue to hold the office until his Successor enters upon his office";

(vi) With regard to the fundamental rights, some basic principles agreed between the parties were enunciated: it was accepted that the people of the State were to have fundamental rights. But in view of the peculiar position in which the State was placed, the whole chapter relating to 'Fundamental Rights' of the Indian Constitution could not be made applicable to the State, the question which remained to be determined was whether the chapter on fundamental rights should form a part of the State Constitution or of the Constitution of India as applicable to the State;

(vii) With regard to the Jurisdiction of the Supreme Court of India, it was accepted that for the time being, owing to the existence of the Board of Judicial Advisers in the State, which was the highest judicial authority in the State, the Supreme Court should have only appellate jurisdiction;

(viii) There was a great deal of discussion with regard to the "Emergency Powers": the Government of India insisted on the application of Article 352, empowering the President to proclaim a general emergency in the State: the State Government argued that in exercise of its powers over defence (item I on the Union List), in the event of war or (item I on the Union List), in the event of war or external aggression, the Government of India would have full authority to take steps and proclaim emergency but the State delegation was, however, averse to the President exercising the power to proclaim a general emergency on account of internal disturbances.

Appendix-5

Kashmir Accord of 13 November, 1974

The state of Jammu and Kashmir, which is a constituent unit of the Union of India, shall, in its relations with the Union, continue to be governed by Article 370 of the Constitution of India.

The residuary powers of legislation shall remain with the State, however, Parliament will continue to have power to make laws relating to the prevention of activities directed towards disclaiming, questioning or disrupting the sovereignty and territorial integrity of India or bringing about cession of a part of the territory of India or secession of a part of the territory of India from the Union or causing insult to the Indian National Flag, the Indian National Anthem and the Constitution.

Where any provision of the Constitution of India had been applied to the State of Jammu and Kashmir with adaptations and modifications, such adaptations and modifications can be altered or repeated by an order of the President under Article 370. each individual proposal in this behalf being considered on its merits: but provisions of the Constitution of India already applied to the State of Jammu and Kashmir without adaptation or modification are and Kashmir without adaptation or modification are unalterable.

With a view to assuring freedom to the State of Jammu and Kashmir to have its own legislation on matters like welfare measures, cultural matters, social security, personal law, and procedural laws, in a manner suited to the special conditions in the State, it is agreed that the State Government can review the laws made by Parliament or extended to the State after 1953 on any matter relatable to the Concurrent List and may decide which of them, in its opinion, needs amendment or repeal. Thereafter, appropriate steps may be taken under Article 254 of the Constitution of India. The grant of President's assent to such legislation would be sympathetically considered. The same approach would be adopted in regard to laws to be made by

Parliament in future under the provision to clause 2 of that Article. The State Government shall be consulted regarding the application of any such law to the State and the views of the State Government shall receive the fullest consideration.

As an arrangement reciprocal to what has been provided under Article 368, a suitable modification of that Article as applied to the State should be made by Presidential Order to the effect that no law made by the Legislature of the State of Jammu and Kashmir, seeking to make any change in or in the effect of any provision of the Constitution of the State or Jammu and Kashmir relating to any of the undermentioned matters, shall take effect unless the Bill having been reserved for the consideration of the President, receives his assent: the matters are:

(a) the appointment, powers, functions, duties, privileges, and immunities of the Governor; and

(b) the following matters relating to Election, namely, the superintendence, direction and control of Elections by the Election Commission of India, eligibility for inclusion in the electoral rolls without discrimination, adult suffrage and composition of the Legislative Council, being matters specified in sections 138, 139, 140 and 50 of the Constitution of the State of Jammu and Kashmir.

No agreement was possible on the question of nomenclature of the Governor and the Chief Minister and the matter is therefore remitted to the principals.

Sd/— Mirza Mohammad Afzal Beg

Sd/— G. Parthasarthi

After signing the documents, Mirza Mohammad Afzal Beg wrote the acknowledgement letter to Mr. G. Parthasarthi on the same day, 13 November, 1974.

Camp New Delhi.

November 13, 1974

Dear Shri Parthasarthi,

I have today signed the document containing the points on which we have reached agreement.

As you may recall, in the course of discussions we had on the various issues. I made proposals regarding the following matters:

(i) The provisions relating to the fundamental rights to incorporated in the State Constitution.

(ii) The superintendence, direction and control over elections to the State Legislature by the Election Commission should be removed.

(iii) Article 356 should be modified to require the consent of the State before an order is issued thereunder, or some similar safeguard should be provided.

After prolonged discussions you did not agree to these proposals.

Kindly acknowledge receipt.

Yours Sincerely.

(Sd) Mirza Mohammad Afzal Beg

Shri G. Parthasarthi

31, Aurangzeb Road

New Delhi.

Appendix-6

The Exceptions and Modifications Subject to which the Constitution of India Applies to the State of Jammu and Kashmir

(1) The Preamable

(a) In the first paragraph, omit "SOCIALIST SECULAR",

(b) In the penultimate paragraph, omit "and INTEGRITY"

These terms were not there in the original Constitution but were added in the Preamable-by the Constitution (Forty-second Amendment) Act, 1976.

(2) Part I: The Union and its Territory

Article 3.—Formation of new States and alteration of areas, boundaries or names of existing States.

(a) Add the following further proviso, namely: —

"Provided further that no Bill providing for increasing or diminishing the area of the State of J & K or altering the name or boundary of that State shall be introduced in Parliament without the consent of the Legislature of that State."

(3) Part II: Citizenship

Article 7.—Rights of Citizenship

Add the following further proviso, namely:

"Provided further that nothing in this article shall apply to a permanent resident of the State of Jammu and Kashmir who, after having so migrated to the territory now included in Pakistan, returns to the territory of that State under a permit for resettlement in that State or permanent return issued by or under the authority of any law made by the

Legislature of that State, and every such person shall be deemed to be a citizen of India."

(4) Part III: Fundamental Rights

In Article 19.—Right to Freedom

After sub-clause (e), insert the following clause, namely: —

"(f) to acquire, hold and dispose of property; and" ;

It was omitted by the Constitution (Forty-Fourth Amendment) Act, 1978.

In Article 22.—"Protection against arrest and detention in certain cases". In clauses (4) and (7), for "Parliament", substitute "the Legislature of the State".

After Article 30, insert the following, namely: —

"Right to Property *Article 31. Compulsory acquisition of property.*—(1) No person shall be deprived of his property save by authority of law. (2) No property shall be compulsorily acquired or requisitioned save for a public purpose and save by authority of a law." 'Right to Property' omitted by the Constitution (Forty-fourth Amendment) Act, 1978. But in case of Jammu and Kashmir it is still a Fundamental Right.

Add Article 35 A. Saving of laws with respect to permanent residents and their rights.—Notwithstanding anything contained in this Constitution, no existing law in force in the State of Jammu and Kashmir, and no law hereafter enacted by the Legislature of the State, —

(a) defining the classes of persons who are, or shall be permanent residents of the State of Jammu and Kashmir; or

(b) conferring on such permanent residents any special rights and privileges or imposing upon other persons any restrictions as respects —

(i) employment under the State Government;

(ii) acquisition of immovable property in the State;

(iii) settlement in State; or

(iv) right to scholarships and such other forms of aid as the State Government may provide,

shall be void on the ground that it is inconsistent with or takes way or abridges any rights conferred on the other citizens of India by any provision of this Part."

(5) Part IV: Directive Principles of State Policy

This part is not applicable to the State of Jammu and Kashmir.

(6) Part IV: A Fundamental Duties

Added by the Constitution (Forty-second Amendment) Act, 1976;

This Part is not applicable to the State of Jammu and Kashmir.

(7) Part V: The Union

Chapter I—The Executive (The President and Vice-President)

Chapter II—Parliament

Chapter III—Legislative Powers of the President

Chapter IV—The Union Judiciary

Chapter V—Comptroller and Auditor-General of India

(All the chapters are applicable to the State of the Jammu and Kashmir with very minor exceptions and omissions.

(8) Part VI: The States

Chapter I—General

Chapter II—The Executive

Chapter III—The State Legislature

Chapter IV—Legislative power of the Governor (All these Chapters are not applicable to the State of Jammu and Kashmir.

Chapter V—The High Courts in the State

Chapter VI—Applies to the State of Jammu and Kashmir with minor exceptions.

(9) Part VII—The States in Part B of the First Schedule. (Repealed by the Constitution (Seventh Amendment) Act, 1956.

(10) Part VIII—'The Union Territories'. This Part is not applicable to the State of Jammu and Kashmir.

(11) Part IX—The Panchayats (Amended by the Constitution (Seventy-third Amendment) Act, 1992).

(12) Part IXA—The Municipalities (Amended by the Constitution (Seventy-fourth Amendment) Act, 1992). Both this Amended Parts are not applicable to the State of J&K.

(13) Part X— The Scheduled and Tribal Areas.

This Part is not applicable to the State of Jammu and Kashmir.

(14) Part XI—Relations between the Union and the States.

Chapter I—Legislative Relations.

In Article 248. Residuary powers of legislation— Substitute the Article, namely, Parliament has exclusive power to make any law with respect to—

(a) prevention of activities involving terrorists acts directed towards over-awing the Government as by law established or striking terror in the people or any section of the people or alienating any section of the people or adversely affecting the harmony amongst different sections of the people;

(aa) Prevention of other activities directed towards disclaiming, questioning or disrupting the sovereignty and territorial integrity of India or bringing about cession of a part of the territory of India or secession of a part of the territory of India from the Union or causing insult to the Indian National Flag, the Indian National Anthem and this Constitution; and

(b) taxes on —

(i) foreign travel by sea or air;

(ii) inland air travel;

(iii) postal articles, including money orders, phonograms and telegrams.

(bb) Article 249, in clause (I), Power of Parliament to legislate with respect to any matter in State List if a Proclamation of Emergency is in operation for "any matter enumerated in the State List specified in the resolution", substitute any matter specified in the resolution, being a matter which is not enumerated in the Union List or in the Constitution List."

(c) Art. 250 'for any of the matters enumerated in the State List' substitute also to matters not enumerated in the Union List.

(15) Part XII: Finance, Property, Contracts and Suits

Article 266 Consolidated Funds....

Article 282 Expenditure defrayable by the Union or a State out of its revenues.

Article 284. Custody of suitors ....

Article 298. Power to carry on trade, etc.

Article 299. Contracts.

Article 300. Suits and proceedings.

(In these articles references to the State or States shall be construed as not including references to the State of Jammu and Kashmir.

Article 300A. Right to Property.

Added by the Constitution (Forty-fourth Amendment) Act, 1978 is not applicable to the State of J&K.

(16) Part XIII: Trade, Commerce and Intercourse within the Territory of India

Not applicable to the State of Jammu and Kashmir.

(17) Part XIV: Services under the Union and the States

Except in article 312, (All India Services) reference to "State" in this part does not include the State of Jammu and Kashmir.

(18) Part XIVA: Tribunals

This Part is not applicable to the State of Jammu and Kashmir.

(19) Part XV: Elections

(a) *Article 324*—Superintendence, direction and control of elections, the reference to the Constitution shall, in relation to elections to either House of the Legislature of Jammu and Kashmir, be construed as a reference to the Constitution of Jammu and Kashmir.

Article 325.—Electoral roll.

Article 326.—Elections of the House of the People and to the Legislative Assemblies of the State.

Article 327.—Power of Parliament to make provision with respect to elections to Legislatures.

Article 328.—Power of Legislature of a State to make provision with respect to election to such Legislature.

Article 329.—Bar to interference by courts in electoral matters.

In all these articles the references to a State shall be construed as not including a reference to the State of Jammu and Kashmir.

(20) Part XVI: Special Provisions Relating to Certain Classes

Article 330.—Reservation of seats for Scheduled Castes and Scheduled Tribes in the House of the People.

Article 331.—Representation of the Anglo-Indian community in the House of the People.

Article 332.—Reservation of seats for Scheduled Castes and Scheduled Tribes in the Legislative Assemblies of the States.

Article 333.—Representation of the Anglo-Indian community in the Legislative Assemblies of the States.

Article 334.—Reservation of seats and special representation of cease after.

Article 335.—Claims of Scheduled Castes and Scheduled Tribes to services and posts.

Article 336.—Special provision for Anglo-Indian Community in certain service.

Article 337.—Special provision with respect to educational grants for the benefit of Anglo-Indian community.

Article 338.—Special Officer for Scheduled Castes and Scheduled Tribes, etc.

Article 339.—Control of the Union over the administration of Scheduled Areas and the welfare of Scheduled Tribes.

All these articles are not applicable to the State of Jammu and Kashmir.

Article 340.—Appointment of a Commission to investigate the conditions of backward classes.

Article 341.—Scheduled Castes.

Both these articles are applicable to the State of Jammu and Kashmir.

Article 342.—Scheduled Tribes, is not applicable to the State of Jammu and Kashmir

(21) Part XVII: Official Language

The provisions of this part shall apply to the State of Jammu and Kashmir only in so far as they relate to —

(i) the official language of the Union;

(ii) the official language for communication between one State and another, or between a State and the Union; and

(iii) the language of the proceedings in the Supreme Court.

(22) Part XVIII: Emergency Provisions

Article 352. Proclamation of Emergency. (National) (a) For article 352, substitute the following article, namely:—

"352. *Proclamation of Emergency—(1)* If the President is satisfied that a grave emergency exists whereby the security of India or of any part of the territory thereof is threatened, whether by war or external aggression or internal disturbance, he may, by Proclamation, make a declaration to that effect.

"(2) A Proclamation issued under clause (1)—

(a) may be revoked by a subsequent proclamation;

(b) shall be laid before each House of Parliament;

(c) shall cease to operate at the expiration of two months unless before the expiration of that period it has been approved by resolutions of both Houses of Parliament.

No Proclamation of Emergency made on grounds only of internal disturbance or imminent danger thereof shall have effect in relation to the State of Jammu and Kashmir (except as respects Article 34) unless —

(a) it is made at the request or with the concurrence of the Government of that State; or

(b) where it has not been so made, it is applied subsequently by the President to that State with the request or with the concurrence of the Government of that State:"

Article 353. Effect of Proclamation of Emergency

The proviso is not applicable to the State of Jammu and Kashmir.

Article 356. Provisions in case of failure of constitutional machinery in States.

This proviso shall in relation to the State of Jammu and Kashmir, be construed as including references to provisions or provision of the Constitution of Jammu and Kashmir;

Article 357. Exercise of legislative powers under Proclamation issued under Article 356 and Article 358. Suspension of provisions of Article 19 during emergencies and Article 359 are applicable to the State of Jammu and Kashmir with very minor exceptions.

Article 360. Provisions as to financial emergency.

This proviso is not applicable to the State of Jammu and Kashmir.

(23) Part XIX: Miscellaneous

Article 361A—Protection of publication of proceeding of Parliament and State Legislatures.

This article is not applicable to the State of Jammu and Kashmir.

(24) Part XX: Amendment of the Constitution

Article 368.—Power of Parliament to amend the Constitution and procedure therefor—

(a) In clause (2) add the following further proviso, namely:—

"Provided further that no such amendment shall have effect in relation to the State of Jammu and Kashmir unless applied by order of the President under clause (1) of article 370.

(25) Part XXI: Temporary, Transitional and Special Provisions

(a) Omit article 369.—Temporary power to Parliament to make laws with respect to certain matters in the State List as if they were matters in the Concurrent List.—

Except Article 370.—Temporary provisions with respect to the State of Jammu and Kashmir.—All other Article 371-A to Article 371-1 are not applicable.

And Articles 372A, 373 and articles 376 to 378A and 392 are not applicable.

(26) Part XXII: Short Title etc. Applies to the State of Jammu and Kashmir

Schedule

The Indian Constitution has 12 Schedules only some of which apply to the State with or without modification related to some of the Articles of the Constitution of India. Each Schedule, which is applicable to the State of Jammu and Kashmir being fathered by a specific Article in the Constitution of the country, will naturally suffer modification, change /substitution depending upon what that Article contains in regard to its application to the State of Jammu and Kashmir.

Appendix-7

J&K Government Order To Set Up The State Autonomy Committee

(Government of Jammu and Kashmir)

General Administration Department

Subject: Setting up Committee to examine the question of restoration of autonomy to the State of Jammu and Kashmir.

Ref: Cabinet Decision No. 11 dated 25/11/1996

Government Order No.:1164-GAD of 1996 Dated 29/11/1996

Sanction is accorded to the formation of the following committee to examine the question of restoration of autonomy to the state of Jammu & Kashmir:

1.	Dr. Karan Singh	Chairman
2.	Shri Mohi-ud-Din Shah	Member
3.	Shri Abdul Ahad Vakil	Member
4.	Shri Abdul Rahim Rather	Member
5.	Shri Piyaray Lal Handoo	Member
6.	Shri Bodh Raj Bali	Member
7.	Moulvi Iftikhar Hussain Ansari	Member
8.	Kushok Thiksey	Member
9.	Shri Teja Singh	

The Committee shall have the following terms of reference:

(i) To examine and recommend measures for the restoration of autonomy to the State of Jammu & Kashmir consistent with the Instrument of Accession, the Constitution Application Order, 1950 and the Delhi Agreement of 1952.

(ii) To examine and recommend safeguards that be regarded necessary for incorporation in the Union/State Constitution to ensure that the Constitutional arrangement that is finally evolved in pursuance of the recommendations of this Committee is inviolable.

(iii) To also examine and recommend measures to ensure a harmonious relationship for the future between the State and the Union.

By order of the Government of Jammu & Kashmir

G.M. Thakur

Commr./Secretary to Government

Copy to:

1. Dr. Karan Singh, Chairman of the Committee
2. Shri Mohi-ud-Din Shah, Member of the Committee
3. Shri Abdul Ahad Vakil, Member of the Committee
4. Shri Abdul Rahim Rather, Member of the Committee
5. Shri Bodh Raj Bali, Member of the Committee
6. Shri Piyaray Lal Handoo, Member of the Committee
7. Moulvi Iftikhar Hussain Ansari, Member of the Committee
8. Kushok Thiksey, Member of the Committee
9. Shri Teja Singh, Member of the Committee

Copy also to:

1. Principal Secretary of Chief Minister.
2. Principal Secretary of Governor.
3. Private Secretaries of all Cabinet Ministers/Minister of State/ Deputy Minister.
4. Private Secretary of Chief Secretary.
5. Government Order file

Composition of Jammu & Kashmir State Autonomy Committee

1. Dr. Karan Singh — Chairman
2. Shri Mohi-ud-Din Shah — Member
   Minister for PWD, Jammu & Kashmir Government
3. Shri Abdul Ahad Vakil — Member
   Minister for Revenue, Jammu & Kashmir Government
4. Shri Abdul Rahim Rather — Member
   Minister for Agriculture, Jammu & Kashmir Government

5. Shri Piyaray Lai Handoo — Member
   Minister for Law, Jammu & Kashmir Government
6. Moulvi Iftikhar Hussain Ansari — Member
   Minister for Housing & Urban Development
   Department, Jammu & Kashmir Government
7. Shri Bodh Raj Bali — Member
   Minister for Industries & Commerce,
   Jammu & Kashmir Government
8. Kushok Thiksey — Member
   Deputy Minister of Tourism, Jammu &
   Kashmir Government
9. Shri Teja Singh — Member-Convenor
   Former Addl. Chief Secretary and Chairman,
   Jammu & Kashmir Public Service Commission

Appendix-8

J&K Government Order To Set Up The Regional Autonomy Committee

(Government of Jammu and Kashmir)

General Administration Department

Subject: Regional and Sub-Regional Autonomy within the State Constitution of Committee.

Ref: Cabinet Decision No. 7 dated 13-11-1996 and Cabinet Decision No. 11 dated 25-11-1996.

Government Order No.: 1166-GAD of 1996 Dated: 29-11-1996

With a view to examine the question of regional and sub-regional autonomy within the state, sanction is hereby accorded to the constitution of the following Committee:

(1)	Chief Minister	Chairman
(2)	Shri Balraj Puri	Working Chairman
(3)	Maulana Attaullah Soharwardy	Member
(4)	Shri Pintoo Norboo	Member
(5)	Shri Mubarak Gul	Member
(6)	Shri Mushtaq Ahmad Bukhari	Member

Shri G.A. Lone, Ex-Secretary to Government, as Secretary of the Committee.

The Committee shall have the following terms of reference:

(i) To examine, consistent with the integrity of the State and to promote better involvement and participation of people in different regions for balanced, political, economic, educational, social and cultural development, evolving of instrumentalities, like local organs of power, at all levels.

(ii) To examine the powers that such organs need to be vested with to achieve the objectives set above.

(iii) To examine whether any change in the State Constitution structure, obtaining as at present, is required.

The Committee will submit its report within a period of six months.

By order of the Government of Jammu & Kashmir.

Sd/-

(G.M. Thakur)

Commr./Secretary to Government

General Adm. Department

Dated: 29-11-96

Appendix-9

The State Autonomy Committee: Recommendations

Jammu, April 1999 (Excerpts)

Chapter XIV: Summary of Recommendations

1. *Temporary, Transitional and Special Provisions (Part X)*

   (i) The word 'temporary' is deleted from the title of part X of the Constitution of India and the word 'temporary' occurring in the heading of Article 370 be substituted by the word 'special'.

2. *Legislative Relations (Part XI)*

   (a) Matters in the Union List not connected with the three subjects of Defence, External Affairs and Communications and/or Ancillary thereto, but made applicable should be excluded from their application to the State.

   (b) All modifications made in Article 246 in its application to the State subsequent to the 1950 order should be rescinded.

   (c) Articles 248, 249, 250 and 251 whether applied in original or substituted/modified form should be omitted from their application to the State.

   (d) As in 1950 and 1954, List II (State) and List III (Concurrent) of the Seventh Schedule should not be applicable to the State.

   (e) Article 254 should be restored to the position it had in its application to the State in 1954.

   (f) Articles 262 and 263 which were not applicable under 1950 Order but were subsequently extended to the State should cease to apply.

3. *Elections (Part XV)*

Changes brought about in this Part be reversed and consequential changes in other Articles in this Part be effected.

4. *Emergency Provisions (Part XVIII)*

(a) The following should be added to C 1.6 of Article 352 in its application to the State:-

'Provided that this request for concurrence of the Government of the State shall be subject to whatever decision the State Assembly may take within two months of declaration of emergency and failing any such decision, the proclamation of emergency shall be deemed to have been revoked.'

(b) Sub-clause 9b) of C 1.6 of this Article should be deleted.

(c) Articles 355, 356, 357, 358, 359 and 360 should be made non-applicable to the State as was the position in 1954.

5. *Fundamental Rights (Part III)*

This part should be deleted. A separate chapter on Fundamental Rights be included in the State Constitution.

6. *The Union (Part V)*

(a) Articles 72 (1) (c), 72 (3), 133,134, 135, 136, 138,145 (1) (c) and 151 (2) should be made non-applicable to the State as was the position in 1950 Order.

(b) Articles 149, 150 and 151 should apply to the State in the form in which they were in 1954.

7. *The States (Part VI)*

(i) Article 218 be omitted in its application to the State and the position as it existed before the Jammu & Kashmir Constitution (First Amendment Act) of 1959 restored.

(ii) Articles 220, 222 and 226 should also be omitted in its application to Jammu & Kashmir State.

8. *Finance, Property, Contracts and Suits (Part XII)*

The matter may be discussed between the state representatives and the Union Government as agreed to during the talks in 1952 (Delhi Agreement).

9. *Services Under the Union and the States (Part XIV)*

In Article 312, the brackets and words 'including the State of Jammu & Kashmir' inserted by the Constitution (Application to Jammu & Kashmir) Order 1958 be omitted.

10. *Special Provisions Relating to Certain Classes (Part XVI)*

Application of Articles 338, 339, 340, 341 and 342 to the State should be omitted and corresponding provisions made in the State Constitution.

11. *Amendment of the Constitution of India (Part XX)*

(i) Clause (4) of Article 368 added vide C.O. 101 be deleted.

(ii) Clause (2) of the Article should apply with the proviso already introduced by 1954 order and clause (1) thereof which was not in existence in 1954 and was introduced in 1971 should remain omitted in its application to the State.

12. *Schedules*

In the Seventh Schedule, entries in the Union List not applied to the State by the Constitution (Application to Jammu & Kashmir) Order, 1950 should be omitted. Concurrent List which was not applicable to the State in 1950 but was applied by subsequent orders should cease to apply to the State.

13. *Changes in the State Constitution*

All amendments in the Constitution of Jammu & Kashmir made vide:

(i) Constitution of Jammu & Kashmir (First Amendment) Act, 1959 in so far as they relate to superintendence, direction and control of elections to the State Legislature and to the State High Court; and

(ii) Constitution of Jammu & Kashmir (Sixth Amendment) Act, 1965 relating to change of nomenclature of the Head of the State and State Executive, mode of appointment of the Head of the State and other consequential amendments should be repealed and the original provisions of the Constitution of Jammu & Kashmir restored.

To sum up, the provisions of the Constitution of India specified in the Second Schedule and the matters specified in the First Schedule to the Constitution (Application to Jammu & Kashmir) Order, 1950 and the matters agreed to by the representatives of the State and the Union vide Delhi Agreement of 1952 should continue to apply to the State subject to the same exceptions and modifications as are specified in the said Order and the Delhi Agreement. All Orders issued thereafter under clause (1) of Article 370 of the Constitution of India by the President, applying various provisions and matters of the Constitution of India to the State whether in full or in modified form or making any change in the provisions or matters already applied by 1950 Order or agreed to under Delhi Agreement should be rescinded and the provisions or matters so applied to the State should cease to apply.

Also the changes made in the State Constitution vide Constitution of Jammu & Kashmir (First Amendment) Act, 1959 and Constitution of Jammu & Kashmir (Sixth Amendment) Act, 1965 be repealed and the original provisions of the Constitution of Jammu & Kashmir as adopted by the State Constituent Assembly on November 17, 1956 be restored.

Bibliography

1. Primary Sources

Government of Jammu and Kashmir, *Report of the State Autonomy Committee* (Srinagar/Jammu), July 2000.

Government of Jammu and Kashmir, *Report on the 1996 Assembly Election in Kashmir*, Srinagar, 1996.

Constitution of India, New Delhi, Ministry of Law.

Report of the Committee on Centre-state Relation under Chairmanship of R.S. Sarkaria, Govt. of India, 1987.

Census of India, Jammu and Kashmir provision population total, Series 2 of 2001, Published by the Controller of Publication, Delhi, 2001.

Report of the Commission of Inquary, Jammu and Kashmir Government, Srinagar, 1987.

Directorate of Economic and Statistics, 2000-01, Economic review of Jammu and Kashmir Government.

Indicators of Regional Development, Govt. of Jammu and Kashmir.

Govt. of Jammu and Kashmir, *Directorate of Economics and Statistics*, "Diggest of statistics"

J & K–A statistical report on the general election to the Jammu and Kashmir assembly election, 1996.

J and K, Assembly election report, 2002.

Census of India, Report on the Jammu and Kashmir state, 1951, 1961, 1971, 1981, 2001.

Report of the Commission of inquary, P.B. Gajendragadkar Commission, 1968.

Regional autonomy committee report, 1999.

Department of Information, *Jammu and Kashmir: Economic development in figure*, Government Press, 1989.

2. Secondary Source

1. Books

Abdullah, Farooq, *My dismissal*, Vikash Publication, Delhi, 1985.

Anand, A.S., *The Constitution of Jammu and Kashmir; its development and Comments*, Universal Book Traders, New Delhi, 1994.

Anand, A. S.,*The development of the Constitution of Jammu and Kashmir,* Life and Light Publication, New Delhi, 1980.

Arora, Balbir and Verney, Douglus, V., *Multiple identities in a single multiple state: Indian federalism in comparative perspective.* Konark Pub, New Delhi, 1995.

Austin, Granville,*The Indian Constitution Corner Stone of a Nation*, Clarendon Press, Oxford, 1966.

Working in a democratic Constitution – the union experience, Oxford, 2000.

Bakshi, S.R. *Kashmir – History and People,* Sarup Publication, New Delhi, 1997.

Basu, D.D., *The Constitution of India*, Prentice Hall of India, New Delhi, 1978.

Basu, Sajal, *Regional movements: Politics of Language, ethinicity, identity,* Indian Institute of advanced study, Simla, 1992.

Bazar, PremNath, *Kashmir is Crucible*, Pamposh Publication, New Delhi, 1980.

Behera, N.,C., *state, identity and violence-Jammu and Kashmir, Manohar,* Pub., Delhi, 1999.

Bhambri, C.P., *Bhartiya Janata Party – Periphery to Centre*, Shipra Publication, New Delhi, 2001.

Bhatia, B.L.,*Jammu and Kashmir – Art. 370 of the Constitution*, Deep Publication, New Delhi, 1997.

Bhattacharjea, Ajit, *Kashmir –the wounded Valley,* UBS Publication, New Delhi, 1994.

Bombwall, R.K., *The foundation of Indian federalism*, Bombay, 1967.

Brass, Paul, R., *Ethinicity and Nationalism. Theory and comparison,* sage Pub., New Delhi, 1991.

Dr. Chanderpal *State autonomy in Indian federalism*, Deep Publication, New Delhi,1984.

Problem of State autonomy –Emerging trends, Cochin University, New Delhi, 1981.

Cyhthia, H., *Entoe, Ethinic comflict and poluted development,* Little Brown Publication., Boston, 1973.

Dasgupta, Sukomal, *Kashmir problem re-examined,* by Socialist Unity Centre of India, Calcutta, 2002.

Dhar, Somnath, *Jammu and Kashmir*, National Book Trust, New Delhi, 1976.

Divatia, Kumud, *The nature of inter-relation in India in the 20th Century*, Popular Book, Bombay, 1957.

Dutt, Jogesh Chander, *Kings of Kashmir,* Mittal Publication, New Delhi, 1990.

Fazili, Mansoor, *Kashmir Government and Politics*, Gulshan Publication, Srinagar, 1982.

The constitution of Jammu and Kashmir, A Stair Publication, Islamabad, 1984.

Gandhi, D.V., *Leaders of India – A profile of eminent public figures of the country*, Indraprastha Pub, New Delhi, 2000.

Ganai, Abdul Jabbar, *Kashmir and National Conference Politics (1975-1980).* Gulshan Publication, Srinagar, 1984.

Gehlot, N.C.,*Trends in Indian politics*, Deep and Deep Publication, New Delhi, 1988.

Grover, Verinder (ed), *Encyclopaedia of India and her state – Himachal Pradesh, Jammu and Kashmir and Punjab,* Deep and Deep Publication, New Delhi, 1996.

Gupta, Sisir, *Kashmir a study in India-Pakistan relation*, New Delhi, 1966.

Gupta, U.N., *Indian federalism and unity of nation*, Vohra Publication, Allahabad, 1988.

Hari, Ram and Sharma S.D., *Politics of autonomy in Jammu and Kashmir*, Kunad Publication, Jaipur, 1999.

Hari Om, *Special status in Indian federalism – Jammu and Kashmir*, Seema Publication, New Delhi, 1982.

Hassnain, Fida, *Encyclopaedia of India – Kashmir,* Deema publication, New Delhi, 1992.

Ian Copland and *John Richard, federalism-comparative perspective from India and Canada,* Manohar Pub., New Delhi, 1999.

Jagmohan, *My Frogen turbulance in Kashmir,* Allied Publication, New Delhi, 1991.

Jai Singh, Hari, *Kashmir—a tale of Shame*, UBS Publication, New Delhi, 1988.

Jana, Anil Kumar, *Indian Politics at the Crossroads,* Commonwealth Publication, New Delhi, 1998.

Kak, B.L., *Kashmir Problem and Politics,* Seema Publication, New Delhi, 1991.

Kashyap, Subash, C., *Reforming the Constitution,* UBS Pub, New Delhi, 1992.

Kaul, M.N., *Encyclopedia of India; Jammu and Kashmir,* Seema Publication, New Delhi, 1992.

Kaul, Pyarelal, *Crisis in Kashmir*, Suman Publication, New Delhi, 1991.

Kaul, Santosh, *Kashmir's Constitutional Status*, Anmol Pub., New Delhi, 1999.

Kashyap, Subash C., (Ed.), *Union-State relation in India*, Institute of Constitution and Parliamentary Studies, New Delhi, 1969.

Khar, GulamHassan, *Freedom movement in Kashmir,* Light and Life Publication, New Delhi, 1980.

Khurshid, Salman, *Beyond Terrorism–New Hope for Kashmir,* UBS Publication, New Delhi, 1991.

Kumar, Dev, P., *Kashmir Return to democracy*, Cosmo Publication, New Delhi, 1996.

Kueck, Gert. W., Mathur, Sudhirchander and Schudilur Klaus (ed), *Federation and decentralisation – Centre state relation in India and Germany*, Oxford publication, London, 1999.

Lakhanpal, P.L., *Essential documents and notes on Kashmir dispute, International publication*, New Delhi, 1986.

Lamb, Alastair, *Kashmir – a dispute legacy (1846-1990)*, Oxford University Press, London, 1991.

Livingstone, W.S., *Federalism and Constitutional Change,* Oxford University Press, London, 1956.

Madhok, Balraj, Jammu, Kashmir and Ladakh, Reliance Publishing House, New Delhi, 1987

Kashmir – Centre to new alignment, Deepak Prakashan, Delhi, 1953.

Mahajan, M.C., *Accession of Kashmir to India* (The inside story). Sholapur Institute of Public Administration, New Delhi, 1977.

Mathew, George, *Panchayati raj in Jammu and Kashmir,* Institute of Social Science, New Delhi, 1990.

Misra, R. N., *Regionalism and state politics in India,* Ashish Pub., New Delhi, 1984.

Nagar, G.R., *Kashmir Accord, 1975 – A political analysis,* Gulshan Publication, Srinagar.

Nanda, K.K., *Conquiring Kashmir – A Pakistani Obsession,* Lancer Publication, New Delhi, 1994.

Narain, Eqbal *State politics in India*, Meenakshi Publication, Meerut, 1976.

Narang A.S., *Ethnic Identities and federalism*, Shimla, 1995.

Palmer, Normen, D., *The Indian political system,* Boston, 1971.

Puri, Balraj, *Regional Autonomy Committee Report,* Gyan Publishing House, New Delhi, 1999.

Puri, Balraj, *Jammu – A clue to Kashmir tangle,* New Delhi, 1966.

Jammu and Kashmir – Triumph and tragedy of Indian federalism, New Delhi, 1981.

Simmering Volcano – study of Jammu's relation with Kashmir, New Delhi, 1983.

Abdullah era, University of Kashmir, Srinagar, 1982.

5000 years of Kashmir, Ajanta Publication, Delhi, 1997.

Raghwan, G.S., *Warming of the Constitution*, Allahabad, 1986.

Rao, H.S. Gururaj, *Legal Aspects of Kashmir problem,* Asia Publishing House, New Delhi, 1967.

Ray, Amal, *Tension areas in Indian federal system,* World Press, Calcutta, 1970.

Ready, G., and Sharma, B., K., *Regionalism in India,* Concept publishing house, New Delhi, 1979.

Santhanam, *Union State Relation*, Bombay, 1963.

Sharma, S.D., *Kashmir autonomy – an exercise in centre state relation*, Subhi Publication, New Delhi, 2000.

Sheshadri, Indian politics-Then and now, Pragati Prakashan, Delhi, 1976.

Singh, Balbir., *The working of the Jammu and Kashmir Legislative Assembly, 1967-72*, Jammu, 1973.

State politics in India – Exploration in political process in Jammu and Kashmir, Macmillan India Limited, New Delhi, 1982.

Singh, Bhavani, *Regionalism and Politics of Separation,* Prinwell Jaipur, 1993.

Singh, G.B., *Encyclopedia of India – Jammu,* Reema Publication, New Delhi, 1992.

Singh, M., P, and chandra. Mohan (eds.) *Religionlism and National identity canadian and Indian perspective,* pragati Publication, Delhi, 1994.

Sinha, Manoj, *Cooperative federalism in India and the U.S.A*, National Books Publication, New Delhi, 1998.

Sawhney, Karan, R., *Kashmir – How far can Vajpayee and Musharraf go?* Peace Publication, New Delhi, 2001.

Teng, Mohan Krishan, Bhatt, Ram Krishan and Kaul, Santosh, *Kashmir-Constitutional history and documents,* Light and Life Publication, 1977.

Thakur, C.P. and Kumar, Dev, P., *India under Atal Bihari Vajpayee–The BJP era,* UBS Publication, New Delhi, 1999.

Thakur, H.K, *Jammu and Kashmir; Integration and Alienation*, Aalekh Publication, New Delhi, 2001.

Thomus, Raju, G.C., *Perspective on Kashmir – the roots of Conflict in South Asia*, Westview Press, New Delhi, 1992.

Turner, Barry (ed), *The Statemens Year Book,* Published by Sara Loyed, Josie Lixon, 2002.

Umashanker, *Kashmir; Triumph and tragedy,* India Publishing House, New Delhi, 1970.

Vashishth, Satish, *Sheikh Abdullah Then and Now*, Maulik Sahitya Prakashan, New Delhi, 1968.

Verma, Ramesh, Kr., *Regionalism and sub-regionalism in state politics-social, economic and political bases,* Deep Publication, New Delhi, 1994.

Wadhwa, K.K.,*Alienation and integration in Jammu and Kashmir,* Aalekh Publication, New Delhi, 2001.

Wallace, Paul. (eds.), *Region and Nation in India,* oxford, New Delhi.

Watts, Ronald, *New Federalism – Experiment in Commonwealth,* Oxford, London, 1966.

Weiner, M. (ed), *State politics in India,* Priston University Publications, New Jersey, 1968.

Wheare, K.C., *Federal Government,* Oxford, London, 1953.

2. Journals / News Magazine / Newspapers etc.

Ahmad, Rashid "Omar takes over, attack centre", *Hindustan Times*, 23 June, 2002.

Ali, Asgar,"Can autonomy be a solution", *Economic and Political Weekly*, 7 July, 2000.

Banerjea, Sumanta, "Beyond the autonomy debate", *Economic and Political Weekly,* 22 July, 2000.

Chaudhary, Rekha, "Autonomy demand – Kashmir at crossroads," *Economic and Political Weekly*, 20 July 2002.

Chaudhary, Rekha and Kumar, Ashutosh "Regional autonomy Committee Report for Jammu and Kashmir" – A critique, *Mainstream* 12 August, 2000.

Dang, Satyapal,"Breaking Kashmir impasse", *The Times of India*, 25 August, 1994.

Francois, Berincen,"Twist with destiny", *India Today*, 10 July, 2000.

Hariom, "Jammu and Kashmir autonomy Report – Disastrous Consequences of pre-1958 position", *Kashmir Samachar,* June 2000.

Hussain, Nazakat, S., "Kashmir elections – Ballots defeat bullets", *Rashtriya Sahara,* October 2002.

Iyyar, Lakshmi, "Polls apart", *India Today,* July 8, 2000.

Iyyar, Shanker "Great shop story". *India Today,* 14 Oct. 2002.

Khare, Harish, "New move to Engage separatist groups in Jammu and Kashmir", *Hindu*, 17 July, 2000.

Kumar, Ashutosh "Kashmir – Dominant concerns and possible solutions" *Mainstream,* Vol. 10, No. 39, Sept. 14, 2002.

"Kashmir – Dominant Cancerns and possible solution", *Mainstream*, 14 September, 2002.

"Reflection on the report of the state autonomy Committee for Jammu and Kashmir", *Mainstream*, 10 June, 2000.

Mohammad, Gul, "Case for restoration of autonomy for Jammu and Kashmir," *Mainstream*, Vol. 10, No. 38, Sept. 7, 2002.

Matto, Amitabh "Dangers of dividing Jammu and Kashmir" *Hindu,* 16 July, 2002.

Lifschultz, Lawrence,"Death in Kashmir: Perils of Self determination," *Economic and Political Weekly*, August 3, 2002.

Narain, T., "A classic Batch-up", *Outlook*, 17 July, 2000.

Puri, Balraj, "Emerging contours of peace in Jammu and Kashmir", *Mainstream*, 27 July, 2001.

"The Farooq's Doctrine – Kashmir's relations with New Delhi", *Economic and Political Weekly,* 24 June, 2000.

"How not to be debate issue of Autonomy", *Economic and Political Weekly*, 19 October, 2000.

"Jammu and Kashmir: After the collapse of ceasefire", *Mainstream,* Vol. 39, No. 27, June 23, 2001.

Saraf, Pushp, "Jammu and Kashmir alienation- A sign of political maturity", *Rashtriya Sahara,* Oct., 2002.

Sharan, Shankar, "By bullet of by ballot in Jammu and Kashmir".

Sachar, Rajinder,"Kashmir – the ignition points", *Mainstream*, 25 May, 2002.

Vinayak, Ramesh,"Vote against dynasty", *India Today,* Oct. 21, 2002.

Singh, M.P.,"Toward a more federalized parliamentary system in India; Explaining functional change", *Pacific Affairs*, Vol. 74, No.4, University of British Columbia, Canada, 2001-02.

Swami, Pravin, "The RSS game", *Frontline*, 2 October, 2002.

"Jammu and Kashmir; Turning the Tide". *The Times of India,* 9 October 2002.

"Kashmir's puppet regime autonomy demand", *Information Times*, 26 June, 2000.

"The Autonomy Report", *India Today*, June, 2000.

"Autonomy is a political slogan of National Conference", *Kashmir Opinion Magazine*, 21 July, 2002.

"State Continues to be in the relentless grip of terrorism", *Kashmir Opinion Magazine*, 21 July, 2002.

"Terrorist outfits change the strategy", *Kashmir Opinion Magazine,* 10 February, 2002.

"Autonomy for Jammu and Kashmir; Little to fear", *Asian News Digest*, July 8-14, 2000.

Newspaper, Digest, etc.

The Hindu, (Madras)

The Statesman, (New Delhi)

Times of India, (New Delhi)

The Hindustan Times, (New Delhi)

Asian News Digest, (New Delhi)
Koshur Samachar, (Srinagar)
Kashmir Opinion, (New Delhi)
Outlook, (New Delhi)
Mainstream, (New Delhi)
Economic and Political Weekly, (New Delhi)
World Focus, (New Delhi)
India Today, (New Delhi)
Cronicle, (New Delhi)

Index

B

C

D

E

N

O & P

Q & R

S